OTHER BOOKS BY THE SAME AUTHOR

Religious Faith, Language, and Knowledge

Faith and Moral Authority

Symbols of Religious Faith

Moral Principles in the Bible

Language and Religion

The Principles of Moral Philosophy

The Philosophy of Schopenhauer

Hegel's Philosophy of History

Kant's Critique of Pure Reason

Nietzsche's Beyond Good and Evil

A Philosophy of Zen Buddhism

Emily Dickinson as Philosopher

Philosophies of Life of the Ancient
Greeks and Israelites

To the memory of my loyal friends

The Carrigans

Catherine
Helen
Frank

Contents

in the world were unrelated to some determinant of them. An underlying motivation of religions, which includes appeals to divine realities, is conditioned by a belief that what human beings do in their worship of divine realities can make essential differences in what takes place in affecting human life.

That there is some "necessity" in sequences, regarded as causal, is a basic conviction of Greeks and Israelites alike. But what accounts for such necessity in causal sequences is interpreted differently in these two cultures.

A Greek term, transliterated, "ananke", has the nonspecified connotation of "necessity"; but when further specified, it is equated with "Fate". Events for which the Greeks presumed no explanation--regarding them as incapable of reasonable accounting--were sometimes referred to as "chance", a Greek term for which is transliterated "tyche". But the use of this term was not for explanatory purposes. Is was rather an acknowledgment that no reasonable accounting could be ventured for them. Greene points out, "chance (tyche) is excluded from serious consideration, as merely a cause (which is) inaccessible to man's reckoning".[1] But whether it should even be referred to as "a cause" is questionable, since as Aristotle later maintained, it is not a cause, but is rather a denotation for those ccurrences for which no accounting can reasonably be proposed. When so interpreted, the Greek use of this term does not imply a doubting of a basic causal order in the world, but rather an admission that the causal order underlying some occurrences is beyond understanding, and therefore, beyond any reasonable analysis.

So basic to Homer's reflecting is his conviction that the world is essentially ordered, that he, for instance, does not even acknowledge a place for Dionysus and his irrational attendants, the maenads. Any such deity resembling later versions of Dionysus was irreconcilable with his version of the world as ordered. Otto explains this disinclination of Homer to admit a deity, celebrated by the excesses of orgiastic rites, as radically contradictory of his beliefs about a world that is fundamentally rational, in the sense of being capable of being reasonably understood and intelligibly explained. And as Otto points out, "The excess" which is characteristic of later versions of Dionysiac rites would not "tally with the clarity which "must...distinguish all that is truly divine".[2]

A fundamental conviction of Homer is that there are divine agencies in the world, which is ordered. In other words, they do not account for its essential order, but rather act in conformity to it; and occurrences for which they are responsible do not go counter to its ordered nature. As Otto also points out, the Odyssey's interpretation of the gods is that they often "operate as a power of fate",3 when such "fate" is regarded as prior to the role of such gods in the ordered world. When so interpreted, the nature of the world, and therefore, the nature or physis of particulars in the world, are equated with Fate, which is also referred to as Moira. "Moira", as Chase points out, is "the order of things."4

Such Fate or Moira in Homer's metaphysic is single. In Greek reflecting subsequent to Homer's time, however, it became plural, and was referred to as "the Fates" or "Moira", as was the case with Hesiod, who introduced a personification of the Fates or Moirai as three principal ones. Since Clotho determines the length of life of living beings, her appellation is "the Spinner", when such imagery is implied in the notion of life as a "thread". Amplifying this imagery includes an identification of another Fate who specifies its length, who, also according to Hesiod, is Lachesis, whose role is characterized as "dispenser of lots". And the personalized fate which "cuts off the thread of life" and "cannot be turned" back from doing so, is Atropos. The fact that such Moirai cannot be influenced in their determinate roles explains why there would be no rites directed to them, and no appeals made to them to alter what is essentially unalterable. It is this property of their nature which accounts for their exclusion from a religion, basic to which is a belief that divine realities can be influenced by human appeals, who in turn, can change what otherwise would have occurred. What such divine realities do in response to human worship thus is accommodating reality to human desires.

2. Both religions maintain that there is an immanence of divine reality in the world

Whatever the literary features may be which indicate more than a single authorship in the writing attributed to Homer, they are, however, of negligible significance in the consistency with which a basic philosophy of history is affirmed in both of these Greek classics. A comparable generalization may be made about the fundamental interpretations of human history which are affirmed in the first five books of the Old Testament, traditionally referred to as the Pentateuch, as well as in the books which follow in the traditional order of the Bible. The distinguishable versions or "strands" in these biblical documents do not impair the consistency of the basic point of view which is affirmed in the Bible that the history of the Israelites is under the final sovereignty of a reality to whom Abraham declared his fidelity, which fidelity remained the spiritual norm of religious life during the long history of this people.

The traditional terminology of "immanence" and "transcendence" for interpreting the relation of a divine reality and an order in the world, which is distinguishable from it, is not satisfactory for understanding the view of the ancient Greeks about these two realities. That they are distinguishable is evident in the very clarity with which Homer and Hesiod refer to deities within the world. The world, however, is not separable from them, as if it had a nature apart from them. They are rather integral to its nature, and are distinguishable within its totality, just as one particular in the world is distinguishable from another particular. And it is in this sense that each is transcendent of the other.

The world for the Greeks is a totality, internal to which are the gods, which are essential to it; and as identifiable within its totality, each is other than it, and in this sense alone are the Greek gods transcendent of the world

The pictorial imagery of Olympus contributes nothing of conceptual significance for arguing the "transcendence" of the gods to the topography of Thessaly, to say nothing of their transcendence of the total world, comprised of the sky, the seas, and the earth. They are internal to this totality of realms, and apart from them, there would not even be the type of sky, land, and sea in which Homer and the ancient Greeks believed.

There is no Greek version of "immanence" of the gods which parallels the Old Testament interpretation of an epiphany or manifestation of the god to whom the Patriarchs oriented their worship. For the Patriarchs, the god whom they trusted for guidance was transcendent of the world in a sense of existing apart from it, since as its creator, it was prior to it, and totally separable from it. In other words, the world would not be without the divine Creator's act, and it is in this sense that the Old Testament idea of the transcendence of the Creator to the world has no parallel in the reflecting of Homer and Hesiod, as well as for Greeks whose reflecting did not differ essentially from theirs.

The foregoing discussion may be summed up in Otto's generalization that "the divine is the fundamental basis of all being and happening" according to Homer and the ancient Greeks. But, as stated, this may also be affirmed of the Old Testament's reflecting on the total dependence of the world upon its Creator, and upon the continued indwelling of the Creator's concern in the world. The parallel, however, cannot be pressed further. Therefore, what Otto affirms about the Greeks' belief that "no part of life is wholly without the divine",5 cannot be said about the Old Testament's interpretation of the relations of the Creator to the world. The Old Testament is consistent in maintaining that the world is under its creator's sovereignty; and its nature, as dependent, is radically other than the divine ultimate upon which it is dependent for its existing and for the manifestations of it immanent providential guardianship.

The providential guardianship of the god who was trusted in the tradition of the Patriarchs is, however, not "self-evident", in the sense that the Divine is always immanent in the world, such as the ancient Greeks believed. The Patriarchs were aware that they were recipients of divine guidance only on condition of their fidelity and their scrupulous fulfilment of their obligations to their god.

"The self-evidence of the divine in the Greek world"6, of which Kerenyi speaks, has no parallel in the Old Testament version of the divine creator of the world. The providence of God, according to the Patriarchs, is contingent upon a loyalty of the people whom their god is not "self-evident", since there are unalterable conditions for meriting it, which are respecting their obligations to fulfil the contract of the Covenant which their god made with them. The nature of the Covenant, for which there is no parallel in Greek religions, will be discussed later. The very meaning of the "guardian god" of the Israelites is inseparable from all that constitutes the nature of the Covenant which was negotiated by their god with them, demanding unqualified integrity in their conformity to its conditions.

30

The very nature of the contractual character of the Covenant with a people, upon whom a providential guardianship is granted, is contingent upon their fidelity to their god. In light of this obligation of a people, as a condition for receiving the guardianship of their god, there is no parallel in what Kerenyi characterizes as Homer's "special religiosity" as "everyone recognis(ing) the divine in what is natural".7 In the Old Testament's account of the religious tradition of the Patriarchs, the divine being is not coextensive with the "natural"; and it is not ubiquitous in the world. Whoever are not respectful of the divine requirements of the Covenant are under judgment for their infidelity, and are judged as deserving of destruction, such as in the Flood or by fire, as the faithless Sodom was destroyed. The infidelity of Israelites, and non-Israelites alike, was regarded in the Old Testament interpretation of human history as responsible for their being cut off from divine providence and left to their own follies. There is no parallel of such uncompromising moral requirements of human beings by the ancient Greek's

The gods, in whose reality and in whose influence in the world the Greeks believed, are, as Otto maintains, "contrasted to the human race" because it is they "who determine the human lot".8 The Old Testament also maintains that "the human lot" is determined by the one divine ultimate in human history; but there is no parallel of the contractual demands upon human beings in a Greek version of religion, such as there is in the Old Testament's. According to the Old Testament, the guidance of god is contingent upon human fidelity to conform to commandments of the Creator, as requirements for being worthy of his providential guardianship.

One parallel, however, which is incontrovertible, is stated by Otto in his characterization of "the Homeric world" in which "every decisive factor' is associated with "the divine".9 The same generalization characterizes the philosophy of history which is affirmed throughout the Old Testament. And this Greek version of the world receives its noblest expression in Cleanthes' "Hymn to Zeus": "Lo! younger heaven, that round the earth is wheeled, follows thy guidance."10

Apart from this particular cosmology, such as is taken for granted by this third century B.C. Stoic philosopher, the religious meaning of this metaphysic underlies the entire Old Testament's interpretation of

31

the world. Cleanthes' reference to what the divine
"purpose brings to birth...on land or in the sea...or
in high heaven's immensity" could, therefore, be
adapted to a scriptural text without alteration, since
it formulates a cosmology that underlies the Old
Testament's interpretation of the world. The Old
Testament, of course, maintains that the world, which
manifests divine purpose, expresses its creator's
intention for it. Such a belief about a creator,
antecedent to the world, is not a Greek cosmology. A
"purpose" immanent in it, such as is believed by some
Stoic philosophers, is the full development of its
rational order, especially in human achievements. The
purpose, on the other hand, which is regarded by the
Old Testament writers as central to the history of the
Israelites is the fulfilment of a covenant obligation,
regarded as binding upon the Israelites, such as it is
not binding upon other peoples. It would, therefore,
not be defensible to maintain that Cleanthes' great
Hymn parallels, in all respects, an Old Testament
interpretation of purpose in the world. The Old
Testament interprets the purpose in the world as
centering especially on the history of one people, to
which the histories of all other peoples are
subordinate in significance.

The world, according to the Old Testament, is a medium
for its creator's guardianship of those who are
faithful to his requirements, as they were believed to
be decreed to those especially qualified to receive
divine disclosures. If this particular aspect of the
Old Testament's interpretation of the Creator's
relation to the world is stressed, it is evident that
divine disclosures of requirements to human beings are
relatively infrequent. These divine epiphanies, as the
disclosure of the ten commandments in the Old
Testament's account, are the high points in human
history; and subsequent history is judged in light of
them. Infidelity in failing to conform to them is
divine judgment, which is always in relation to a human
failure to fulfil divine requirements. This point
explains why Kerenyi's generalization that "the nature
in Homer's religion is the divine",[11] cannot be
affirmed about an Old Testament's point of view about
the relation of the world and human history to the
ultimate divine reality. Otto's generalization about
Greek religion that "The deity is one with the world"
likewise cannot be affirmed about an Old Testament
interpretation. But Otto's statement that "The
deity...approaches man out of the things of the
world"[12] characterizes, in its nonspecified way, a

relation which is basic to the Old Testament's interpretation of human beings in their relation to the divine creator of the world.

3. Both religions affirm that divine reality is ambivalent

A characterization of divine reality as a determiner of occurences in the world is a metaphysic, such as Aeschylus maintains is the nature of Zeus, as "the dispenser of all things".13 This metaphysic of Zeus inplies, as Richard Patrich points out, that he is, therefore, "the dispenser of good and evil in the fortunes of men."14 The nature of any such causal factor in human history implies its ambivalent nature, in the sense that it is capable of radically different acts, which indicate a nature that is not consistent in conforming either to doing good or to doing its opposite. This duality of capacities is its essential ambivalence.

Such a metaphysic of Zeus in Greek mythology and religion is, as will be pointed out in reference to the Old Testament, the nature also of the Creator, as interpreted in passages in Scriptures.

An ambivalence in the nature of a reality to which trust is directed in worship acounts for an emergence of disbelief in its dependability as an ultimate source of human help. This metaphysic of a deity disturbs a reflective person who seriously thinks about the unpredicable character of a reality which is capable of contradictory acting. And it is this type of reflecting which underlies the increasing scepticism of Euripides toward the traditional beliefs which were basic to popular Greek religions. This type of disbelief is affirmed in his drama Heracles, when the wife of Heracles declares: "How uncertain are God's dealings with men!"15 Or another translation of this same assertion of disbelief is that "God's way with men is past finding out!"16

A human being's awareness of an inability to understand what is essentially "past finding out" implies also an acknowledgment of the "uncertain" aspect of all human relations to such a reality. And this uncertainty weakens a religious faith or trust in the predictability of a god's acting. When unpredictable, the basic need in human life for being oriented to a trustworthy reality is unfulfilled. A consequence of

33

this failure to satisfy an elemental motive for directing one's life beyond human undependability to a dependable reality is that the very motive fundamental to a religious orientation is cancelled. A disbelief in the trustworthiness of a god, to whom popular religion is oriented, is expressed in Euripides' Iphigenia in Tauris, when Orestes declares: "Nor are these gods, that have the name of wise, less false than fleeting dreams."17 Another translation accuses such a deity of being no "less deceitful than fleeting dreams".18 Both of these mentioned dramas of Euripides affirm bases for his disillusionment in popular notions of gods who are interpreted as "dispenser of all things". And there is a comparable disinclination in any reflective person to trust a reality which in no more predictable than phenomena in the world which are denoted as "chance". A fundamental need in human life to turn for trustworthy help to a dependable reality is left unfulfilled; and this denial of fulfilment of an essential need supports the arguments for the futility of a religious worship which can assure no greater dependability than can life without such a religious orientation.

A tolerance of any contradictory aspect of reality, whether divine or human, supports a reasonable individual's disinclination to respect it. Highly regarded Athenian law, for instance, permitted a practice which Douglas MacDowell characterizes as "one of the most startling features of Athenian life and society". It was permitting or authorizing the "torture" of "an innocent man or woman in order to check the truth of information about someone else's offence".19 An estimate of this as "wanton" impairs respect for an entire system of law, notwithstanding its otherwise admirable character. The same response follows a reflective person's disinclination to respect a religion which tolerates a belief about an ambivalent deity whose nature is manifested in contradictory acts, no matter how such contradiction is rationalized, in an attempt to reconcile it with a religious trust in a deity.

The reflective Greek was aware of contradictions internal to human beings, and this ambivalent nature of people inevitably conditions anthropomorphic imagery in interpretations of gods.

The fact that human beings are ambivalent is discouraging, but it need not qualify a religious trust of divine reality, when such a reality is free from the moral deficiencies that qualify the consistency of human morality.

Reflective Greeks were not unaware of the commonly contradictory characters of human beings, as Kerenyi points out: "To the Greek idea of mankind there belongs...the half Titanic, half Silenic, comic aspect" as well as "the heroic aspect". What is significant about this version of human nature is its "kinship with the gods".[20] This qualification of a so-called "theology" by a popular "anthropology" entails a disparagement of beliefs about gods as these are basic to a popular version of religion.

The Greeks' acknowledgment of the composite or mixed characters of human beings has a history at least as ancient as Homer and Hesiod. Hesiod, for instance, characterizes human beings as "hav(ing) good mingled with their evils".[21] It is this ambivalent character of human nature which is basic to the "Greek idea of humanity" as essentially "tragic".[22]

In the **Antigone** by Sophocles, for example, the Chorus of Elders of Thebes declares, with obvious regret: "Passing the wildest flight of thought are the cunning and skill that guide man now to the light, but now to counsels of ill."[23] If the disappointment of human beings with themselves could be confined to themselves, and to other human beings, their religion would be unaffected, provided they were not to include in it anthropomorphic traits of a god. Yet, the Greeks, with only rare exceptions, did not divorce their versions of gods from an imagery determined by their own natures. But any religion which characterizes a god in anthropomorphic imagery impairs a faith in a reality which is believed to be thoroughly worthy of trust because unqualifiedly dependable.

When every type of occurence, such as a destruction of one people by their enemy, is attributed to a god, the malice of warfare is projected onto the character of the god which is believed to have brought it about.

The Odyssey, for example, attributes the destruction of Ilium and its people to the preference of Zeus for "the Argives' and the Danaans' venture".[24] And Odysseus tells Eumaeus: "Our fleet was scattered by a god"[25] on its return from the ten-year seige of Troy. When Demodokos, the blind singer of the Phaiakians, told Odysseus a tale of how Poseidon, god of the sea, acted in relation to his people, he commented that "the god might either bring it to pass, or it might be left undone, as the god's heart pleases".26 And, as Plutarch describes the attitude of Greeks towards Poseidon, they acknowledged that he both destroyed them by earthquakes, and also could grant them "security against earthquakes". Ignoring, as it were, his destructive capacities, they attributed the epithet "Asphaleios" to him, which means "securer".27

People's need to seek help from some god to spare them adversities, which a god is believed to be able to bring about, tends to make them ignore the cruel aspect of the god, provided they can somehow persuade him to spare them the adversities he could as readily direct to them. The pathetic plight of human beings has a way of paralyzing the clarity of their thinking so that they overlook or ignore the ambivalent character of a god who is capable of doing them the greatest injury, provided there is some way they can take advantage of the aspect of his composite being to help them, rather than injure them.

The apparent indifference with which such a deity can express one aspect of its nature, rather than another, is indicated in Hesiod's comment about Zeus, that "easily he makes strong, and easily he brings the strong man low".28

The Iliad's version of the indifference of Zeus to what he permits to occur is expressed in the appeal of defeated Priam of Troy to Achilles, when he declares: "Upon the floor of Zeus stands two jars of the evil gifts that he giveth, and another of blessing.29 The characterization of these mutually exclusive fortunes for human beings, as contents of pithoi, stresses the nature of these two types of occurences as external to the nature of Zeus. As if he were unmoved by their contents, he distributes them without concern for human plight. The cynical attitude basic to this analysis in th Iliad underlies an interpreting of occurrences in human history as brought about by divine beings who are indifferent to human suffering which is entailed. Priam expresses this attitude in speaking to Felen: "I bear you no ill will at all." He declare: "I blame the gods. It is they who brought this terrible Achaean war upon me."30

The Iliad characterizes Zeus as so capricous that no reflective person would both believe this characterization as defensible, and also trust him for his consistent wisdom in determining events in human history. Agamemnon attributes to Zeus the tragic loss of his fleet on its return after the ten year long war, declaring: "The cruel god, who once assured me solemnly that I should bring down the walls of Ilium before I left this spot, has changed his mind."[31]

The Iliad characterizes Apollo with the same basic ambivalence as it interprets Zeus. Apollo, who was believed to have power to spare people the curse of plagues, was also believed to have a power to destroy people by sending them such a curse. Taking the side of his priest, Chryses, against Agamemnon, he inflicted "a deadly plague on Agamemnon's army",[32] thereby destroying men who were in no way responsible for the acts of their commander. Although Apollo in subsequent centuries was often esteemed for the justice of his relation to human beings, he was differently interpreted in the Iliad, because imposing suffering and death upon some people for the wrongs committed by others.

The same unpredictable acting is also attributed in the Iliad to Aphrodite, who in anger turned to Helen, declaring: "I might...hate you as heartily as I have loved you."[33]

It is no less surprising that the Iliad should characterize Ares as being as capricious as Aphrodite, since the natures of the god of war and goddess of love are unpredictable. The Iliad refers to Ares as "double-faced", having promised to aid the Argives in the war against the Trojans, but then he "forgot" his agreement, and aided the Trojans instead.[34]

If the turn of events in wars were not explained as a deity's responsibility, there would have been no discrediting of the trustworthiness of gods in Greek mythology, which conditioned what was thought about them in Greek religions. But such a version of any reality regarded as divine, and yet as capricious, by virtue of its essentially ambivalent nature, impairs and also destroys a people's confidence in its dependability. One of the Greek deities, for whom people would ordinarily have greatest need was Hekate, who as Prothyraia, "stood before the doors" of houses in which women were in childbirth, and rather than being trusted for helping them, was also regarded as being responsible for doing the very opposite.[35]

Although the Hymns, once attributed to Homer, were most likely composed by rhapsodists, they express a belief about Greek gods and goddesses which reaffirm the same versions of them as are affirmed in the earliest classics. The Homeric Hymn dedicated "To Earth the Mother of All", declares: "To you it belongs to give means of life to mortal men and to take it away."[36] The Hymn "To Demeter" characterizes her in the same way, sending to "mortals" what they must "bear", even though they suffer; acknowledging that the "gods are much stronger" than they are.[37]

The ease with which, as it were, there is one source for disparate occurrences in human life impairs the tendency of some people to trust such realities. Such impairment of trust weakens a basis in human life for orienting itself to such deities. Even a religion oriented to Athena could not have been unqualified in trusting her, since she was interpreted both as "destroyer or cities (persepolis) and also as "guardian of cities"(erysiptolis).[38] The Homeric Hymn "To Athena" refers to her as "guardian of the city", and yet, "Dread is she", since she, no less than Ares, "loves...the sack of cities."[39] The same ambivalence is attributed to Hermes, in the Hymn dedicated to him, who "occompanies all men and gods", and yet, is not worthy of trust, since although "he bestows benefits, yet beyond measure, he deceives mortal men".[40]

So integral to Greek culture was the version of the duality of divine beings that its earliest historian, Herodotus, claims to record a belief which Solon affirmed that "there are many to whom heaven has given a vision of blessedness, and yet afterwards brought them to utter ruin".[41] Although no particular deity is accused of these opposed occurrences in the lives of some people, they are nevertheless, attributed to what was regarded as the ultimate reality which controlled human destinies.

The major Greek dramatist of the sixth and fifth centuries B.C. reaffirmed this duality or duplicity of the gods. The Messenger in Aeschylus' The Persians explains the destruction of a Persian fleet as "some power divine that swayed down the scale of fortune with unequal weight".[42]

Philoctetes, in Sophocles' drama of the same name, declares that evil is "fostered...by gods" who, in total disregard for human moral merit, "speed the righteous on their downward way".[43] The manner in which Sophocles characterizes the injustice of this indifference of divine agencies to human moral merit

38

indicates his disinclination to accept the earlier versions of a divine endorsement of evil. He thus indicates a criticism of the popular Greek belief of the ambivalent nature of their gods, as making them unworthy of an unqualified human trust.

Euripides presses this critique more persistently, although in his earlier dramas, he conforms to the popular points of view that gods are capable of bringing about occurrences in human life with total disregard for human merit. In his drama, The Suppliants, the ruler of Athens declares to the king of Argos: "...the deity" often destroys one "who never sinned nor commited injustice."<u>44</u> It is such a version of divine determinants of human history which accounts for Aristotle's estimate of Euripides as the "most tragic of the poets".<u>45</u>

The unmerited misfortunes which impair human well-being are dramatically effective, but theologically pernicious and religiously disastrous. They inevitably result in a disbelief in those who are capable of reflecting and recognizing the unsoundness of trusting realities which are essentially unpredictable, and whose dependability is no more consistent than much human behavior. This is a penalty which a religion of a people suffers for interpreting divine realities in the imagery and character of human beings.

William Nickerson Bates maintains that a dramatist is concerned to "interest his audience" in the injustices which human beings suffer, without offering "explanations of it".<u>46</u> William Chase Greene, on the other hand, maintains that "tragedy presents a spectacle of suffering that is explained, though not necessarily justified."<u>47</u> Yet, some explanation is offered in a drama when a misfortune takes place in human history that is attributed to a divine source, such as a god's malice or a god's apathy to human virtue.

Recognizing not only his own, but everyone's, inabilities to give a cogent explanation for evil in human history, Euripides concludes not less than five of his tragedies with an acknowleadment of the futility to lament or protest unmerited misfortunes. The closing words declare the profoundest of Stoic resignation: "Whoso is but mortal needs must bear the fate of heaven sent."<u>48</u> Variations of this sense of futility to complain about what occurs is the closing in <u>Andromache</u>: "... the things that we looked for, the gods deign not to fulfil them."49 Although this point of view about the wisdom of not complaining is a thoroughgoing Stoicism, it does, nevertheless, discredit a popular religious belief that by means of human beings' prayers and their worship of the gods, they can somehow influence the gods to take account of human desires.

Euripides left Athens when Plato was nineteen years old, and when Plato began his philosophical career in writing, he continued to affirm a critique of popular versions of the gods, which is comparable to Euripides'. The relation of Plato to earlier mythology and popular versions of religions is very much a parallel of some of the prophets in the Old Testament to some of the preceding versions of the nature of divine reality. Plato, however, is more consistent than most of the Old Testament prophets in rejecting any notion of the ambivalence of the ultimate divine reality. He uncompromisingly maintains that what is not good, is not of God; and whatever may soundly be attributed to God is necessarily good.

The third century B.C Stoics continued an intellectual confrontation with adversities in human life, but rather than entailing divine realities for their explanations, formulated a consistent moral philosophy. The basic premise of their moral philosphies is that whatever occurs, which cannot be altered, should be accepted. This, therefore, was reaffirming the point of view which Euripides maintained in several of his greatest dramas.

The third century Stoic philosopher Cleanthes reaffirms the metaphysic of Plato that evil which occurs in human history is not caused by divine reality. The role of divine reality in the world is rather "harmonizing things evil with things good", to the end that "there should be one Word through all things everlastingly".50

With very few exceptions, whatever has been said about the Greeks' interpretations of their ambivalent gods may also be said in commenting about the Old Testament's version of an ambivalent god, when such interpretations likewise are conditioned by anthropomorphic imagery. Whenever features of human behavior condition predications about the nature of divine realities, such realities are reduced to the moral level of human interpreters.

The sixth century B.C. Eleatic philosopher, Xenophanes,

affirmed a critique of such anthropomorphic imagery for interpreting divine realities when he censured "Homer and Hesiod" for attributing to "the gods all things which are disreputable and worthy of blame when done by men".51 He was aware enough of what is included in anthropomorphic versions of a deity to point out that "Ethiopians make their gods black and snub-nosed, Thracians red-haired and with blue eyes".52

The Greeks interpreted their gods from a perspective conditioned by their own morality of what they regarded compatible with deities, whose natures were regarded as ambivalent as their own. The same may be said of Old Testament versions of the god of the Isreaelites. The authors to whom the books of the Old Testament are attributed affirms traits of their god which reveal their own characters; and only rarely are their interpretations so transcendent of their own character limitations that their affirmations about a divine reality of the stature of a Creator of the world are commensurate with such a cosmic being.

The following references to Scripture are typical of interpretations in each biblical book, with infrequent exceptions. According to the priestly authors of Genesis, the god whom they indentify with the Creator of the world is regarded as both the purposive giver of life, and when he decides such a life is undeserving of continuing, also terminates it. Such a decision is illustrated in the Israelites' god in relation to Er, the first-born of Judah, who offended their god, and who thereupon "brought about his death"(38:7). The same type of decision of their god was made about an act of Onan, which the priestly writers characterized as "offensive" to their god, and on this basis, their god, "brought about his death also"(vs. 10).

The authors of Exodus attribute to their god an instruction to Moses to deliver to the Israelites that they "are stubborn people" and "at any moment" their god "may annihilate" them (33:5).

The same basic unpredictability of a human being is attributed to the god of the Israelites by the authors of Leviticus, who interpret their god to declare to them that he would "turn against" them, and instead of defending them against their enemies, would permit them to be defeated. To add to this anthropomorphic version of a radical change of attitude toward his people, their god is credited with doing to them what the Greek Pan did, when he instilled panic in people. The

41

authors of Leviticus attribute such a deceitful acting to their god when they declare that in combat, the Israelites shall "take flight when there is no one pursuing" them (26:17). And to add to such a malice, credited to a deity, they attribute to their god a judgment upon his people that they "shall wear out (their) strength in vain" in working a land which "shall not yield its produce any longer nor the trees fruit"(vs.20). This particular attribution to a god is one which was also attributed by the Greeks to Demeter.

The priestly authors of Numbers attribute to the god of the Israelites a radical change of attitude toward his people when he asked Moses: "How long will this people insult me?" And then in anger, their god declared that, as punishment, he "will strike them with pestilence and disown them"(14:11-12). The ambivalence so attributed to their god is the identical trait attributed to Apollo and to Athena, as well as to other gods of the Greeks, such as Hera and Aphrodite.

This ambivalence of a deity is portrayed, as graphically as such duality of nature can be characterized, when the authors of Numbers point out how the charity of their god for his people expressed itself in driving "quails in from the West", when the Israelites were hungry. But as this account continues, eat this food "when the Lord's anger broke out against the people and he struck them with a deadly plague". As if their god were incapable of understanding their hunger, after having had no food, and therefore, were eager to eat, it is credited to their god that he destroyed his people "because (they) had been greedy for meat"(11:31-34). The place they were buried, after having been destroyed in the anger of their god, was "called Kibroth-hattaavh", which means "Graves of Greed".

The frequent practice of the Greeks to invent a myth to account for a practice, a rite, or a name of a place, is paralleled in this particualr name of a place referred to in Numbers because remembered in the tradition of the Israelites, and transmitted orally before having been written.

The ambivalence of radically disparate capacities is attributed to the god of the Israelites by the priestly authors of Deuteronomy, when they affirm that their god, who has no comparable equal among the gods of their neighbors, has the capacity to "put to death" and "to keep alive"; to "wound" and to "heal". And then, as if totally unaware of the religous consequence of what they credited to their god, they attributed to him the declaration: "There is no rescue from my grasp"(32:29). This is the frequently repeated judgment of the ancient Greeks about the unalterability of a decree of Fate. Whatever is so regarded as such a decree is, therefore, excluded from a religious orientation of a person or a people, since neither prayer nor sacrifice, nor any rite in worship, could alter what is by its nature unalterable.

The Book of Job is one of the best known of all literary efforts to struggle with the problem of evil. Basic to this discussion is a belief that whatever takes place in human life is with the consent of the god whom Job trusts for unfailing justice. It is, therefore, evident that both blessings, as well as handicaps to well-being, are explained as brought about by this divine reality. Even after Job's wife tried to dissuade him from retaining his trust in divine justice, he continued to affirm his faith in the god whom he trusted, although he regarded the deity's nature as ambivalent, being capable of permitting evil to occur in the lives of those who trust him, as well as granting them benefits.

Job affirms his basic attitude toward evil, as well as toward the god whom he trusts for his justice, when he asks:"If we accept good from God, shall we not accept evil?"(2:10). This reaffirms his basic religious faith that the same divine reality which "gives" benefits, can also take them away (1:21). In this declaration of faith, he thus affirms a theological premise that the ultimate source of all that occurs in human life is ambivalent, or is capable of permitting the occurrence of radically different manifestations of his ultimate sovereignty. Job's friend, Eliphaz the Temanite, affirms in the first cycle of discourses, the same theology as Job, that "though god wounds, he will bind up"; and basic to this theological premise is the anthropomorphic image of a human hand which can both "smite" as well as "heal"(5:18).

Job repeats the same anthropomorphic imagery in arguing that the "hands" of his god gave him "shape" and "made" him; and, as human hands can do with its own creations, his god can also "turn and destroy". This imagery of human hands which are capable of creating, suggests to Job the analogy of a human potter who molds clay with his hands. Job thereupon reminds his Creator: "Thou

43

didst knead me like clay", and then completing the parallel of a potter with his creator, he asks: "Wouldst thou turn me back into dust?"(10:8-9). Thus the otherwise profound reflecting in the Book of Job on the problem of evil is impaired by the anthropomorphic imagery with which the presumed nature of divine reality is interpreted. There is also another equally serious impairment of this literary masterpiece, devoted to understanding evil occurring in a world believed to be under the sovereignty of a just god. This grave defect thereby converts a profound and sustained reflecting on evil into what would be regarded as a "tragic-comedy". In so doing, it dilutes the gravity of human suffering, which is tragic, into a glid ending. This Epilogue, which is an unfortunate addition to an otherwise very great tragic drama, describes how "the Lord restored Job's fortunes and doubled all his possessions". It describes how his relatives came to celebrate the radical change in the drama of his suffering and "feasted with him", consoling him for all the misfortunes which the Lord had brought on him. The Epilogue thus attributes to deity a rewarding of Job for his fidelity of faith. Evidence for such a benefaction, sanctioned by the god, is that at "the end of Job's life" he had "more than (at) the beginning". The spectacular evidence to substantiate this contrast is that he finally "had fourteen thousand head of small cattle and six thousand camels, a thousand yoke of oxen", and much more in addition, including daughters whose beauty surpassed all other women "in all the world". This appended comment to an otherwise superior masterpiece is what William Chase Greene refers to as "poetic justice", which he censures as "immoral".53 Its immorality may be analyzed as glossing over religious faith, and submerging such a spiritual triumph under a clutter of materialistically minded values.

The major prophets continue the conviction of the earlier books of the Bible in affirming the ambivalence of the ultimate divine reality. Isaiah characterizes the guardian god of the Israelites as "healing as he strikes"(19:22). Thus one divine reality acts with the same type of opposite behaviors as do people, from whose composite characters scripture borrows images of divine reality. This ambivalence of deity is stated by Isaiah as a basic premise of his theology when he declares that the guardian god is "author alike of prosperity and trouble". And this dual type of acting, which is attributed to the nature of deity, is implied in the prior premise that the ultimate determiner of what takes place in human history is responsible for "all these things"(45:7). The fact that even the great Prophet Isaiah is not free from attributing ambivalence to the ultimate sovereign over human history accounts for his anthropopathic interpretations of divine nature as alternating between "wrath", in which the guardian god "strikes down" his people, the Israelites, and then shows them "pity and favour"(60:10).

Jeremiah continues the same type of interpretation of the guardian god of the Israelites as Isaiah affirms. He attributes to their guardian deity the judgment upon them that he "will scatter them among nations" and "will harry them with the sword" until he has "made an end of them"(9:16). Although their guardian god, Jeremiah maintains that this divine reality declares: "I will hand over all Judah to the king of Babylon", and this will enable him to "deport them to Babylon and put them to the sword"(20:4-5). No expression of human anger with another could exceed the violence of anger which Jeremiah attributes to the guardian deity of the Israelites, maintaining that the deity declared: "I have set my face against this city (Jerusalem), meaning to do them harm, not good." And although Jerusalem was the center of his worship in the great sanctuary, he, nevertheless, condemns it to destruction, declaring: "It shall be handed over to the king of Babylon, and he shall burn it to the ground"(21:10).

The character of this prophet is obviously projected into his version of deity when he attributes to deity the anger and hate which he himself experiences in his outrage against the practices of his people, which he construes as infidelity to their god. The Prophet then attributes to their god the decree that "All in this city who survive pestilence, sword, and famine", shall be handed "over to Nebuchadrezzar the king of Babylon, (and) to their enemies" who "would kill them"(21:7). The radical opposites of acting of which the guardian god is capable, according to the Prophet, is that after having "scattered Israel", he "shall gather them again and watch over them as a shepherd watches over his flock"(31:10).

The anthropomorphic parallels with which Jeremiah interprets a deity accounts for the duality or ambivalence he attributes to the guardian god of the Israelites. Rather than reflecting on which properties would be compatible with the nature of a reality that is worthy of trust, because having a nature of unqualified trustworthiness, the Prophet confines his

45

theology to a level commensurate with human behavior, which vascilates between anger and forgiveness, between hate for another and regret for one's acting. Such oscillatng of emotions, underlying contrary ways of acting, is basic to his characterzation of the Israelites' guardian god as turning his own people's "mourning into gladness"; and after "relenting", deciding to "give them joy to outdo their sorrow". The Prophet thereby expresses a very low level of spiritual sensitivities when he declares it "is the very word of the Lord": "I will satisfy the priests with the fat of the land and fill my people with my bounty"(31:13-14).

Jeremiah thus reduces his theology to a level comparable to the low level of the Epilogue to the Book of Job. The Prophet continues to claim that it "is the very word of the Lord" that the guardian god of the Israelites expressed his ambivalent nature in referring to his role as guardian: "As I watch over with intent to pull down and to uproot, to demolish and destroy and harm, so now will I watch over them to build and plant"(31:28). No person who is capable of contrasting such disparate actions, attributed to a god, would be worthy of unqualified trust for understanding the pathetic contraditions internal to human motivations; and instead of pitying and forgiving, would first "destroy and harm"; and after doing so, would "watch over them". A duality of personality can be understood in human beings, but it is totally unconvincing for serious religious life to believe that the nature of a divine ultimate reality is as unpredictable as many human beings are.

Jeremiah seems to be incapable of recognizing the anthropopathic nature of his characterization of god, since he reaffirms such disparate motivations to what he regards as the sovereign ruler of "the whole earth". He attributes to such a divine reality, contrary acts, declaring that "These are the words of the Lord": "What I have built, I demolish; what I have planted, I uproot"(45:4).

It is such contradictory acting which Plato condemns as intolerable in the mythology of Homer; maintaining that such tales about gods must be deleted from the literature with which children are instructed. Jeremiah, however, has a capacity to entertain radical opposites in ways of acting, such as is seldom equaled in the Homeric mythology which Plato censures. The Prophet attributes to deity a claim worthy of a human being when he maintains that the "Lord" claims: "I

46

have broken Moab like a useless thing"(48:39). And the ambivalent nature of the Prophet's version of deity is expressed when he attributes to his god the promise: "Yet in days to come I will restore Moab"s fortunes"(48:47). This duality is reaffirmed when the Prophet refers to another people and their kingdom, such as when he attributes to the god of the Israelites, a promise as a prediction: "I will set my throne in Elam, and there I will destroy the king and his officers." The contrary way of a deity's acting is then affirmed by the Prophet: "In days to come I will restore the fortunes of Elam." And to argue the point of his prophecy as beyond any questioning, reaffirms the wearisome presumption which is characteristic of his prophecy: "This is the very word of the Lord"(43:98).

What has been attributed to Jeremiah as his "Lamentations" may be questioned as his writings for various reasons, such as scholars in the Jerusalem Bible point out.54 Yet, the personality of its author is the same as the author of the Book of Jeremiah. In reading both of these books of the Bible, one cannot help recall the sound insight of John Locke when he maintained that "God does not unmake the man when he makes the prophet". The person who wrote the Lamentations attributes the same type of ambivalent nature to deity as does the Prophet. He declares of the guardian god of the Isreaelites: "With his strong arm he slew all those who had been his delight; he poured his fury out like fire on the tent of the daughter of Zion"(2:4). The only parallel of this in Greek literature is Euripides' Medea.

A scripture which declares that "both bad and good proceed from the mouth of the Most High"(3:38), such as Lamentations maintains, could not convince a reflective person that such a deity, which is capable of such radical ambivalence, would be worthy of trust. It is,therefore, a disservice to earnest religious people, who seriously seek instruction about divine reality, to be expected to regard a scripture of this type as "inspired" or "true".

Some of the most distressing characterizations of a divine reality are affirmed in the so-called "Twelve Minor Prophets". Amos, for example, attributes to the guardian god of the Israelties a negation of its trustworthy property when he credits this deity with the claim: "I sent plague upon you...I killed with sword your young men...I made your camps stink in your

47

nostrils." Presuming that this duality of attitude toward the Israelites is declared by their own guardian god, Amos maintains that this expression of heartless cruelty "is the very word of the Lord"(4:10), Intended as a declaration of deserved punishment for their infidelity, it actually constitutes a basis for an unrelenting antagonism to such a deity.

The prophet Nahum characterizes the tutelary deity of the Israelites in essentially the same way that Amos does. After asking the rhetorical question: "Who can resist his fury?", Nahum declares: "His anger pours out like a stream of fire." And to intensify the threat of their god's anger against them, the Prophet maintains that even "the rocks melt before" his fury. Then Nahum makes a radical shift in his characterization of the god by declaring: "The Lord is a sure refuge for those who look to him in time of distress" and "cares for all who seek his protection"(1:6-8). A person would have a short memory span to understand what is affirmed in one verse and also believe the contradictions are consistent with a theology which interprets a god as ambivalent to such an extreme extent that "he makes a final end of all who oppose him", and yet, he is also said to "care for all who seek his protection". Even though people, in their blindness of what is good for them, fail to seek a trustworthy help from a divine reality which is capable of giving it, such a realty would be a genuine guardian of a wayward people if he were to seek _them_ in _their_ follies, and were to do so as "The Hound of Heaven", with ceaseless mercy, pursue those who turn from his goodness.

No person who is capable of reflecting could both believe that a deity was a trustworthy guardian of his people, and also believe that his charity toward them was so qualified that those who deny themselves his guidance are thereupon "burnt up like tangled briars"(1:6-9). Even though human beings are, as Nahum points out "fickle", and many are unworthy of being trusted as loyal, the very possibility for their redemption is destroyed when they are turned from a divine source of help, whose charity has been denied in scripture to which such people might have turned for enlightened guidance. Few people who intelligently read a scripture for its enlightening help would believe what is affirmed in a short verse, such as the twelfth in chapter one of the Prophet Nahum, which is attributed to the god of the Israelites, who acknowleges: "I have afflicted you"; and then also affirms the promise, "but I will not afflict you again". This is neither sound theology nor sound human psychology. If a novelist understands human psychology when he declares: "one quarrel loseth wife and life and all", then surely no person who has once trusted what he regarded as a divine guide, and later believed that he was handicapped by the same reality by being severely punished, would turn with trust to such a reality again. It is tragic that scripture should attribute to divine reality traits of ambivalence of human beings, capable of perfidity and qualified charity; but it is senseless that the nature of human beings should be disregarded who read such scripture.

The prophet Habakkuk qualifies the ambivalent nature of deity when he addresses the god of the Israelites, declaring: "...in thy wrath thou didst remember mercy"(3:2). A very different _religious_ response to this scriptural assertion would, however, be more likely if such a theology were to affirm that divine mercy awaits those who, in _their_ "wrath" turn away from a trustworthy guidance of a divine wisdom that could save them from wasting their lives in the blindness of anger.

The prophet Zechariah is no more effective than Nahum or Amos are in reconciling two emphases, one stressing the effect of human infidelity upon their god, and the other, their god's response to them for such ingratitude for his trustworthy wisdom to guide them with an enlighteded way of living. The prophet Zechariah attributes the very injustice to his god which the prophet Ezekiel repudiates, when Zechariah attributes to God: "I resolved to ruin you because your ancestors roused me to anger"(8:14). Ezekiel declares that "it is the words of the Lord"(Vs.1) that "a man shall not die for his father's wrongdoing"(Vs.17). The profounder moral philosophy of Ezekiel is responsible for crediting to God the decree: "It is the soul that sins, and no other, that shall die; a son shall not share a father's guilt, nor a father his son's"(vs.20).

After attributing to the god of the Israelites a type of injustice in dealing with his people, the deity, according to the prophet, promises his people: "I have once more resolved to do good to Jerusalem and to the house of Judah." A feeble assurance, "Do not be afraid", which concludes this verse, would persuade no serious human being to forget all that had preceded it in this passage in scripture.

The theologically unconvincing ambivalence attributed by Zechariah to the god of the Israelites is: "I will restore them...and they shall be as though I had never cast them off"(10:6). "Casting off" a people, with the injury which such rejection would entail for those who had once trusted their god, would leave so indelible a memory that few people could forget it and forgive it. After all, human beings have to forgive an injury to them before they can again trust the one who had previously injured them; and this fact in human psychology cannot be ignored when a scripture affirms an ambivalence to a god, credited with unfailing charity, but who also declares an unwillingness to "relent" in turning away from those whose folly in living indicates that they are in need of the very redemptive help from which they turn away.

The prophet Malachi repeats the same bewildering version of theology as the other prophets do when he attributes to "the Lord", the declaration: "I love Jacob, but I hate Esau; I have turned his mountains into a waste"(1:3-4). As has been argued in the foregoing discussion, such radically disparate emotions as "love" and "hate", when directed toward the same person or people, is an indictment of human instability, and it is a property of a type of life which cannot be respected. When such ambivalence, therefore, is attributed in a scripture to a divine reality, both the scripture and also the reality it so interprets are regarded with disbelief. This is the inevitable tradegy with a religion to which such a scripture is basic. It is the tragedy of interpreting a divine reality with properties that are characteristic of some human beings, when such ambivalent properties in human beings are handicaps to a well-being from which they themselves turn, with hope, to a reality transcendent of such undependability of duplicity.

A reason for considering some of the deutero-canonical books, often referred to as "The Apocrypha", which are not included in the Hebrew canon of the Scriptures, is that they indicate how deeply ingrained these concepts are of a god's ambivalence, even in the later centuries of the pre-Christian era.

The author of First Esdras reaffirms the long established belief that the god, who had been the guardian of the faithful descendants of the Patriarchs, radically changed his ways in relation to all those in this tradition who were not worthy of his continued guardianship, by virtue of their infidelity to commandments he had delivered to Moses. The priestly author of this text, Ezra, declares: "When our fathers sinned against the heavenly Lord of Israel,...he delivered them over to Nebuchadnezzar, king of Babylon", who destroyed the great temple in Jerusalem, and "took the people into exile"(6:15-17). This belief that "the Lord", whom the earlier Israelites had trusted for his guidance, abandoned their descendants because of their infidelity, reaffirms a theology that persists throughout the canonical Hebrew Scriptures. This belief that the deity, whom the faithful of the Israelites worshiped, had later "handed them all over to their enemies", expresses the theological version of an ambivalent deity, capable of permitting a foe of his people, the king of Babylon, to kill tens of thousands of the very people who had defended the Holy City under Babylonian attack (1:54-56).

When the priestly author of Second Esdras wrote the account of exile in Babylon, he declared that his "heart sank" when he "saw" how the god whom his ancestors had worshiped could "tolerate sinners", and "spare the godless", and yet, "destroy" his "own people", while "protect(ing) their "enemies"(3:28-30). This priestly author admits that such ambivalence of a god is something which he cannot understand, and he addresses an acknowledgment of his bewilderment to the divine reality, declaring: "You have given no hint whatever to anyone to understand your ways"(vs.31).

This admission of his bewilderment is profoundly significant since it expresses the tragic consequence of maintaining the theological doctrine of an ambivalent deity. Even this devout and highly learned priest was crushed by a perplexity of reconciling what in principle is incapable of being reconciled, because when this concept of ambivalence is affirmed, it becomes a logically contradictory assertion. It declares that a divine being is a guardian god of his people, and yet, is not their guardian, because he destroys them instead of guiding and protecting them. The inability of this priestly author of Second Esdras expressed a response of every reflective person to this theological concept of an ambivalent deity. The basic reason, however, for this is not essentially theological, but rather logical. It is the inability of a human mind to comprehend the meaning of a proposition which both affirms and denies the same concept. The way to be spared bewilderment in thinking about such a theological doctrine is rejecting it from

51

a serious interpretation of a divine reality which is believed to be a trustworthy source of guidance in human life. If, instead, a god were interpreted as having unqualified wisdom to understand the tragic duality constitutive of so much human life, such a god would also be interpreted as pitying such confused human beings, floundering in their follies. Sustaining such understanding toward human beings would, in the unalterable wisdom worthy of a god, pity them for bringing upon themselves the judgment of their own folly.

The priestly writer of Ecclesiasticus, indentified as "Jesus, son of Sirach", points out in his reflecting on another version of theology, what is logically implied in maintaining that whatever takes place in human history is explainable in terms of one reality. After it is declared that there is one ultimate cause for every occurrence in the world, it logically follows, as this priestly writer points out: "Good fortune and bad, life and death, poverty and wealth, all come from" this one ultimate cause, whom, as a religious monotheist, he refers to as "the Lord"(11:14).

Another equally instructive feature of a theology which characterized deity in anthropomorphic imagery is also pointed out in this same deutro-canonical book. The foregoing concept of ambivalence of a deity would readily be inferred from an anthropomorphic version of deity, such as this writer suggests: "Blow on a spark to make it glow, or spit on in to put it out; both results come from the one mouth"(28:12).

One other such deutero-canonical book, Second Maccabees, may be considered as illustrative of the persistence through centuries of priestly reflecting on theological concepts which are basic to canonical books in the Hebrew Scripture. This reflective priestly writer is bewildered about the historical fact that Anthiochus Epiphanes, although one of the cruelest of men, was chosen by the guardian god of the Israelites, to destroy eighty-thousand people in Jerusalem in the same military campaign in which he "enter(ed) the holiest temple on earth", desecrating its "sacred vessels"(5:15-16). The commentary of this priestly writer on this tragic destruction of the temple, and the murder of tens of thousands of the inhabitants of Jerusalem, is simply a repetition of the concept, repeated and repeated, in the canonical books, that all this occured as their god's judgment upon "the people of Jerusalem" who had been "angered" by their "sins", and because "angered...for a short time...left the temple to its fate"(vs.18).

The capacity of a religious interpreter of human history to attribute such massive destruction of sacred art, and a slaughter of people, to a plan of a god, demonstrates how blind even the most intellectual of human beings can be when so brain washed by an idea, drilled into their mentally from infancy, and sanctified by the belief of its scriptural truth. Rather than having the religious integrity and the intellectual stature to rethink the defensibilty of this blashphemous concept, even though reaffirmed tirelessly in Scripture, this highly learned writer resigns himself to reconcilling the destruction of what he himself refers to as "the holiest temple on earth" with the judgment of a creator of the world upon the follies of people who were too stupid to live sensibly. When their stupidity engulfed their religion, and perverted their character so that they no longer revered what had been sacred to their ancestors, their infidelity was regarded as warranting such unimaginable destruction both of people and of what throughout their cultural tradition, had been revered as holy. The idea of the ambivalence of a god is complacently reaffirmed in this commentary on one of the greatest tragedies in human history: "Even the sanctuary itself...was abandoned when the Lord Almighty was angry, but restored again in all its splendour when he became reconciled"(5:20-22).

The lesson of what indoctrination can do, whether religious or political, is one of the sobering phenomena in human life. When, for instance, a scripture, which is esteemed as sacred and all of its affirmations are regarded as true, is reaffirmed through centuries of institutional instruction, the critical mentality of a people, who reveres such an institution, becomes spritually paralyzed and intellectually intimidated to such an extent that they do not challenge or contest what impairs reverence for divine reality, to which devout people turn in their need for enlightened guidance. Instead, they are given versions of a god which would be indictments of a human being who permitted himself to be responsible for what scripture attributes to deity. Only when a scripture itself is challenged for its unworthiness to be regarded as giving enlighted instruction of the ultimate divine reality, will there be a genuine religious mode of life among intellectually enlightened people, who sincerely seek for spiritual orientation of their lives, but who must be persuaded by a characterization which is worthy of its nature, rather than being a projection of the internal contradictions which are chacteristic of so much bewildered and floundering human life.

An ethnological study of cultural contacts of the ancient Israelites enables one to understand that what is affirmed in the Old Testamant about the ambivalent nature of their guardian god is not unique to the Israelites. Israelites had cultural contacts with the Babylonians; and the Babylonian "Epic of Creation" affirms the same type of ambivalence of Marduk, the principal Babylonian deity, as the Old Testament affirms of the nature of the guardian god of the Israelites. According to this Epic, the counsel of gods delegated to Marduk the uncontested sovereignty over gods, both "to promote, and to abase" all who came under his sovereign "power".55

The similarity of concepts in two cultures, even with direct contacts, is not necessarily an expression of cultural borrowing. What is ethnologically significant is that cultures of an historical period indicate parallel types of interpretations. Parallels, for example, of concepts in the cultures of the ancient Greeks and Israelites cannot be accounted for by direct cultural contacts. Rather, such parallels occur in historical periods of approximately the same centuries. Such parallelism, therefore, is explained in some philosphies of history, such as Hegel's. All that is being argued in this discussion, however, is that there are comparable ways of interpreting realities in relatively the same historical eras. The archeological discovery, classified as "The Cyrus Cylinder", for example, declares that Marduk "gave orders" to Cyrus, King of Persia (550-529 B.C.) to "go against his (own) city Babylon". Thus the tutelary deity of Babylon turned against the people who had regarded him as their guardian god, just as the guardian god of the Israelites turned against them. Both were punishing their own people for their negligence in giving less than wholehearted obedience to them as their sovereign rulers. This archeological text furthermore characterizes Marduk not only as commanding the foe of the Babylonians to "take the road to Babylon", the capital of the kingdom, but it declares that this foreign deity "went at his side like a friend and comrade".56

Ancient texts of the Israelites attribute the same type

of perfidity to their guardian god when he turned the "Holy City" of Jerusalem over to the Babylonians, permitting them to desroy it and kill tens of thousands of its defenders.

The Israelites in Palestine were also in cultural contacts with the Moabites. An archeological discovery of a document, classified as "The Moabite Stone", maintains that the guardian god of the Moabites, Chemosh, permitting the king of the Israelites, their enemies, to "oppress Moab many days". And the explanation for this historical occurrence is the same as is repeated time and time again in the Old Testament, when the Israelites were oppressed by their enemies: "Chemosh (their god) was angry with his land."57

The Genesis account (xix.37) that Moab is the son of Lot, who in turn is nephew of Abraham, establishes a relationship of the two tribal confederations. Yet, even this blood relation does not constitute evidence for a cultural borrowing of two parallel concepts of guardian deities, who turn against their own people. It is sufficient, therefore, to take account of the historical era of the eighth century B.C. to appreciated a phenomenon of ethological significance, contacts, have parallel ways of interpreting their gods. It is "as if"--in the terminology of Hans Vaihinger--58 there were some sort of functioning determinant underlying cultures of an historical period. One philosophical hypothesis for such an hypothetical factor which accounts for cultural parallels is the "panpneumatism" of Eduard von Hartman.59 But even without presuming to explain such cultural parallels without direct cultural contacts, it is sufficient to accept the empirical data of archeologists, which demonstrate such parallels in approximately the same historical eras.

When the qualification of trust in a guardian god is not entailed in a concept of a deity's ambivalence, a genuine religious faith in the dependability of a divine reality is then possible. Such genuine faith is affirmed throughout the Old Testament, notwithstanding the repeated introductions in Scripture of a qualification of such faith by virtue of maintaining the ambivalence of deity. Such a genuine religious trust, for example, is also affirmed in the archeological discovery of a Babylonian document, entitled "Prayer to any God", which declares an

55

unqualified assurance of faith that a god whom a person devoutly trusts "will not srike down (his) servant".[60]

If this basic creed of faith were to have remained a living determinant of all that was believed about a guardian god, the pernicious doctrine of ambivalence would not have entered into Scripture. The possibility for preserving religious purity in a cultural tradition is demonstrated as a reality in a Jewish sect, whose religious reflections are preserved in the Qumran archeological discoveries, which are among the purest version of religion of which there are historical records.

The Qumran Sect of devout Jews had its origin in a protest against what was regarded as the widespread infidelity in Jerusalem under the spurious high priest, Hyrcanus II, who received the appointment to this sacred office entirely on political grounds, when his mother, Salome Alexandra, chose him for this supreme office. This event precipitated every imaginable disorder in Jerusalem, including even a civil war waged between the two brothers, Hyrcanus II and Aristobulus II, who was supported by the Roman Pompey. When Pompey seized Jerusalem, the Hasmonaean rule ended, and a Jewish sovereignty, basically religious, was replaced by a political power which destroyed the bases for a theocratic orientation of an ancient culture.

John Allegro believes that "the Qumran Sect" of devout Jews came into being near the Dead Sea location "soon after the reign of John Hyrcanus (Hyrcanus II)" in 135-104, and this devout community later came to a catastrophic "end shortly before the destruction of Jerusalem in A.D. 70".[61] What is significant in taking account of this Essene Sect is the basic creed of its theology that "God is the cause of all good, but nothing evil."[62] It was this interpretation of God which impressed Philo of Alexandria, also known as Philo Judaeus, a Hellenistic Jewish philosopher, who was esteemed as "The Jewish Plato". One reason for this reference to an earlier Platonic influence is his own metaphysic, which reaffirms Plato's. And it was this metaphysic which impressed him in the Essenes' religion.

Many passages from the Qumran scrolls indicate what a normative character of religious faith would be implied in a basic creed that the ultimate divine reality is unqualifiedly good, and therefore, is free from the duality, often as extreme as radical duplicity, such as when ambivalence is attributed to a divine Ultimate. The Essene "Scroll of the Rule" affirms this religious trust that God "has poured forth from the fount of His knowledge the light that enlightens"63 all who turn with trust to his divine help. It is such trust which is compatible with a theological premise of the incapacity of God to do what is a handicap to human well-being, because his divine nature is free from any qualifications of essential goodness. Turning to such a divine reality, which is so interpreted, and therefore trusted, is understandable when a religious orientation is supported by the faith that "without Thee no way is perfect".64

The genuiness of such religious trust is, consequently, expressed in the faith: "Thou hast not deserted my hope." When reverses occur human life, a person, who has such trust in the consistency of a god's goodness, does not explain his handicaps or reverses as caused or sanctioned by his god. He regards them as occurring by virtue of other determinants. Thus his religious faith remains unqualified by an inevitable perplexity how his god could sanction or cause them. In other words, by virtue of not qualifying a faith in the goodness of a god, such as is done in maintaining ambivalence in divine nature, a religious person is spared the tragic qualification of faith in the unfailing goodness in the god whom he is confident is worthy of his trust. When reverses do occur in life, such a religious person can then honestly declare: "In the face of the blows Thou hast made my spirit stand fast."65 This is a very different interpretation of life's difficulties from the interpretation that reverses in one's life are caused or sanctioned by the very divine reality to whom one turns for a reassurance of a dependable help in surmounting such difficulties. The Essene "Scroll of the Rule", for example, indicates what a genuine trust can be when human life is oriented to a divine reality that is believed to be unqualifiedly worthy of trust. It declares that one who so trusts "shall...delight in all that (God) has made", and therefore, all that God sanctions and permits. Such trust is affirmed as the religious faith that "beyond the will of God (one) shall desire nothing".66

4.Both the ancient Greeks and Israelites believed that each of them was central to the concerns of their own gods or god

A feature of the ancient religions which are oriented

to anthropomorphically interpreted gods is a belief that their deities have concerns which are restricted to their own people, either communities or nations. What Herodotus says of the Thracians can therefore be said equally well of other ancient peoples, who also believe "in no other god but their own".67 Such gods are either national or local, and what the priestly writers of Second Kings affirm of them is ethnologically important. This scriptural text declares that "each of the nations made its own god".(17:29). Of course, the priestly authors of this biblical book believed that their analysis of the status of the gods, of other peoples explained only them, and not their own god, which Scripture interprets as having properties essentially the same as all other tribal and national deities.

Such anthropomorphically characterized deities are devoted only to the people whose religions are oriented to them. The same bias is expressed as their literary accounts of the realities which they regard as divine, and therefore, as entitled to their worship. As Lattimore points out, "the Iliad was composed for a Hellenic audience of the upper class". Since many of this cultural stratum "claimed to trace their ancestry back to the heroes of the Trojan War",68 their cultural orientation might be characterized as "chauvinistic", when this term is used with a sense wide enough to include an excessive preoccupation with whatever glorifies a culture, internal to which one himself lives.

The same may also be said of a dominant trait of the ancient Israelites' interpretation of themselves in relation to the god whom they regarded as a guardian exclusively of themselves, and as such, having concern for no other people. Their own importance for their guardian is described in Exodus, in contrasting "all the inhabitants of Canaan" who "were in turmoil" when "terror and dread fell upon them", while the Israelites "passed by", whom thou madest thy own"(15:15). Exodus records another similar event which emphasizes the centrality of the Israelites to their own god's concern: When Moses was leading the Israelites, as the "chosen people" of their god, he addressed their divine guardian, declaring: "So shall we be distinct, I and thy people, from all the peoples on earth"(33:17).

The ninety-fourth Psalm is a reassurance, directed to the Israelites as one people, when it affirms that their god "will not abandon his people nor forsake his chosen nation"(vs.14). A reverse application of excessive devotion, characteristic of a chauvinistic loyalty, is certainly a feature of the deity whom the Israelites regarded as their god, who had concern only for them, and not for other people.

Isaiah makes this chauvinistic type of deity so unambiguous that only the most superificial reading of this scriptural text could gloss over its actual meaning. Presuming to speak for the god of the Israelites, the Prophet declares to them: "You are more precious to me that the Assyrians, you are honoured and I have loved you, I would give the Edomites in exchange for you"(43:4). No one could really understand what is affirmed by the prophet Amos without also understanding the chauvinistic orientation of the deity for whom he presumes to speak. Addressing the Israelites, he says: "Listen, Israelites, to these words that the Lord addresses to you...For you alone have I cared among all the nations of the world"(3:1-2). The prophet Joel declares the same scope of concern of the deity whom the faithful among the Israelites worshiped, assuring them that "the Lord is a refuge for his people and the defence of Israel"(3:16). This version of a god's concern for one and only one people is likewise stressed by Joel when he attributs to the guardian god of the Israelites the prediction of his judgment upon other nations, when he "will gather all the nations together and lead them down to the Valley of the Lord's Judgement, and there bring them to judgement on behalf of Israel, my own possession"(vs.2). The reassurance of the Israelites that they will be compensated, and thereby, possibly consoled, for all reverses they suffered by the antagonism of other people, is affirmed in the deutero-canoncial book, attributed to Ezra, who presumes to speak for the god of the Israelites: "I will do to them as they are doing to my chosen people"(II Esdras 15:21). This attempted type of compensatory consolation is again affirmed when Ezra, presuming to speak for "the Lord", assures his people, the Isrealites: "All nations shall envy you, but shall be powerless against you"(2:28). Then reassuring them of their centrality to their deity's concern, Ezra tells his people that their god "said" to him "It was for Israel that I made the world"(7:11).

A feature characteristic of the ancient literatures of both the Greeks and the Israelites is the belief that each people is "chosen" by some god as his own special concern. The Iliad attributes to Zeus an address to the Trojans: "For all the cities that men live in under the sun and starry sky, the warmest of my heart was holy Ilium, with Priam and the people of Priam."[69] This interpretation of Zeus as favoring the Trojans above all other people is reaffirmed in Aeschylus' The Suppliant Maidens, when he expressed the Trojans' belief that "Zeus (is) the author of our race".[70]

The priestly authors of Leviticus attribute to the god worshiped by the Israelites a reassurance addressed to them: "I am the Lord your God: I have made a clear separation between you and the nations"(20:24-25). The prophet Isaiah, who ordinarily is regarded as affirming the universality of the god whose nature he interprets, nevertheless, attributes to "the Lord...the Holy One of Israel", an assurance which is limited to the Israelites: "I have formed this people for myself"(43:21). It is this verse which is the key to the meaning of the preceding assertion: "I am the Lord, your Holy one, your creator, Israel, and your king"(vs.14-15). No rationalizing of this verse in Christian centuries, by redefining the denotative meaning of "Israel", can defensibly diminish the nonuniversal character of the deity to which reference is here made. The divine reality which is so interpreted is not a universal god, but is one whose preference is for a particular people.

A god who prefers one people or nation to others also has preferences for rare individuals among such people. Moses alone was selected from among all the Israelites then living to be given the honor by the god of the Israelites to receive his commandments, formulated as the Decalogue. Psalms 106 charecterizes Moses as "the man he had chosen", not only for this honor to receive the Commandments, but also as a spokesman for his people, who had extraordinary influence with their god. When the faithless among the Israelites "made a calf" of metal "at Horeb"(vs.19), this Psalm declares that it was the god's "purpose...to destroy them", but it was "Moses" who "threw himself into the breach to turn back his wrath lest it destroy them"(vs.23). When faithless Israelites again deserted their god, and "joined in worshiping the Baal of Peor", they were punished by their god with a "plague (which) broke out among them". It was Phinehas (who) stood up and interceded; and so influential was he in the esteem of his god, that "the plague was stopped"(vs.29-30).

The same type of expression of a god's preference for some individual among an entire people is affirmed in

Greek literature. The Iliad includes an account of Athena's intervention in the Trojan War, when she "decended from the sky", having been sent by Hera, to prevent Achilles from killing Agamemnon, whom Hera loved, as she also loved Achilles. Since both were favorites of the goddess, she could not permit death of one by the "great sword" of the other.[71] The Trojan prince, Hector, was favorite of Apollo, and when the archer Teukros (Teucer) aimed at Hector "and sent an arrow flying from his string", it was "Apollo (who) turned his dart aside".[72] The special concern of Aphrodite for one particular Trojan was for Aeneas to whom she refers as "my own beloved son...my favourite".[73] Another translation characterizes her love for him as "who beyond all else in the world is dear to me".[74]

Both the ancient Greeks and Israelites regarded the principal centers for their own most sacred relations to divine realities to be the most important locations on earth. Aeschylus refers to Delphi as "earth's central shrine".[75] Euripides reaffirms the common reference to the temple of Apollo at Delphi as "the navel of the earth". [76] He also characterizes it as "the World's Heart".[77] So esteemed was Athens, with its citadel on which the great temple honored Athena, that Sophocles refers to it as "the city built by gods".[78] Other locations in Greece which were esteemed by Greeks, include Argos, where the celebrated temple was dedicated to Hera, and Olympia, where her prominence was later shared, if not eclipsed, by Zeus. A complete inventory of sacred sites for the Greeks would include other areas, such as Epidaurus, where Asclepius was revered.

There is, of course, no parallel for such a wide distribution of sacred sites in the history of the Israelites. In their history, after they established a "homeland", promised to them by their god, there was one central sacred site, the "Holy City" of Jerusalem. When Jerusalem became the focal center of worship, the theology of the Israelites had already transcended the properties of nonuniversality for the divine reality. This spiritual achievement did not, however, occur in popular religions of Greece, which were oriented to a plurality of divine beings. This polytheistic feature of Greek religions is, therefore, without parallel in the history of the Israelites, for whom their god was intolerant of any other deity, such as the neighbors of the Israelites worshiped.

What, however, is a parallel in the religions of the
Greeks and Israelites is especially evident in the
sacred rites conducted in Eleusis, in which the
Mysteries admitted no so-called "barbarians". "The
great Eleusinian festival" was "a pure Hellenic
institution". An inflexible condition "for admission
to the secret events of the great festival" was
"Hellenic language".79 A comparable intolerance of the
Israelites for other people is explained in Scriptures
as the precaution against the introduction of elements
of a foreign religion into their religion, thereby
corrupting not only its purity, but also alienating
their god from his guardianship and guidance. The
consistent focus upon one deity in the long history of
the Israelites, therefore, accounts for a radical
difference in the religious cultures of the Israelites
and the polytheistic Greeks.

There is, however, a partial parallel of the antagonism
of the god of the Israelites to other gods, in the
contest between Greek gods, such as between Athena and
Poseidon for sovereignty over Attica.80 This notion of
an antagonism of gods is a trait of the anthropomorphic
imagery with which deites are interpreted. The
hostility of one Greek god for another, whether Hera or
Aphrodite, is consistent with anthropopathic versions
of deities. Jealousy is a trait of much human life,
and therefore, an acknowledgment of such a trait also
in the god of the Israelites is an expression of a
theology conditioned by modes of human emotions. But
in addition to this factor, the intolerance of their
god for other gods is integral to the necessity of a
people for preserving its religious tradition. The
tradition of the Patriarchs, with the exemplary
fidelity of Abraham to the guardian god to whom he was
loyal, could not have continued had there been a
tolerance for the religions of other peoples.

Even the polytheistic Babylonians acknowledged the
supremacy of Marduk to other gods of the pantheon.
"The Epic of Creation" describes the "circle" of gods
who sought to test the merit of Marduk to become
sovereign over them. When he demonstrated his
superiority by means of miracle or magic, he was
unanimously acclaimed by them as their "king".81

Concepts which are primarily political determine the
religious factor of the necessity for a centrality of
sovereignty when gods are regarded as imposing
requirements upon people. If every god in the
Babylonian pantheon, for instance, were to have had a

right to proclaim demands to which the Babylonians were
expected to conform, there would have been no political
alternative to anarchy. This political consideration
is also a factor in the theocracy, such as the
Israelites revered. If more than one god were to have
been acknowledged as having authority to impose
commands upon the Israelites, an absoluteness of the
Decalogue would never have been a feature of their
religious history. If one set of commandments or
requirements for a people is to be accepted as final,
it necessarily must be acknowledged as established by
an uncontested sovereign over a people, for whom the
requirements are obligatory; and any infraction is
punishable without appeal to another authority of equal
sovereignty.

"The Moabite Stone", which has an origin about 830
B.C., records an autocratic version of a supreme god of
the Moabites. This deity, Chemosh, gave unchangeable
commands to his people, basic to which was the
political necessity to preserve their kingdom from its
destruction by other people, such as the Israelites.
For military effectiveness, therefore, any people who
struggle for their preservation depend upon an
autocratic rule which cannot be challenged. The king
of Moab derived his unchallengeable authority from
Chemosh, who commanded the King to go "against Israel".
The success of his military campaign included,
according to this archeological record, killing "seven
thousand men, boys, women" and many others. The sacred
vessels which were dedicated by the Israelites to their
god were taken by the Moabites, and were rededicated to
Chemosh.

When religions interpret their deities as supreme
sovereigns over their people, it follows that when such
people engage in warfare, their sovereign gods become
their supreme military commanders. The national god of
the Moabites, for instance, was their military
commander, just as "the national god of Israel"82 was
the supreme commander of the Israelites in their
military encounters with other people.

In Greek religions, Athena, as Polias or Poliouchos,
was The Protecting Goddess" of her city, Athens, and
when the Athenians engaged in war, she assumed the role
of "goddess of war", with the title, "Athena Areia".
As a leader in combat, she became "the goddess who
fights in front", with the title" Athena Promachos".
As the one to whom military victory was accorded, she
was "Athena Nike", "goddess of victory".

63

Not only was Athena trusted by the Athenians for her guardianship, but Zeus also was so trusted. As "Zeus the Saviour", he was revered as "a protector of cities".83 In such guardian role, Zeus had a sovereignty of wider scope than Athena, as tutelary goddess of Athens. By the sixth century B.C., as Kerenyi points out, "the Greeks saw in Zeus the god of their history"; 84 and in this respect, "Greek religion was primarily Zeus religion". 85 In one very restricted sense, this property of Zeus parallels the property of the god of the Israelites. But the dominance of Zeus in Greek history is always within a polytheism, and in this respect, there is , of course, no parallel in the religious tradition of the Israelites.

In the Athenian festival of Hecatombaion, which took place in the first month of the Attic year, "the magistrates and council" members, who were completing offices held in the past year, appealed "to the gods for the protection of Athens in the coming year". 86 The various roles of various gods in a polytheistic culture, such as the Greeks, were consolidated into a single divine sovereignty in a monalatry or a monotheism, such as the religious tradition of the Israelites may be classified. A monalatry is a type of religion which worships one deity, but acknowledges the existence of other deities of other people. The Old Testament, as will be pointed out in a later discussion, refers many times to the gods of other people, who were neighbors of the Israelites, but it always maintains that the one god, which is supreme over other gods, is their god. A commonly made interpretation of the Old Testament regards this theological concept as "monotheism". And from the point of view of the faithful among the Israelites, their god was the only divine ultimate being, and the gods in which other people believed were delusions, expressions of their ignorance.

Chapter Three

GODS IDENTIFIED BY PROPERTIES

1. The properties of a reality regarded as a deity constitute its religious significance, and not the name by which it is denoted

The set of properties designated by a name is the significant reality of which account should be taken in a comparative study of religions, since such a set of properties is the sign-function of a name. Whereas a name is a peculiarity of a particular language, the properties with which a reality is interpreted often are not so restricted, and may have universality of application. It is the universality of such properties, therefore, which makes a comparison of religions possible.

Properties which constitute an interpretation of a reality--such as a deity, which is the object of a people's worship--are the ideational content of religious interpretations of what are regarded divine realities. Even "the most primitive religion", as Kerenyi argues, "has an intellectual content",[1] which constitutes the meaning that is associated with whatever is believed to be the reality to which worship is directed. One type of ideas which are included in corporate worship, as he points out, is an account of "the divine inauguration of the cult itself".[2] Such accounts, for example are included in the Old Testament's explanation for the divine sanction of the name by which a patriarch is to be revered, as well as the name of a divinely chosen people, such as the Israelites.

Every religious cult-activity among the Greeks includes "mythical tales", which account for the institution of the cult, and such accounts are the "ideas" which specify the procedures of the cult itself. As Kerenyi also explains, "cult procedures", which "are accompanied by a festive quality", as among the Greeks, are defined "by a system of powerful ideas".[3] What is meant by this feature of ideas is their persisting effectiveness in a religious tradition. Generations of a people my well suceed each other, and yet, the cultic explanation itself persists. The scriptural account, for instance, of the Passover has persisted for centuries, and the explanation for its origin is the religious significance which accompanies its celebration. It is such ideas which are understandable to others who are not internal to a cult or a religion, and such intelligibility of practices which are included in religions is the basis for a comparative study in which parallels are acknowledged as empirical evidence for a universality of religion as a human phenomenon, even though features of particular religions are unique to a particular culture. Such properties include a human awareness of its helplessness in some circumstances in life, and a belief that there is a source of help to which human beings in their need can turn, which can do for them what they could not do for themsleves apart from such help, is made available by means of their religious practices.

The complex set of beliefs about the nature of whatever realities are trusted by a people for such help, constitute the idea-content of a religion. As Hocking points out, "ideas are what a people in their religious practice think with, not what (they) think of".4 What, therefore, is of primary importance in any understanding of a religion and its practices is understanding what a people, who includes such practices in their religion, believe about the reality to which they are directed, as well as what they believe about the effectiveness of such practices to achieve what they seek in relation to the reality which they believe is capable of providing them with the benefits which they seek through their religious orientation to it.

A reality to which a religion is directed is in some way denoted, such as by a name, which is always unique to the culture in which a religion is included. But what is important in any comparative study of religions in what is thought about such a reality. What is so thought, constitutes the properties which are believed to be the nature of the reality to which such a religion is oriented. Herodotus, for instance, was aware of this fundamental condition for a comparative study of religions when he points out that "Amum is the Egyptian name for Zeus".5 In other words, the realities denoted by these two names were regarded by two cultures as having properties which are similar. If Herodotus had not acknowledged their similarites in the denoted realities, the parallelism he points out would be meaningless. He points out another parallelism of the gods of two civilizations when he maintains that the deity named "Horus" by the Egyptians was the son of Osiris, and their "Osiris is, in the Greek language, Dionysus".6

The parallelism which Herodotus acknowledged thus indicates his understanding of the ethnological importance, not primarily of names of realities which are worshiped by peoples, but rather the properties of such worshiped realities. Such properties are the nature of the realities thus worshiped; and what is believed about them are people's ideas which are basic to their religious practices.

There obviously is no similarity of names of realities which are worshiped in various cultures, but there is, nevertheless, a similarity of the properties with which such realities are interpreted. If it were not for this parallelism of interpretations of properties of realities to which religions are oriented, there would be no justification for the general classification "religion" for practices which were peculiar to particular cultures. What are not equally unique to different cultures are the generic interpretations of an order other than their own resources, and which is accessible to them on conditions which they respect in the practices that constitute their own religion.

What, for example, the Greeks thought about Aphrodite, goddess of love, parallels what other civilizations thought about a comparable deity, denoted by various names, such as "Ishtar", "Astaroth", or "Astarte". In this instance alone, it is evident that the mere linguistic device for denoting a deity is not of fundamental importance. Rather, the properties which constitute the designative meaning of a reality are what is of basic significance for a study of a parallelism of religions.

"The historian", as Kerenyi declares, "must never cease to ask what the transmmitted names of the gods meant in any specific epoch".7 When the properties of such realities are understood, then it is possible to appreciate the underlying religious intention of practices, even though they include features which are unique to a culture. Their uniqueness to a culture, however, is not a handicap in a comparative study, when it is recognized as a peculiarity of a particular religion, features of which are not equally unique to it.

2. Names for denoting gods have a history, as well as the people who believe in their reality as a source of dependable help

Herodotus affirms a basic principle for a study of a history of religions when he maintains that "wellnigh all the names of the gods came to Hellas from Egypt". There were some exceptions, as he acknowledges, such as "Poseidon", the source of which name, as he believed, was the Libyians, who had "the name of Poseidon from the first",[8] which, therefore, was, at least for a time, unique to them.

A denotative linguistic device which likewise was unique to the Israelites' religious tradition is the tetragrammaton "YHWH", of which there are several variations of four consonants, transliterated from the Hebrew. What again is significant in a study of comparative religions is how this linguistic formation was regarded in the religious tradition of the Israelites. From their point of view, this tetragrammaton should be incapable of pronunciation as any other regular name, since any linguistic identification of a divine reality would, according to their belief, disclose its nature. They believed that a Supreme Being, which was transcendent of all that it had created, should be regarded with utmost reverence, and presuming to call it by a name, would be a sacrilege, thereby treating it as capable of being known by means of its name.

This early sense of awesome regard for the holiness of their god, as was acknowledged by the unpronouncable four consonants, deteriorated in the centuries when the awesome aspect of Divine Being was no longer as integral to their religion as it had been in previous centuries, when the Israelites were aware of their total dependence upon the ultimate reality, their Creator, for every condition making their survival possible, as well as the preservation of their religious tradition, as the distinguishing feature of one people's relation to divine reality.

In a sense, an attempt to pronounce a name by substituting terms such as Jahweh, Jahveh, Jahvah, Jahve, for the unpronouncable tetragrammaton, was more than a linguistic alteration in a religious tradition.[9] It was rather a change in their sense of the awesome nature of the reality which once believed ought not to be named, since such a presumed attempt was, from this earlier religious orientation, blasphemous. Something, therefore, of the very holiness and sacredness of the reality worshiped by the later Israelites was sacrificed by the nonreligious desire to pronounce a linguistic denotation for their deity. This later, and actually perverse version of a former religious awe, is made evident by the profound account in Exodus (3:13-15), according to which Moses addressed himself to the god of "their forefathers", saying that if "they ask me his name, what shall I say?" The priestly authors of Exodus showed that they were aware of what was involved in such a demand of a people for the name of their god; and they showed their sound understanding when they declared, as they wrote this scriptural account, that "God answered, 'I AM'". The god thus instructed Moses, the leader of his people, to tell them that their god is what their god is, and not what they, in their human limitations, may think he is, since such limited understanding would then become the denotative significance of the names, or its sign-function for denoting the divine reality. For these priestly Israelites, who were the authors of Exodus, this was also a precaution against reducing a religiously critical linguistic device to the level of magic, since a knowledge of a reality which has power to do what a people wants to have done, is a control over such a reality, because, according to an ancient belief, knowing its name, is knowing its essential nature. Hence the wisdom expressed by the priestly authors of Exodus includes their understanding of the primitive motivation among some people, under the gloss of religion, to practice what amounts to magic.

The later revisions of the earliest texts of Scripture inserted the addition, "and God said further, you must tell the Israelites this that it is Jehovah". This obviously is a concession to the curiosity of those who were unaware of the profoundity of understanding of the earlier priestly authors, both of the nature of the divine Ultimate Reality, and also of the nature of some people, who, without a capacity for an awesome sense of a sacred reality, want primarily to talk about it, and thereby reduce its sacred nature to a level commensurate with their own low level of religious life.

The wisdom of the earliest priestly authors of this book in the Pentateuch, in declaring that "God is what God is", and not what people think God is, is the same wisdom which Aristotle expresses in maintaining that "A reality is what it is", by which he means that its nature does not adapt itself to what people think it is.

Even if it is the case that "Yahweh...is an archaic form of the verb 'to be'"10, its pronouncability is the very aspect of the word which the tetragrammaton was originally intended to prevent, and which the profoundly sensible earlier priests of the Israelites wanted to avoid. Thus what may appear to some people as a mere linguistic detail, may actually, have had a religious significance which was lost in later centuries by its substitution. This loss would, however, have been prevented by another tautologous expression, such as "The Lord is God". This expression is as repetitious as the expression, "I am that I am".

Whatever deviation there is from such tautologous expressions losses sight of the earliest use of such expressions in the religious tradition of the Israelites. Neither "Yahweh", and its various spellings, or "Jehovah", and its various spellings, are in any way equivalent to the unpronouncable tetragrammaton, or even the unnamed "I AM".

Using the expression, "The Lord", in translating Yahwistic terminology (such as is used in the Davidic group of Psalms 1-41), as well as the Elohistic terminology (such as is used in the second Davidic group in Psalms 42-83), is a way of preserving some of the original intention of the earliest priestly authors of Exodus.

Later priestly traditions maintain that the god worshiped by the Israelites was revealed to the Patriarchs as El-Shaddai. The priestly authors of Genesis 17:1, for example, identify the god whom Abram worshiped as El Shaddai, declaring: "When Abram was ninety-nine years old", the god whom he served "appeared to him and said, 'I am El Shaddai'". This name, which probably means "Mountain God",11 was rarely used in Scripture other than in the Pentateuch (except in Job). It is thus characteristic as a designation for the god worshiped by the Israelites in the patriarchal period, and preserved in the priestly tradition. The preference for this appellation "El Shaddai" in the priestly account of the patriarchal succession is indicated in Exodus 5:3, when the god of the Israelites appeared as "El Shaddai" to "Abraham, Isaac, and Jacob".

Various terms are acknowledged in the Old Testament for

the gods which were worshiped by other people, but whose properties paralleled properties of the god worshiped by the Israelites. The term "Bel", for example, denotes a Western Semitic deity, also referred to as "lord". "Bel" was a general title for many Babylonian gods, but was later restricted to Marduk, as "the Lord".

What is ethnologically significant, as has been argued, is not the names of deities, but their properties. "The Father of Men" for the Canaanites, for instance, was denoted "El", and it is significant that a cultural contact of the Israelites with the Canaanites is indicated in Genesis, when after the patriarch Jacob "arrived safely at the town of Shechem in Canaanite territory...he erected an altar which he called 'El, God of Israel'", according to the translation in The Jerusalem Bible, or "El-Elophey-Irael", according to the translation in The New English Bible.

A parallel property of El was identified as "Bel" in the oldest of Babylonian inscriptions. A property which constitutes the basic meaning of "Bel" or "Baal" is "King of gods", referred to in the Ras Shamra texts as "Thou who Mountest the Clouds", which is a property of both Zeus of the Greeks and of the god of the Israelites. The same texts refer to Baal, "Thou shalt subdue thine adversaries",12 which is repeatedly attributed in the Old Testament to the guardian god of the Israelities, who accompanied them in thier military campaigns, and on whom they depended for victory.

In concluding this section, it may be said that an ethnological principle which might well introduce all studies in comparative religions is stated in Cleanthes' great Hymn to Zeus: "O God most glorious, called by many a name." When the meanings of these many names are comparable, the religious signification of the name is understood; and the various terms for denoting deities so interpreted are of incidental importance in an ethnological study of religions.

3. Reverence for a name which denotes a deity is one type of religious experience

Prohibitions against speaking the name of a god were integral to the cultures of both the ancient Greeks and Israelites, as well as integral to the cultures of their neighbors. Herodotus, in giving accounts of the religions of various peoples, acknowledges that he is not permitted to utter the names of their gods.

Kerenyi points out that "scruples against uttering the real name" of a deity "were no less powerful in early times than in late" in the history of Greek religions. The principal goddess of Lykosoura, for example, was "referred to only as the 'Mistress'".13 The comment of Pausanias, in later centuries, when he recorded the beliefs and practices of the Greeks, acknowledges that "The true name of the Mistress I fear to communicate to the uninitiated".14 The fear which Pausanias, as a reporter of religious beliefs, experienced was obviously not the same mode of fear as was experienced by people who were internal to a religion whose sense of the awesome majesty of their deity was basic to their reason for not articulating its name. Parke points out that the "names of Demeter and Persephone" were regarded by all who had respect for the Eleusinian Mysteries as "too sacred to utter," and therefore, they referring to them. The Greeks also "feared to name Pluto", and instead, mentioned him by one of several descriptive titles, such as "Host of Many".15

This sense of the awesome character of the names of divine realities extended even to artefacts which were associated with the worship of such realities, to whom temple services were dedicated. Parke also points out that a frequent reference occurs in Athenian inscriptions, as well as in ancient dictionaries, "to carry the unspoken things (arrephorein)". The young women, chosen from aristocratic families to conduct religious rites in honour of Athena Polias, guardian of Athens, lived in a residence near her temple on the Acropolis. Their role in her worship was indicated by the expression to which they were referred: "The Carriers of the Unspoken Things".16

Identifying a name with a reality denoted by it, was, as has been mentioned in the preceding discussion, a feature of ancient religions. And it may also be pointed out that Plato seriously discusses this aspect of language, in which a name is regarded as disclosing the nature of a reality denoted by it, when in the Cratylus, Socrates maintains "that speech which says things as they are is true".17 In this case, this way of regarding language, especially for denoting a sacred reality, is not by any means confined to so-called "primitive" mentality, and it likewise is not regarded seriously only in a practice of magic. Whereas a

72

sophisticated attitude toward language regards the equating of a sign for the signified, and a denoting name for a denoted reality, as a "linguistic fallacy", classified as "metonymy", the awesome hesitancy or fear to name a god, or to denote even anything associated in its worship, was certainly not considered to be a misunderstanding of the nature of language.

Ancient religions, which identified language for denoting a deity as equivalent to the deity, believed that whatever was done with such language was also done to the god. When, for example, the Egyptians rejected the imposed worship of Amon-Re, they not only suppressed the priesthood which was dedicated to the worship of this deity, but they also effaced the "name of Amun wherever it appeared", and the reason for doing so, as has been mentioned, is that they regarded "the name itself as possessing the very essence of the one bearing it". The destruction of the name of this god, in other words, was regarded by the Egyptians as a way of "wiping out the god's existence".18 And the identification, by the Egyptians, of the name for a god with the reality of the god, was evident in the widespread reform initiated in order to change a religious system or entire temple organization. The name "Amum" was removed from the royal titulary, and the ruler who instituted this reform changed his own name from Amenhotep to Akenaten, and did so to declare his fidelity to the god whose worship he endeavored to establish as an imposed obligation upon his people. Even the evidence for the deity which he sought to displace, such as his statues and names in the capital of Thebes, became offensive as sacrilege to the young ruler, and he thereupon moved his capital from Thebes to Tell el-Amarna.

In light of the fact that Egyptian civilization was certainly one of the most extraordinary on the entire earth, it is highly instructive to take account of the Egyptian attitude toward language and its function in religion, when it was presumed that the name for denoting a god was equivalent in meaning to the properties constitutive of the nature of the god. It would, therefore, be indefensible to regard the awesome attitude expressed by the ancient Israelites as either primitive or superstitious. The most advanced of contemporaneous civilizations identified the connotation of a term as equivalent with the properties of a reality identified by the term, and regarded the name for a reality as sacred as the reality itself which was denoted by the name.

Although speaking a holy name was forbidden to human beings in ancient cultures, since they were of an order below the status of gods, one deity was believed to be permitted to articulate the name of another, such as was the privilege accorded to Anshar in the Babylonian pantheon, by virtue of his nature as "father of gods", and thus as a senior of Marduk, who was confirmed by the many gods of the pantheon as "overlord of the gods of heaven and earth". The Epic of Creation includes a reference to Anshar, extoling Marduk for his merits, and "proclaim(ing) his name 'Asalluhi'". So holy was this real name of Marduk that, according to the Epic, "upon the opening of his mouth be all other gods silent".19

From a point of view dominant in both the Babylonian and Egyptian civilizations, with which the Israelites had cultural contacts, it can obviously not be maintained that their attitude toward the name of their god was an expression of an aspect of their culture which was peculiar to them. It was, as has been argued, neither peculiar to them nor to the ancient Greeks. It was rather an interpretation of the presumed nature of the noetic, or knowledge aspect, of language, which was regarded as its informative function in relation to nonlinguistic realities. Only when language was regarded as purely conventional, as in critical philosophies, such as Cynicism, was its noetic function rejected. And with this change of interpretation of language, the last vestige of religious awe for language denoting gods met the same fate as the religious belief itself in gods.

4. The religious significance of the term "god" differs radically from its significance in speculative philosophies.

The religious meaning of a general theistic term, such as the Greek "theos", is included in its use for referring to a reality which is acknowledged as having supreme importance for human life, such that its role in the world is revered as indispensable for sustaining human life, as well as for making its well-being possible. A connotation of such a theistic term which is not so defined is excluded from the religious aspect of human life, but may, nevertheless, have importance for individuals who reflect about a reality to which they refer with theistic terminology. Such a use of this terminology, however, is not basically religious, even though some existentialists maintain that a speculative activity which has unconditioned importance in a person's life may be regarded as a religious experience.

No purely speculative thought about a reality which is referred to with a theistic terminology is, as such, an acknowledgment of a total dependence upon such a reality. The centrality of such a reality in speculative effort is a philosophical interest; and although a philosophy about reality is included in the religious life of people who are capable of reflecting for purely nonpractical purposes, their philosophical reflecting about reality is very different from a religious acknowledgment of their total dependence upon it. Speculative activity is essential to the well-being of some people, but such well-being comes within the scope of morality, rather than of religion. That is, it is an indispensable good in their lives which is within their own control, such as Stoic philosophers point out. Although it is essential to the quality of life which some require for what they regard as a justification itself for living, it is very different from the type of thinking which acknowledges the relation of human life, in its need, to a reality which is revered for its presumed capacity to fulfil such a need, as no other realities are capable of doing.

A purely speculative use of a theistic terminology does not include a grammatical vocative, which is addressing a theistic reality, such as is affirmed in the well-known expression in religions, "O Lord", or "Domine," as a title expressing reverence for the reality so addressed. A Semitic vocative for the deity Adonis is "Adoni", which is equivalent in meaning to "My Lord".[20] This address had religious significance among the Phoenicians, with whom the Israelites had cultural contacts. Since the Phoenician Adonis is in every essential respect the Babylonian Tammuz, who, in turn, is the Sumerian Dumuzi, it is understandable that even Abraham was acquainted with this religious address when he lived in Chaldea. And since the worship of Dumuzi as Tammuz and also as Adonis extended throughout northern Semitic peoples, the cultural contacts of the Israelites with a worship of this deity persisted throughout the centuries following Abraham's search for a new homeland for his descendants.

The grammatical vocative for addressing a reality which is revered as a god presupposes an interpretation of it in anthropomorphic imagery, as being capable of hearing an address, as well as prayers which appeal for mercy and for help. There are no such appeals or prayers in any purely speculative use of theistic terminology. Such appeals as are made in prayers that are addressed to realities which are revered as divine, and are worshiped as gods, were universal in the entire area in which the Israelites lived throughout their long history. The Babylonian king, for example, addressed Shamash, the god worshiped in Assyrian and Babylonian religions as the ultimate source of order in the world and of moral order or righteousness in human life, appealing to this god for fullness of life for himself and "for Belshazzar", to whom he refers as "my first born". The prayer that his son's "days be long" and that "in his heart (there may be) reverence for thy high divinity",[21] is integral to a religion which is oriented to a divine reality that is regarded as the ultimate source for what is cherished as the supreme blessings in human life. Such an essentially religious address to a god in prayer is foreign to any strictly philosophical or speculative thinking about the nature of a reality entitled "god" in such reflecting.

No Greek philosophies, as will be mentioned in the following analysis, include anything which is even remotely related to the language that is characteristic of the Greek religious festival on the seventh day of Boedromion, which was dedicated to Apollo, as an expression of gratitude for his role in helping the Greeks in their warfare. Since this month in the Attic calendar is September, it marked "the close of the campaigning season", including whatever successes the Greeks had, for which they acknowledged their indebtness to their god. The name itself of the month indicates this religious significance, since it is derived from the Greek term, "Boedromios", which is translated "to run to help in response to a shout".[22] The god Apollo was so trusted by those who celebrated this festival as a religious act. He was trusted for his response to the appeals for help, which they regarded as indispensable in defending them in relation to their foes.

Kerenyi affirms a profoundly important fact about the Greek use of the general term "theos" when he points out that "in the whole Greek language, so far as it is not spoken by Jews or Christians, theos has no vocative", and the reason is evident, since Greek culture, from its earliest centuries, includes philosophies in which theistic terminology is used.

76

Even identifying "Zeus" with "theos", or the reverse, is not necessarily of religious significance, unless the properties of Zeus are specified as integral to his worship as a deity for its essential role in the life of those who orient themselves to him, acknowledging their final dependence upon him for whatever they acknowledge that they cannot secure from any other source.

The sixth century B.C. Greek philosopher, Xenophanes, for example, uses theistic terminology in his speculating about the nature of reality, and although such terminology is also integral to Greek religions, the reflecting of Xenophanes cannot be regarded as religious in any sense, such as is expressed in the many Greek festivals which are dedicated to their gods. Everyone of these celebrations in the Greek calendar was, at least at some time, religiously important for the Greeks, even when the celebrations in later times continued without any particular religious significance, such as Christmas and Easter continue in contemporary cultures, when such celebrations have little more than nominal religious significance for many people.

In reflecting about reality as one, and not as plural, such as the Greek gods, Xenophanes objectifies this numerical term as One, meaning by this the totality of all that exists. He thereupon analyzes properties of the One which are logically consistent with a numerical property of unity. For purely logical or linguistic reasons, therefore, the One is exclusive of essential plurality, and as One, it is incapable of internal differentiation, such as would be the nature of movement. As one, there would, in purely spatial imagery, be no place in which it could move! And in comparable temporal terminology, it would be free from alteration, such as is possible only in a temporal sequence. As free from such sequence, it is eternal; and, in this respect, is characterized by a property which religious reflecting attributes to <u>theos</u>.

But the logical meaning of "eternal", as nontemporal, is implied in a strict definition of "one", as free from internal differentiation. Hence, although the terminology of "one" and "eternal" are also used in referring to a deity (<u>theos</u>) which is worshiped, and thus is addressed in appeals for mercy and help, there is no such religious meaning in the speculative "One" of the sixth century B.C. Eleatic Greek philosophers, Xenophanes, Parmenides, and Zeno.

Aristotle declares that "Xenophanes first taught the unity" of all that is ordinarily regarded as "many". This proposal for grouping multiplicity in a category of unity becomes the premise of his philosophy. This is purely a linguistic procedure, on the basis of out what logically is implied in this premise. This, of course, is a standard metaphysical procedure. A metaphysical premise is affirmed, and an entire philosophy is derived from reflecting on its logical

implications. Such reflecting, therefore, does not refer to an ultimate reality, such as religious rites or religious appeals do. It is confined rather to linguistic meanings of the basic terms in the premise, account of reality other than what is initially affirmed.

No behavior obviously would qualify as a religious act with such a restriction. Religious life, rather than purely reflective activity, is oriented to a reality,

which as single or as one, would be revered as "the One". And as being the one source to which appeal for help is directed, it is revered as "ultimate", or as "the ultimate One". Since it is regarded as available

so regarded, it is revered as "eternal", in distinction to the world of temporal order in which human struggling occurs, and in which human beings are

confronted with unpredictable vicissitudes. Such an interpretation is basic to religious life, whether in corporate rituals or in the appeals made by individuals in the solitude of their devoted praying.

Since, for purely linguistic reasons, the one reality is the "Universe", there is no reality other than it. Xenophanes and Parmenides, therefore, limit their reflecting to this linguistic equation, and their philosophies are simply logical derivations of the meaning assigned to the numerical terminology of one, hence of universal".

As One, it cannot become other than what its unitary nature is. Hence, as fragment 26, attributed to Xenophanes, maintains: "It always abides." This could be replaced by a terminology of "eternal" or "changeless", such as is common in religious discourse. But the meaning of "changeless" in religious discourse is totally different from its meaning in Eleatic metaphysic, which can be reduced to the proposition: "What is, is"; and as such, is not anything other than what it is. Parmenides declares: "'What is' cannot also be 'What is not'". This is purely redundant, and is merely another logically admissible way of reaffirming the one basic Eleatic premise that there is reality, which as "Reality", is not "realities"; and as "one reality" is "One"; and as such is, and always is, what it is. That is, it is eternal. But the meaning of this "eternal", which is implied for purely linguistic reasons, is far from the religious meaning that the one ultimate source of divine help is always or eternally dependable, and therefore, is justifiably trusted by those who turn to it with a reverent confidence in its unfailing nature, because as "changeless", it always provides help to those in need, who turn to it, trusting it as they trust no other comparable source of help.

Xenophanes disregards both the linguistic meaning of "one", which is basic to his premise, and also basic to his logic, when he predicates anthropomorphic traits to the One, declaring: "The Whole sees; the Whole perceives; the Whole hears."[23] The properties of "seeing", "perceiving", and "hearing" are predicated to gods in religions of anthropomorphically interpreted gods, to which religious orientations are directed; but such religious ways of acting are not directed to what the speculative Eleatics refer to as "the Whole" or "the One". A religious orientation, whether addressing a god in prayer or in making an appeal in a ritualistic sacrifice, is to a reality that is distinguished from all other realities. There is, however, no such distinction or differentiation admissible in logically consistent Eleatic reflecting.

In considering only the premise of Parmenides, as interpreted by Aristotle, the basic Eleatic philosophy is oriented to reflecting on what may logically be affirmed after the premise is affirmed: "Being is one and...there is nothing else."[24] Aristotle sums up the entire philosophical meaning of the Eleatic philosophers when he maintains that they affirm the "opinion about the universe that it is one in its essential nature".[25]

Although Parmenides declares in "The Way of Truth" that "Destiny has bound it so that it is whole and motionless",[26] it is evident that Destiny need not be cited for this property, but only philosophical analysis, which is logically consistent with a linguistically unambiguous initial premise, on which subsequent reflecting points out what is implied in its grammatically assigned usage.

What becomes a source of possible confusion in this Eleatic philosophy is Aristotle's comment about Parmenides, when he says that Parmenides "gazing at the whole heaven,...said, 'the One is God'".27 In saying this, Parmenides, of course, follows conventionally established meaning of the term "god", which is a reality that is (i) one (ii) always one, and as such is eternal; and (iii) as an eternal, is changeless, which, for a religious faith, is an assurance of absolute trustworthiness of dependability. But, as has been argued in the preceding, this philosophical analysis proposes an interpretation of an ultimate and eternal reality which could not be appealed to as one reality which is separable from less dependable realitites, and could not initiate a change in events in the world in responding to the appeals of religious human beings, who direct their worship, with its prayers, to such a reality, having as they believe, properties which neither they nor any other reality on the entire earth has.

Very much of the above analysis of Eleatic speculation can also be said of the speculative character of Aristotle's own metaphysic, which also contains theistic terminology of "god". What Aristotle regards as "First philosophy", was later termed "Metaphysics", in which he maintains that there both is an eternal reality, and also temporal realities other than it, whose nature as changing, is eternally assured by the eternal Unmoved Mover, to which he refers as "God". But the theistic term which he so assigns to this reality has little similarity to a religious belief about deity in the practices of prayer and ritual, so that it can be said to be without religious meaning. If, however, account is taken, as Aquinas does, only of the terminology used by Aristotle, which is also used in religious discourse, then the purely speculative significance of Aristotle's metaphysic is disregarded.

Aristotle identified the one changeless, and therefore, eternal reality as Pure Actuality. As such, it is incapable, by its nature, of becoming. That is, it is eternally the same, such as is predicated by Artistotle of God, as well as in the metaphysics of the Eleatics, which also appropriated the terminology of religious use, but for a purely speculative purpose. The eternal or changeless nature of God, according to the metaphysic of Aristotle, follows logically from his definition of "Pure Actuality", which is devoid of "matter", or potentiality for becoming. That is, it is incapable of becoming other than what it is. As so incapable, it is changeless, although its pure actuality or pure form is the telos or goal of every other reality, which, as other than pure form, includes a factor of potentiality to become another stage in its process of actualizing its possiblilities, which are its so-called "matter". Such "matter" is the principle of its identity as an individual, which is distinguishable, therefore, from other individuals that may have the same formal nature, but whose material nature is unique to each natural body. Since it is the nature of every individual with a material ingredient to become actualized, the possibility for this process of actualizing cannot terminate, and the condition for its ceaseless or eternal nature is the eternal Pure Actuality of God. In other words, God the Unmoved Mover, is the ideal of the complete actualization of the immanent form in each individual. The norm of complete actuality is pure form, and thus the nature of what Aristotle speculatively defines as God, is Pure Form. It is the telos to which the entire world moves. As its ideal goal or objective, God, as it were, attracts every reality other than itself to actualize its potentialities.

This is a profound basis for a normative morality, and also it could well be regarded as the most intellectually, and even spiritually, impressive version of normative human endeavor, but it has no similarity to any ritualistic form of religious behaviors which are oriented to divine realities as means to establish favorable relations of human beings with such realities. Aristotle's metaphysic has no spiritual equal as a profound moral challenge to actualize one's own possibilities for well-being, which is living to the utmost of one's rational capacities. But such a moral challenge would impose upon a person the obligation to aspire to the unrealizable ideal of God as the normative telos. And furthermore, such a devotion of one's life, primarily to his own nature, obviously has nothing in common with the corporate religious practices of either the Israelites or the Greeks. The role of God in such a moral enterprize of self-actualization is an ideal, and certainly a challenge, but as unrealizable for any natural body, does not fulfil a basic feature of a genuine moral ideal, which is its realizability, notwithstsanding its stern conditions.

The spiritual challenge of such a version of God, as

Aristotle formulates, would be capable of appealing only to the relatively few, who, retiring from the ordinary struggles of human life, could devote themselves to a contemplative life, in which their essential nature, as reasonable, would transform every other aspect of their nature. This ideal of such a moral objective would then be pure intellectual actuality, such as is only momentarily realizable in the purest form of rational reflecting, as Aristotle himself acknowledges.

Aristotle's most extended analysis of what he identifies as God is in the seventh and eighth books of his Physics, rather than in his First Principles of Metaphysics. The nature of God he so interprets is the condition for motion in the world which is included within its outermost "sphere" of the eternal nature of God, the Unmoved Mover. As pure form, such a speculative concept of God, is the formal ideal of "enmattered form". Actualizing such potentiality is the identity of every reality other than God.[28]

Aristotle's analysis in De Caelo is another speculative philosophy in which theistic terminology of "God" is used, and it is in this document that the term "Unmoved mover" is a primary concept of the Pure Actuality of God. Since no reality in the total universe has the same nature as God, the Unmoved Mover, it is in this sense alone that Aristotle's concept of God has a property in common with the properties with which genuine religions interpret their divine realities with a theistic terminology. But realities so interpreted are regarded as moved to compassion for them to help them in response to their appeals, either in rituals or in prayers, and there is no such movement of God toward human appeals as Aristotle interprets the ultimate reality which he refers to as "God".

Even though the Unmoved Mover is other than every other reality, and in this sense, is "transcendent" of the physical world, Aristotle's version of its transcendent nature is essentially different from such transcendence as the property of the theistic reality to which religions are oriented in ritualistic sacrfices and in prayers which appeal for divine help. As Professor Randall soundly maintains, the Unmoved Mover which Aristotle identifies with God is a "logical explanation",[29] and is without any meaning which constitutes the connotation of "god" in religions which are oriented to a reality that is revered as other than the unpredicatable order of circumstances which confront human beings with problems from which they turn with a trust that the divine reality can do for them what they, and all other available resources, cannot do.

When Aristotle introduces in <u>De Caeloa</u> spatial imagery of God, the Unmoved Mover, as "the uppermost" or as the "circumference" of the cosmos, his metaphysic resorts to an imagery in common with mythology, in which gods are identified with localities or places. As Professor Randall again soundly points out, this metaphorical or "mythological" imagery and terminology, which is included in Book Lambda of <u>First Principles</u>, "has no real place in Aristotle's metaphysics",<u>30</u> and it may well be that it was included in <u>First Principles</u> by Alexander of Aphrodisias in the third century A.D., when Neoplatonism was dominant. If, however, it is not so interpreted, but is regarded as genuine Aristotlelianism, it would be most instructive as indicating how easily it is even for the most enlightened terminology about God's nature to pass into a version which is impaired by spatial imagery, that thereby reduces the spiritual character of a divine reality, which in all respects and properties, is unlike temporally and spatially limited realities.

5. <u>The meanings of names for divine and semi-divine realities in polytheistic cultures are fluid, such as they are not for the god of the Israelites</u>

The properties of the Babylonian deity Bel, god of the earth, who, according to the oldest inscriptions, was revered as the principal god, were transferred to Marduk when Babylon became politically dominant. Such politically conditioned meanings of deities is a feature primarily of religions in which many realities are regarded as divine or even as semi-divine. And this is a marked feature of the religions of the Greeks, but not of the more unified religious tradition of the Israelites, as this is interpreted in the Old Testament.

Although various names of the guardian god of the Israelites are used in the priestly versions of the Old Testament, their meanings are, nevertheless, relatively consistent. The same type of consistency of meanings is not, however, a property of the polytheistic religions of the Greeks. The term "pallas", for instance, associated with Athena, has a fluidity of meanings, which are so extreme that they may be construed as denoting either a masculine or a feminine nature of deity.31

The Orphic version of Zeus as "the breath of all things"32 explains why a customary identification of "male" was not attributed by the Orphics to Zeus, who regarded the nature of Zeus as both male and also as female, but not as one, exclusive of the other. Since the universality of this deity in all living beings was regarded as the deity's primary property, a customary identification of it as having one property, which is exclusive of its complementary property, would not be consistent with the initial predication of the deity's universal manifestation in all living beings.

A comparable fluidity of properties is characteristic in Greek paintings of realities which are less in divine nature than gods, such as the Sirens. Such fluidity of properties is also a characteristic of deities, properties of which at one time are associated with one deity, and at another time are transferred to other deities. The property of being remote from human beings, as well as from other gods, which was regarded as a trait of Hekate, "the Distant One", was also attributed to Apollo as "Hekatos", and to Artemis as "Hekate".33

No deities when anthropomorphically interpreted have only one property, but often have as many properties as human beings have, which are as fluid as their complex personalities.

6. **Properties of deities are their identities, which differ from images of them**

A symbol of considerable antiquity in Greek culture is the aegis, which Homer identifies as an accouterment of Zeus, and describes as "shaggy" and as having "golden tassels". If Zeus were to have been the only deity in Greek religious traditions so identified, it would have been as unambiguous an identification as was his name. But since it later also became associated with Athena, appearing as a breastplate ornament on statues which portray her, she could likewise have been referred to as "aegis bearing". Such an epithet could then have been ambiguous, since it would have had at least a twofold application in Greek culture for denoting deities. By virtue of its twofold denoting function in the Greek pantheon, its referent would have been uncertain if referred to as "aegis bearing". In so far, on the other hand, as a Gorgon's head had been included on his breastplate, very likely as an apotropaic device for averting harm or evil, and the same type of gorgoneion was included in the ornaments Athena also wore, then it would have been sufficient to distinguish Zeus and Athena, even though both were "aegis bearing". In other words, only if a symbolic identification is as unique in being associated with a reality as the individuality of the reality itself, would it be an unambiguous identifying sign for such a reality, as for a deity.

A dove, for example, was associated by the Greeks with Aphrodite, since both her property and also the property of the dove, were symbolic of fertility. But the dove was also a symbol of fertility for other goddesses in other cultures, who likewise were characterized with the properties of Aphrodite, such as Astarte, Ishtar, or Ashtarath. Thus the property of fertility among human beings, as a consequence of the love-inducing capacities of these several goddesses, is a property which they have in common. And since they also are associated with a dove, their general nature as fertility agencies could be recognized by this would then be indicated by the name by which each of these goddesses of love and fertility was identified in several civilizations. But the dove as symbolic of the gentle aspect of love, and also of its goddess, would be inappropriate for goddesses of love in ancient civilizations which were also goddesses of warfare. Although Aphrodite was not identified with such a role among the Greeks, she, nevertheless, was regarded by them as closely related to Ares, by virtue of the properties which she had in common with him.

The jealousy with which the Greeks characterized Hera, by virtue of her relation to the promiscuous nature of Zeus, would qualify her vindictive anger as a property to be identified with the Mesopotamian goddesses of war, whose ambivalent natures were also acknowledged in the civilizations which identified them with goddess of love and war.

The essential need of ancient peoples to have adequate food, and also adequate resources for military purposes, accounts for the preoccupation in such civilizations with fertility in vegetation, in cattle, and in human beings. A common symbol for the fertility of crops was a sheaf of wheat or a single head of grain; which was associated with various fertility deities, such as Demeter and also Kronos, who originally was worshiped as "a god of the grain harvest". The Kronia festival, on the 12th of the first month of the Attic year, the Hecatombaion, was dedicated to Kronos by virtue of his fertility role as a condition for the harvest of grain. The fourth Attic month, Pyanepsion, was introduced with a festival that was dedicated to Demeter, the name of which was "Proerosia".34 It also was oriented to acknowledging appeals for her fertility role, by means of which people live and also are brought into being.

Since the reaping hook was commonly associated with Kronos, but not with Demeter or with other deities who also shared his fertility property, it was a sufficient device for his unambigous identification, such as a sheaf of grain would not have been.

Although Dionysus was worshiped in every imaginable orgiastic manner, and as a consequence, also had fertility powers associated with his nature, his identification by the epithet "Eleuthereus"--derived from a small community between Athens and Boeotia35 --would have been an unequivocal identification for him, even though he shared the fertility role with other deities in Greek religions, had it not been that Zeus also was so referred to, but not for the same reason of his origin. It was rather for the meaning of the name as "The Deliverer".

Since there was only one deity worshiped by the Israelites as the ultimate source of every good essential to the life of his people, it is obvious that there was no special symbol for acknowledging the fertility role of their god, as the ultimate explanation for the fertility of people, their cattle, and their crops. (The fertility role of their god will be considered in a subsequent discussion, when it will be pointed out that one of the principal functions of a guardian deity is proividing his people their fertility for their crops, their cattle and themselves.)

Even the prohibition among the Israelites for making a "graven" image of their god, could, when extended to other graphic symbols, have accounted for the disinclination, in the most representative of their religious culture, to identify their deity and its fertiltiy role with any particular symbol, such as was common among other peoples.

7. The intended meaning with which an image is used in referring to a deity is its religious intension

A selection of a reality which is believed in some way to be a representation of a trait of a god is an expression of a religious aspect of human life. Human life, which endeavors to enter into relation with a divine source of help, also has a motivation to perceive it, just as is also an experience which is understandable when one person loves another. A person who is so related to another regards any reality as having special importance when it reduces the sense of distance from the other who is loved. The function of any object which performs a comparable role in religious life likewise reduces the apparent distance between a human being and a god to whom such a person turns in his need for what he cannot secure in relation to other realities.

Some such motive or want underlies the votive statues which were so widespread throughout the centuries in Greek religions. An association of Zeus with the ultimate power over the heavens, including the awesome lightning which can destroy, as it often did in the mountains of Greece, accounts for votive statues of Zeus, made in clay, as well as in bronze, portraying the deity grasping a zig-zag form, intended to represent lightning. The way the hand of the image clasps the thunderbolt indicates an interpretation of the god as having control over this awesome power.

One property of Zeus was thus portrayed in the imagery with which he was represented, as having ultimate sovereignty over the most powerful aspect of the heavens. The reassurance projected into the imagery of Zeus, holding the lightning in his hand, is the religious significance, or sign-function, of this imagery. The image, therefore, cannot be judged only on the basis of its artistic properties, or on the basis of an aesthetic response to them. It must be understood as a particular vehicle of religious meaning. Its religious role is its sign-function, exhibiting the sovereignty of Zeus, in full control of the most powerful and most feared of meteorological phenomena. As the sovereign of the heavens, Zeus was sovereign over every distinguishable aspect of the heavens, and the worshiper of Zeus, who could grasp his votive statue, even though of clay, had a reassuring experience of help. In times of otherwise unmitigated terror in storms, whether on land or at sea, grasping the votive image was, as if a frightened person was not totally alone when surrounded by the awesome power which could do such destructive havoc. The reassurance of being near the sovereign of the heavens, by the reminder of the image, was a genuine religious experience of being nearer the god than one could otherwise have felt, without the role of the image of the god, also grasping the lightning in his hand.

The thunder itself, associated with the lightning, but distinguishable from it, and for most people, unrelated to it, except incidentally, was likewise a cause of terror. A comparable terror for an agricultural people was the proximity to an angered bull, when one was without protection. The association of the deity, Poseidon, with a bull, therefore, is not only for the fertility association, but also for the frightening bellowing, which asserting the power of the animal, induced a terror under circumstances of being unprotected, which was emotionally a parallel of the terror experienced in thunder storms, in which thunder seems to be a threat to life itself.

Although the sound of thunder could not be portrayed, as was the lightning which was held in the hand of Zeus, the mere association of the thunder, roaring through the vast sky, with the image of Poseidon, was somehow bringing it within an individual's control. A comparable control was representing lightning in a votive image of Zeus, which also gave a reassurance of having some degree of control, as would not have been experienced without the tangible portrayal of holding or hurling the thunderbolt. The parallel imagery of Zeus and Poseidon was natural in the Greek versions of the two gods as brothers, and therefore, as having a family identity. Such a family trait could be portrayed in a physical image as the sound of the thunder could not be. Hence the supplementary imagery of Poseidon as a bull, completed the intended function of artefacts to portray the nature of his sovereignty over meteorological manisfestations of his power, having awesome impact upon human beings, nearly equal to the terror sensed of destructive lightning, under the sovereignty of his brother.

Associating Poseidon, who had sovereignty over the seas, with an animal form, was thus an impoverishment of the mode of awe in the sense of the sublime, with which a spiritual response is made to the power of which great bodies of water are capable in time of their violent agitation. Such a theriomorphic association of a deity, identified with sovereignty over the seas, is an inevitable impairment in human experience, by virtue of having selected one parallel of a deity with an animal, rather then remaining satisfied with the association of the diety with the representation of the thunderbolt.

The association of images in which the features of one suggest the properties of another is illustrated in both Zeus and Poseidon, since their interpretations as sovereigns over heavenly phenomena include rain, the primary association of which by agricultural peoples is the growth of crops. Hence, a fertility aspect of both Zeus and Poseidon is basic to mythological tales, with their imagery that often is difficult to regard as compatible with even the slightest spiritual aspect of human capacities. But as in human life itself, so in the association of images in human imagination, there is no control or limit which is imposed by images upon themselves. It is this aspect of imagery and of their associative character, of which Kerenyi speaks, when he refers to "Poseidon's father image (as) a dark one, enclosing an animal husband image."36 Whereas such an association would not have been objectionable for some people, it certainly would not have contributed to a spiritualizing of the associations identified with Poseidon as god of the sea, or as god of thunder, sharing with Zeus, sovereignty over two of the awesome aspects of the heavens, each of which is capable of inducing a sense of the sublime in those human beings who are capable of such a spiritual version of their religious life.

The religious significance of any image for particular human beings is determined by their own spiritual qualities, and these are cultivated, or left uncultivated. Thus what any image of a deity means to an individual human being is what the individual has done to become spiritually sensitive to the realities in relation to which he lives, which include also imagery in the religions of the culture in which he lives. Some human spirituality acquires a sensitivity which includes an awareness that no image is adequate as a reverent association with a divine reality. And it is this level of spirituality which attempts to satisfy both its religious needs and its spiritual sensitivities by reducing the role of spatial images in its life. Included in this spiritualizing of an individual's religion is either an aniconic rejection of all images of divine realities, such as the Israelites were commanded by their god to do, or reducing specific features of a physical medium so that its anthropomorphic associations are reduced to the barest minimum. This attempt may be regarded as the spiritual motivation underlying the role of xoanoa, or wooden blocks which have only the general outline of a human figure, but have none if its characteristic features. Such a figure is dominated more by features of the block of material from which it is carved than it is by its portrayal of either human or animal features. It has, in other words, a generality which is not unlike a verbal symbol for a divine reality.

It perfoms a religious function, however, which no linguistic symbolism can perform for a religious person, since it is something which can be held, grasped, and clung to for its reassuring security. Such an image with no distinct features has a generality that is commensurate with a spiritiual need for something which is other than the market place or the humdrum circumstances, internal to which one lives so much of his life. It is something even in those circumstances to which an individual can cling, being reassured by it that he is with a reality, free from caprice, free from unpredictable whims, which is a guardian of himself and of his sensitivities.

Any expression of an interpretation in concrete or particular imagery may be classified as a mythologem, when any such spatial representation of an essentially nonspatial reality is attempted. But any such particular imagery impairs the spiritual possiblilites of an experience which is regarded as an awareness of the presence of a divine reality, in relation to which a human being proposes such a graphic interpretation of its nature. The very disparity between a reality, whose nature is a universal presence in the world, and the particular features of an image of it, constitutes a handicap to the development of spiritual possiblities in human life.

8. Rejecting spatial imagery expresses a spiritual awareness of the transcendent nature of divine reality

The Greek philosopher, Heraclitus, characterizes "Wisdom" as "understand(ing) the mind by which all things are steered through all things."[37] This concept of an ultimate reality which is manifested in events that take place in the world to give them direction and order is an essential conviction of religious life.

The way in which Heraclitus interprets this divine reality, which is other than the events to which it gives direction, is free from a graphic imagery which interprets the divine reality in terms of spatial imagery. Heraclitus was so clearly aware of the impairment to a spiritual orientation to divine reality by such images that he maintains that ultimate wisdom should only with utmost hesitancy be identified by a humanly devised name, such as "Zeus". It is for this reason that he declares: "The one thing which alone is wise is willing and unwilling to be called by the name of Zeus."[38] He most likely means by this that since the god named "Zeus" by the Greeks is regarded by them as the supreme of all realities of which they are aware, his name, distinguished from all other names, would be most suitable for denoting the supreme wisdom, which is the ultimate condition for the ordered world. But since the term is a human invention, it, therefore, is unlike the nonhuman divine ultimate to which it is referred in human discourse.

Heraclitus thus anticipated a comparable disinclination of Xenophanes to subscribe to a popular usage of anthropomorphic imagery for interpreting divine realities, and this accounts for his stern critique of Homer and Hesiod for "attribut(ing) to the gods" properties of human beings.[39] Xenophanes' identification of God with the totality of all that is, accounts for his dissatisfaction with all imagery that is incapable of unqualified unity. His premise that "God is one"[40] is itself a highly condensed critique, not only of Greek polytheistic religions, but also of every Greek version of the many gods.

The critiques which both Heraclitus and Xenophanes direct against anthropomorphic imagery in interpretations of realities which are revered as divine, and therefore, as transcendent of human beings, anticipates the aniconic critiques in following centuries, and it is also summed up in the Israelites' prohibition of all "graven images" which would handicap their understanding of the transcendent nature of the the divine reality, and the radical difference of such a reality from human beings.

A profound awareness of the total inadequacy of images for interpreting the nature of the divine Creator is expressed in the association of light with the divine creative act. Reverence for light accounts for this association with the ultimate reality worshiped as the Creator, since in light, as God's first manifestation of his cosmic creativity, an essentially spiritual nature of God is thereby intended.

A parallel reverence for light is expressed in Euripides' identification of the light with truth.[41] For a Greek of the intellectual order of Euripides, there is no reality of a more divine nature than truth, and hence the spiritual association of the two, truth and light. The light to which Euripides refers illuminates the world as truth illuminates human life. In other words, there is a comparable function which cannot be indicated by any concrete imagery, since for the ancients, light is no more a part of the material world than is truth. That is, according to this ancient interpretation of light, it is other than the physical world, and in this sense, is transcendent of it. As transcendent of the physical world, it had for them a property with which they interpreted God, the Ultimate.

A modern interpretation of light, of course, is incompatible with the parallel, which had profound significance for ancient interpretations of the divine ultimate as light. There is, of course, more than one interpretation of nearly every reality, and this principle also holds for light. The physical nature of light, according to modern science, is only one of the meanings of the term "light". A meaning other than this is the spiritual sense that a supreme event in human life is being made aware of a truth of which one had not previously been aware. Such an event in human life is an intellectual illumination, and when this makes a difference in the quality of human life, for its enrichment and its ennoblement, it is a spiritual experience, whose moral order is superseded by no other occurrence in human life. It is this complex sequence in human life which is basic to the religious meaning of illumination in the world by a creative act of God. Illumination in human life, which is an event of redirecting it, is its spiritual significance. Such a new significance irradiates human life as the divine act of bringing light into being irradiates the world. As the irradiation of the world by light eliminates a previous darkness, so the infusion of a new significance in life, to give it direction and purpose, is a parallel elimination of moral or spiritual darkness.

A sense of being enlightened, which occurs as any previously oppressive sense of bewildering darkness is cancelled, is the birth of a new life for a human being. For him therefore, the scriptural account of God creating light becomes a significance internal to himself. A thankfulness for such an enlightening of life is a spiritual experience; and when it is revered as an act of a divine reality, liberating life from a previous restriction, it is a profoundly important religious experience in such a person's life. Such relatively rare occurrences in human life, which cast a new and more encouraging meaning over its entire nature, are frequently interpreted in the imagery of celestial occurrences, such as a sunrise.

The ancient Egyptian "Hymn to Aten", which reveres the god as "the first to live", also associates this divine reality with the sun that "appear(s) beautiful on the horizon of heaven". Aten's illumination of the world, which is also the cancellation of its darkness, is interpreted as an awakening of life of every creature, such as "The birds which fly from their nests", into the light of a new day, which is paralleled in the Hymn to their "adoration" of the soul of Aten, the source of life and its illumination in the world. A further spiritual parallel is then affirmed in the Hymn when it declares that every living being comes into new life when Aten "has risen (for) them".42

Even though the Egyptian Hymn may not have had an influence upon the Israelites' version of their god, it is, nevertheless, ethnologically significant that the Hymn predicates properties to Aten which the Old Testament predicates to the Creator as the "sole god", and therefore, without an equal. In declaring of Aten, "there is no other like thee", the Hymn affirms a property of the Egyptian deity which is likewise predicated as a feature of the guardian god of the Israelites. Both Egyptians and Israelites worshiped a deity which each esteemed as having no equal, and also as the one who "didst create the earth". And both religions likewise revere their own guardian deity as the "lord of eternity".43 When the Hymn does not identify Aten with the solar disc or sun, there is a further parallel in the properties which the Egyptians attribute to their Creator, and which the Israelites attribute to their god, when both acknowledge the illuminating role of the god, as when the Hymn declares: "When thou dost rise", all that lives, "lives through thee".44

9. An interpretation of the nature of a god, worshiped as the ultimate source of human well-being is a religiously significant theology

As has been pointed out in the foregoing analysis, a discourse about the nature of an ultimate reality which is regarded as God, may be purely speculative, constituting one type of metaphysic, which is without religious significance. Hence, it is necessary to distinguish interpretations of God, which are not essentially religious, from those which are.

A commonly accepted definition of "theology" is "a doctrine about the nature of God". Such a doctrine consists of a set of interpretations of such a reality in relation to other realities, of which account must also be taken in considering such a reality upon other realities whose natures are contingent upon it as the ultimate being. Thus, in the concept of "God as Creator of the world", a concept is also included about the world in relation to God. An adequate interpretation, therefore, of such a Creator would include a cosmology, or an analysis of the nature of a cosmos so created, and as such, dependent for its nature upon its relation to the reality without which it would not have had the nature that is its essential being. Such an interpretation is a religious version of its nature when the divine reality to which its origin is attributed, is also worshiped. It is, in other words, the religious significance of acknowledging the dependence of the world upon the ultimate divine reality which is the religious interpretation of the world. All that is included in such a complex interpretation of the ultimate source of the world, including human life, is, therefore, also esential to a theology, when the source of human life is attributed to the reality worshiped as God.

Although a worship, which is so directed, may take account of one reality as uppermost, a reflective interpretation of all that is included in its total nature cannot be so restricted. This fact is illustrated even in the scriptural versions of the scope of divine reality to which human beings are believed to be related in their worship. Such divine reality, as it is interpreted in the Old Testament, is actually not as singular as is indicated in the terminology of "Creator". Instead, it is often interpreted as if plural, not as in any polytheistic religion, however, such as the Greeks', in which there is plurality of deities, but rather, in the sense that there are various divine agencies, often in the service of the one principal deity. The sixth chapter of Genesis, for example, refers to "the sons of the gods"; and the plurality of such a reference is unambiguous. An interpretation of the inclusion, in an otherwise monotheistic or monolatrous religion, of this account in the Old Testament, constitutes a problem, one explanation for which is the plurality of strands in the written form of Scripture; and another is the type of pluralistic interpretations of deities, widespread in the cultures in relation to which the Israelites sought to preserve their highly restricted worship of one god.

The "mythological" character of this reference in Genesis is evident when the account includes the tale that "the sons of the gods saw that the daughters of men were beautiful, so they took for themselves such women as they chose"(vs.2). This story has every element in common with Greek mythological versions of gods, who also were enamoured of human beings. This mythological insertion into Genesis has a story-telling value, but surely no religious significance, since such "sons of the gods" are not realities to which any devout worship was directed. The conglomerate character of such a scriptural text, however, is ethnologically instructive as illustrating how cultural contacts of a people infiltrate into their religious literature, which, in turn, reveals how writers of scripture have a mentality that is conditioned by the cultural contexts in which they live. Hence, what is included in such scriptural accounts of the nature of a god, which accounts are a theology, is as mixed as the cultural strands which influence the mentality of the authors of scriptural texts. This obviously mixed nature of a single chapter in Scripture is illustrated in the verse which follows this mythological tale about the amorous antics of "the sons of the gods". The very next verse (vs.3) is a profoundly spiritual interpretation of the nature of the divine source of life in the world, which interpretation is comparable to the most spiritual of the theological doctrines, when it refers to the "life-giving spirit" of "the Lord". This spiritual version of a theological doctrine, however, is followed by the verse which continues the mythological account of "the sons of the gods" who "had intercourse with the daughters of men". This scriptural account in the sixth chapter of Genesis is a parallel of comparable accounts in Greek mythology. As such, it is obvious that it is no more consistent with a monotheistic theology than are the Greek mythological tales, whose function is for the

95

entertainment of those whose religious sensitivites are not offended by such stories. In other words, the qualified spiritual character of this segment in Genesis reflects the same qualified spiritual character of those who wrote it. And it is their cultural conditioning which impairs serious theological doctrines about the ultimate divine reality.

A very different level of spiritual sensitivity is exhibited in Exodus by its priestly authors, who recognize the value for devoutly religious human beings to be assured of access to divine realities which are less distant from human beings than the awesome Creator. The twenty-third chapter of Exodus is thus an adaptation to this human hunger to be related to a reality worthy of reverence, which is, however, less awesome than God. This chapter attributes to God a merciful consideration for human need in declaring: "I myself will send an angel before you to guard you as you go and to bring you to the place that I have prepared"(vs.20).

The guardian role of the supreme deity worshiped by the Israelites is thus particularized in the guardian angel. The priestly motive for this version of the guardian role of their god is evident also in the scriptural assurance that "My angel will go before you and lead you" to the lands occupied by peoples whom the Israelites endeavored to displace from their own homes, such as "the Hittites, the Perizites, the Canaanites, the Hivites, the Jebusites"(vs.24). The specific purpose of this guardian role of their god, mediated through the "angel", was to "exterminate these" many peoples, in order that "the chosen people" might possess their lands. The spiritual aspect of this scriptural explanation of the guardian role of their god and his guardian angel is, therefore, on the same level of morality as the priestly writers of this scripture, who saw no incompatibility of this attribution to a guardian deity with a divine Creator of mankind. The highly restricted preoccupation of a priesthood with its own religious tradition is, therefore, expressed in this version of a theology, accommodated to tribal or national patriotism (vs.24).

A very different scriptural version of a plurality in a divine order is affirmed in Deuteronomy in an exhortation to the Israelites, attributed to "the song that Moses...recited in the hearing of the people: 'Rejoice with him, you heavens, bow down, all you gods, before him'"(32:43-44). This reference to "gods" is, of course, a so-called henotheistic version of religion, which also is classified as a monolatry, by which is meant that, whereas one god is worshiped by a people, the gods of other peoples are also acknowledged as comparable realities, even though a lower order of merit for being worshiped.

Yet another version of plurality of beings in the divine order, transcendent of the physical world and human beings, is affirmed by Isaiah as Seraphim, "calling ceaselessly to one another, 'Holy, holy, holy is the Lord of Hosts: the whole earth is full of his glory'"(6:3). A comparable plurality is affirmed in Psalms 148 as angels, who exhort: "Praise him, all his angels; praise him all his host"(vs.2).

These types of divine beings share with the ultimate deity his order which is other then the world, including human beings. But they are of a different character from the deity regarded as their sovereign, as well as the sovereign of the world and mankind. They are in his service, mediating his will, and thus subordinate to his unconditioned authority.

As the messianic expectations increased in the turbulent history of the Israelites, apocalyptical writings likewise increased, such as the Book of Daniel. A primary motive for such a messianic emphais upon divine intermediaries is less theological than psychological. It is a means for reassuring troubled and bewildered people in times of political turmoil that they are under a divine scrutiny, and will be guided and guarded in every aspect of their lives. Such reassurance lends an evident support to a religious people in times that otherwise would destroy their hope for any promising future.

The dominant feature of such a messianic assurance continued through the centuries of the turbulent times in the history of the Israelites, as this is indicated in the Quamran literature, such as "The Scroll of the War Rule", in which reference is made to the "Day of Misfortune" for the "lot of darkenss", when "the congregation of the gods and the assembly of men...shall battle together".[45] What is significant in this reference is not only the persistent concept of an apocalyptical ending of human history in a messianic event, but also the reference to a plurality of "gods". Such gods, without doubt, are those in whom other people trusted, who will not, in times of utmost need, be able to do for them what the guardian god of the

Israelites will do for his "chosen people".

The mere mention in scriptural texts of a plurality of divine beings was offensive to the scholars who were devoted to formulating the Massoretic text of the Old Testament. Such references to a plurality of divine beings, as was retained in the Septuagint version of the Old Testament, were, therefore, modified in the Massoretic text. As John Allegro points out, this text "avoids all reference to these heavenly creatures with 'All ye nations'".46

In so doing, of course, the ethnological significance is ignored of scriptural references to such a plurality of divine beings. Such significance also includes an essentially religious significance, as has been pointed out, when a people, who are pressed by adversities, is given assurance by the sense of proximity to divine sources of help and guidance. And in periods of utmost despondency, they are given courage by the hope of more promising days, assured by their god, who will enlist "a heavenly host" to establish their security, which they had so long been denied. Then as the Book of Daniel declares: "The God of heaven will establish a kingdom which shall never be destroyed"(2:44). And the same book continues to assure the religiously devout: "His sovereignty...(will) be an everlasting sovereignty which should not pass away, and his kingly power such as should never be impaired"(7:14).

Chapter Four

GUARDIAN GODS IN ANCIENT RELIGIONS

1. The historical eras are comparable in which the
religions of ancient Greeks and Israelites developed

The earliest type of culture on the Greek mainland is
prehistoric, which is commonly referred to as Early
Helladic, and is regarded as between 2500 and 2000 B.C.
It is the Middle Helladic, between 2000 and 1600 B.C.,
Which is the era on the mainland of Greece, or Hellas,
that is the same as the era in Asia during which the
earliest beginning of the religious tradition of the
Israelites is traced.

Hellas, or "Land of the Hellenes", was a name for
Greece before it was referred to by the latter term;
and for some unknown reason, the term "Graecia" was
used by the Romans to refer to it.

If the religion which is identified with Abraham
(Abram) is regarded as the beginning of a tradition
which persisted through the centuries of the
Israelites, and if the religion of the Hellenes,
oriented to Zeus, is traced to a Mycenaean culture, the
flourishing of which was between 1400 and 1100,[1] then
the antiquity of the worship of Zeus is only a few
centuries later than the type of worship which is
attributed in the Old Testament to Abraham and to those
who traced their tradition to him.

The Old Testament account in Genesis is that Abram,
whose name was later changed to Abraham, was born in
"Ur of the Chaldees"(11:28), a city in ancient Sumer,
whose antiquity dates to at least 3000 B.C. The
elderly father of Abram persuaded his son to leave his
homeland and to set out, with his wife and nephew, Lot,
for Canaan (vs.31). Since the people of Sumer, in this
southern division of ancient Babylonia, were
non-Semitic,[2] it is likely that Abram's father believed
that a more favorable location could be found for the
establishment of a people and their religious
tradition, such as would have been either more
difficult or less likely among a non-Semitic people in
the lower Euphrates valley.

The account in Genesis is that when Abram reached Shechem, a location among the Canaanites, "The Lord appeared" to him, promising the land to him and his descendants". Acknowledging this promise, "Abram built an alter there to the Lord who had appeared to him"(12:6-8). This may be regarded as the beginning of a tradition of worship in the new homeland, for the establishment and retention of which the following centuries were devoted.

If the time of Abraham's stay in Canaan is regarded as about 1850 B.C.,3 then the worship of the guardian god of the Israelites is approximately four hundred years prior to historical evidence for a worship of Zeus in the Peloponnesian center of Pylos.

Mycenaean history came to an abrupt end about 1100 B.C., when the Dorians from the North invaded Hellas, and settled in locations such as Argolis, Messenia, Laconia, establishing their principal capitals in Corinth and Sparta. The Dorians destroyed the principal Mycenaean centers of Mycenae, Tiryns, and Pylos. This abrupt end of the Mycenaean civilization was the beginning of the Greek City States; and what is worship of Zeus continued through the turmoil of these migrations into the Peloponnese, and became a dominant religion in Greece in the following centuries.

Worship of the guardian god of Abraham and his descendants thus had a history not unlike the worship of the principal god of the Greeks. If the Dorian invasion is regarded as "the last wave of Greek-speaking peoples" to enter Greece and to settle in the Peloponnese, and if the earlier invasions of "Greek speaking people" preceded them as early as 1900 B.C.,4 then the historical parallel of these two ancient peoples, the Greeks and the Israelites, is very much the same, provided that the time of Abraham's stay in Canaan is placed at about 1850 B.C. This parellelism is maintained by Kerenyi, who argues that "Uniquely Greek religious experience has a history which...may be specified as late Helladic",5 and this, as has been mentioned, begins about 1600 B.C.

Although this era is many centuries before Homer, which likely is about the ninth or eighth century B.C., the Odyssey, which is one of the earliest of Greek literatures that characterizes religious practices at the time, and also earlier, mentions a parallel to Abraham's sacrifice at an altar to his god, in which he acknowledged his gratitude for the guidance and guardianship of his god during the long journey from the lower Euphrates to Palestine. The Odyssey's account is of an Egytian seer who censured Menelaus for not having "offered rich sacrifices to Zeus, and all the other gods"6 before he embarked on his homeward voyage, and he declared that Menelaus would not again see his home until he made sacrifices to the gods "who hold wide heaven".7

As the guardian god whom Abraham worshiped was believed to have guided him on his long journey, so the Greeks in later centuries believed that Apollo Agyieus, the god of journeys, would do the same for them. Included in the properties of this god in his earliest religious role among the Greeks is "a leader of Colonies", and in this role, parallels the Israelites' long struggle to establish themselves in a new homeland, which their god had promised Abraham before he left Ur of Chaldees. This new home was to enable his descendants to become "a greater nation", as their god had promised for their future (Gen. 12:1-2).

2. The term "Israelite" has an essentially religious meaning

In the fourteenth chapter of Genesis, Abram, later to be named "Abraham", was refered to as "Abram the Hebrew" (vs.13). This linguistic and ethnic identification was subsequently changed in Genesis to a religiously significant apellation, after an event which occurred in the life of his grandson, Jacob. One night, according to Genesis, after Jacob had dismissed others with whom he was traveling, and when he was alone, and anxiously awaiting the morning when he was to meet his brother, Esau, from whom he had been estranged, he encountered a stranger with whom he wrestled. During the struggle, he made a request of the stranger, which was according to an ancient custom, that he bless him before Jacob would release him. The stranger then answered: "Your name shall no longer be Jacob, but Israel", a meaning associated with which term is that he had pevailed in a struggle with both divine and human beings. Thereupon, Jacob named the place of this encounter "Peniel", a meaning of which is "face of god". The religious reason for this particular naming is that he believed he had encountered the god to whom his grandfather had been loyal, to a degree that became a norm of religious life in the centuries to follow the first of the great patriarchs (32:22-32).

Genesis maintains that the guardian god of his forefathers appeared a second time to him, declaring again that his name should no longer be "Jacob", but "Israel"(35:9-10). A reason for the repetition of this explanation for a divine sanction of the religiously significant name of a people is that it represents a different biblical strand of authorship, indicated by the identification of the deity as "El Shaddai". The Patriarch then renamed the place "Bethel"(vs.15), as a memorial to this religiously important event in which the god, who had established a covenant with his father, Isaac, had sanctioned the identification of their descendants, to distinguish them from other Hebrews.

Another religiously significant aspect of this account of the Patriarch is the vow he made with his god that he would give a tenth of all of his property which he religiously regarded as a "gift" of his god's generosity to him and his people. Yet another significant aspect of this same account is that this tithe, characterized as an exchange, was as it were, for the safety which the guardian god of his forefathers had given him on his journey. The bargaining feature of this tithing is made evident in the conditions which the Patriarch stipulated for his accepting the god of his forefathers as his own god, when he declared the vow: "If god goes with me and helps me safe on this journey...if he gives me bread to eat and clothes to wear, and if I return home safely to my father"(28:20-22), then his father's god shall also be his god.

Although a human being here specifies conditions in a contractual arrangement with what is regarded as a divine realtity, the account in Genesis is ethnologically important because it indicates that a deity is chosen by people, as well as such a guardian god chosing people as his own, which is pointed out in the frequently repeated reference in the Old Testament to the "Chosen people". Another ethnologically significant feature of this account is that a guardian god is also a traveler's god, as Apollo Agyieus was for the Greeks.

3. A guardian god is providence for a people who trust it

102

The guardian god of the Israelites declared to Abram that he had "taken care of him" in order that there may be a tradition of those who would be faithful in their worship. The fulfilment of this "purpose", however, was dependent upon "charging his sons and their families after him to conform to the way" of their god (Gen.18:19). This sequence of fathers and sons in the worship of their god is the essential meaning of the patriarchal version of the religion of the Israelites. Isaac, the son of Abram, therefore, did to his son what his father had done to him when he was blessed: He appealed to their guardian god to make his descendants "fruitful", and to increase their descendants until they become "a host of nations".

After Jacob parted from his father, Isaac, he stopped to rest; and during the night, he dreamed that their guardian god stood beside him, identifying himself as "the god of your fathers Abraham and the god of Isaac," who promised that the land on which he rested would be given to him and his descendants. So blessed, therefore, would his descendants be by their god that "They shall be countless as the dust upon the earth". As a memorial to this experience of being in the presence of the god of his people, he set up a "sacred pillar", identified in Hebrew tradition as the matsebah, whose religious significance is a memorial to "the presence of god of the family". Jacob, in turn, told his son Joseph, that the guardian god, El Shaddai, "appeared" to him "in the country of Canaan" and "blessed" him, saying: "I will make you fruitful and increase you in numbers.(48:3-4).

A parallel of Joseph, as an ideal son, is recorded in a Ras Shamra text of the ancient Ugarit, on the north Syrian coast, which dates from about 1400 B.C., and thus is within an approximate era of the sons of Jacob and their relation to the Egyptians. It records an appeal of a royal son that the "Creator of Created Things" bless him by being a son worthy of his father as "a scion in the midst of his palace; One who may set up the pillar of his ancestral god in the sanctuary, the refuge of his clan."[8] The religious significance of such a tradition of a father and his descendants is the assurance of a continuity of worship of the guardian deity throughout a sequence of generations of a family.

Ancient Athenian laws maintained that because a society consisted of "members of a family living together in one house (oikos)", the family unit has obligations to perform "religious ceremonies including observances in honour of its dead menbers". Professor MacDowell points out that "ancient Greek(s) attached great importance to the preservation of his _oikos_, and to its continuation after the death of its present kyrios"("lord","controller"). If there was no son as direct heir, a man's property passed into the possession of another branch of the family, leaving his _oikos_ extinct, and all religious observances honouring him, would likely be discontinued._9_

The guardian god of the descendants of the Patriarchs was their providential source of help during the centuries that they were strangers in the land to which Abraham had journeyed. And their god did for them what Apollo Agyieus, god of journeys, did for the ancient Greeks who trusted him on their travels. An Homeric epigram admonishes people who are in need of providential guidance on their journeying to "observe the reverence due to Zeus who rules on high, the god of strangers"._10_ And the "Homeric Hymm ", addressed "to the Dioscuri", acknowledges the providential guidance of those who travel, and are confronted with its adversities. They, therefore, were trusted as "deliverers of men on earth and of swift-going ships when stormy gails range over the ruthless sea"._11_

Guardian gods are trusted for preserving a family sequence, the increase of whose numbers is sanctioned by their god. And when a people, such as the descendants of Abraham, travel in search of a new home, or a people, such as the ancient Greeks, engage in travel for their livelihood, an acknowledgment of their dependence upon the deities whom they trust for guidance is their religion.

(i) The guardian god of the Israelites assured them that they would become a great nation

Genesis includes an anthropomorphic version of a tutelary deity who said : "The Lord thought to himself, Shall I conceal from Abraham what I intend to do?" His intention for this patriarch was that his descendants "will become a great and powerful nation"(18:17-18). A condition for the possibility of such a "powerful nation" is that there should be land sufficient to support cattle and crops, as well as providing space on which people can build their homes and their cities. Thus the guardian god, referred to in Genesis, assured Abraham: "All the land within sight I will give to you and your descendants for ever"(13:14-15). This promise was declared as a covenant with Abraham, specifying the vast area "from the River of Egypt to the Great...Euphrates" which was occupied by the "Kenites, the Kenizzites, the Kadmonites, the Hittites, the Perizzites, the Canaanites, the Girgashites, and the Jebusites" (15:18-21). A token for having established this contractual covenant with the patriarch was that his name was to be changed to "Abraham", as an acknowledgment that his guardian god had made him "father of a multitude of nations"(17:5-6).

A comparable version of a guardian god, who is the "shepherd" of his own people, and therefore, is devoted to their welfare, rather that to the welfare of other peoples, is attributed to the Babylonian Shamash, who as "the shepherd Shamash guides the people like a god".12 This contract in the covenant which the guardian god made with Abraham remained unbroken even during the years that the Israelites were enslaved by the Egyptians. Exodus declares: "The Israelites were fruitful and prolific", and "the more harshly they were treated, the more their numbers increased." By virtue came to loathe the sight of them", and then "they treated their Israelite slaves with ruthless severity"(1:7-13).

Notwithstanding their suffering during their servitude in Egypt, their increase was a condition for the fulfilment of the covenant that the descendants of Abraham would become a mighty nation. The condition is stated in Genesis that in order for the chosen people to "swarm throughout the earth and rule over it"(or "increase"), they "must be fruitful and increase"(9:7) .Fertility, as a feature of an entire people, implies, according to the Deuteronomic version of the Israelites' guardian god, that "No man or woman among (them) shall be barren"; and a condition for the support of such fertility among many people is that "no male or female of (their) beasts" shall be "infertile"(7:14).

The unqualified fertility among the Israelites is interpreted by the prophet Ezekiel as their god's way of demonstrating to them that he is "the Lord"(36:12).

The fertility of people, cattle, and crops, depends upon moisture, which Deuteronomy characterizes as "the precious things of heaven, for the dew, and for the deep that coucheth beneath"(33:13). An ancient Greek religious ceremony, which included the "night ritual of the Arrephorai", and performed at the time of planting of seeds, is a parallel of the Israelites' acknowledgment of their dependence upon moisture, even in quantities as limited as dew. In this Greek ceremony, "an appeal" was oriented "to the goddess (Erse) to grant life-giving moisture to the thirsty parched soil."13

The providence of a guardian god of an ancient people includes his control over conditions which control all expressions of fertility, whether of land, crops, cattle, or human beings. The Greeks, for instance, interpreted Zeus as Chthonios, the property of whom was "god of the earth and the giver of fertilty".14 It is this version of Zeus as principal factor in the earth's fertility which is acknowledged in the prayer by the Chorus in Aeschylus's The Suppliant Maidens: "May Zeus cause the earth to render its tribute of fruit...may their grazing cattle in the fields have abundant increase."15

Hesiod regards Gaia as the "mother earth by whose designs everything in the growing world was to come into being".16 Even though Homer does not include Demeter in the "family gatherings" of the gods, her worship as a fertility power of crops, nevertheless, was as early as Mycenaean times,17 and this is an era comparable to the period in which the Israelites were confronted with their total dependence upon the fertility of a land to support them. The Greeks thus acknowledged a comparable dependence upon the fertility of land which was expressed in their worship of Demeter, when her fertility role was "limited to the growth of grain".18 Aglauros was another fertility deity worshiped by the Greeks; and a primitive religious significance of Apollo was his role as a fertility god of vegetation, in which role he was associated in the Peloponnese with Hyacinthus, one aspect of whose fertility celebration, the Hyacinthia, was dedicated to him. His role in making a harvest plentiful was also acknowledged in the festival of Thargelia; and as a specific protector of flocks, he was worshiped as Apollo Criophorus (Kriophoros).

Whereas the polytheistic Greeks personified the various aspects of fertility, upon which they were dependent, with particular deities, the Israelites, intolerant of polytheism, identified all various aspects of fertility with their one guardian god, including them in his role which was devoted to bringing his chosen people to the status of "a great nation".

Psalm 104 sums up the various aspects of human dependence upon fertility features of the earth in declaring that all these are within the final control of one god: "...thou dost water the hills; the earth is enriched by thy provision. Thou makest grass grow for the cattle and green things for those who toil for man, bringing bread out of the earth and bread to sustain their strength"(vs.13-14). Leviticus declares that if human beings were without the providence of divine sovereignty over all the conditions which make life possible, they would "wear out their strength in vain; their land would not yield its produce any longer nor the trees their fruit"(26:20).

(ii) <u>The essential properties of the god worshiped by the early Israelites are the same as the guardian deities of other ancient people</u>

The god whom Abraham trusted for his guardianship, when he journeyed from his home in Chaldea, remained for centuries the guardian god of his descendants. The restricted scope of concern for this one people, descendants of Abraham, is affirmed in Genesis: "I will bless those who bless you: I will curse those who slight you"(12:3). The essential qualification for receiving this special benefaction and protection was respected by the first of the patriarchs, when he "put his faith" in the god who promised him and his own people guidance and protection. The effectiveness and adequacy of his faith expressed as trust, is also acknowledged in Genesis: "And the Lord counted that faith to him as righteousness"(15:6).

The significance of such faith on the part of a human being, in relation to a reality regarded as divine, and therefore, of a radically different order of being, is likewise clearly pointed out in the same text, which explains that the providential care offered to the faithful is not only for their advantage, but it serves a purpose which is advantageous for the god who shows them his providential care. In exchange for his guidance for the faithful, his people will, in turn, "charge (their) sons and family...to conform to the way "which is acceptable to their god (18:19). In other words, his relation to a people becomes established by the fidelity which they direct to him; and in doing so, orient the loyalty of their children in the worship of the god who had originally entered into a contractual relation with the founder of their religious tradition. The providence, with which the journeys of Abraham were blessed, continued to bless his son, as this is also narrated in the Genesis account. Since Isaac continued to be faithful to his father's god, as his father himself had been, his father's god became his god; and when he undertook to leave his father's home to find a wife for himself, the god of the family assured him that he would "send his angel to make (Isaac's) journey successful"(24:40). And the intimacy or nearness of a family god to the members of such a family is expressed also in the same narrative that the family god himself had "chosen for his master's son" the wife whom he regarded as most likely to continue a fidelity, comparable to the Patriarch's, and therefore, also in teaching her children to be loyal to their forefathers' god.

On a journey which Isaac undertook, he was encountered by his father's god, who identified himself as "the god of your father Abraham". What is especially significant in this text for understanding what a people's fidelity meant to their own god, is the explanation which the god of Abraham gave to Isaac for continuing to receive his providence: "I will bless you...on account of my servant Abraham"(26:23-24). It is a text such as this which accounts for a later Christian belief that the merit which accrues to the relation of one individual to his god can be transferred to another's credit. There could, therefore, have been no greater kindness which a parent bequeathed to his children than his own fidelity to his god, which would become for them, a basis for receiving comparable blessings from their father's god, as a tribute of respect to their father's fidelity to his god.

Jacob (Israel) "offered sacrifices to the god of his father Isaac", and it was on this occasion that his father's god again identified himself as "the god of your father"(46:3). The same type of identification, "The god of your fathers, the god of Abraham, the god of Isaac, and the god of Jacob"(Ex.3:14), was offered to Moses by the guardian god to whom Abraham had established a relation by virtue of his fidelity, which continued to be providential for Abraham's descendants. This same general way of referring to the guardian deity, to whom early Israelite history is oriented, is reaffirmed in addressing Moses in the account in Deuteronomy as "the god of your fathers"(1:11). And in later Wisdom literature of the first century B.C., even when written in Greek, the Jewish author retains an awareness of the earliest Israelites' version of their god, as "the god of the fathers".

A comparable way of identifying deities worshiped by a people is expressed in Aeschylus' The Seven Against Thebes, in which the Herald announces the "decree of the council of...Cadmus", which forbid the royal Polynices to be buried, but rather left "a prey to dogs", so that "even in death he shall retain the stain of his guilt against his fathers' gods."

4. A guardian god is near his people as a cosmic god is not

The more remote a deity is from human beings, the less accessible it is to them, and the less likely it is that they will turn to it in times of their greatest needs. In such times, however, they will seek help from what they believe is near to them and is capable of responding to their appeals.

A significant commentary on early Greek religions is that although many altars and shrines were dedicated to Zeus, and although he was regarded as sovereign over other deities, there nevertheless, were fewer temples dedicated exclusively to him than to his son, Apollo.[19] The same relation holds in Hinduism, in which there are great numbers of temples dedicated to the sectarian gods, Vishnu, Siva, Shakti, but only one principal temple dedicated to Brahma, the ultimate One. As One, and therefore, as undifferentiated, it is incapable of being conceived; and as inclusive of all differentiations internal to its ultimate unity, no version of worship is possible in relation to it, such as is directed to sectarian deities.

(i) It is an ancient belief that there are guardian gods of individuals, families, communities, and nations

The Mycenaean king, Nestor, assured Telemachus, son of his friend, Odysseus: "I have no thought you will turn out mean and cowardly if, when you are so young, the gods go with you and guide you."[20] Such divine guides are "guardian gods".[21]

The guardian god to whom Homer refers in this passage in the Odyssey is Athene (Athena); and in this role, she is "guardian spirit of the family", which includes its various members, such as the boy to whom the king of Pylos spoke.[22]

The term by which this goddess is denoted is actually not a name, but rather a title, which means "the Athenian one".[23] As such, she was a guardian goddess of Athens. And to distinguish her guardian role over Athens, from a comparable role over other localities, she was sometimes referred to as "Athenaia", which is less general in its denotative significance than the more general "Athene" or "Athena". According to a motion proposed by Themistocles, it was "resolved by the Council and the People" of Athens "to entrust the city to Athena, the Mistress of Athens, and to all the other gods to guard and defend" it.[24] The Chorus in Euripides' Rhesus sums up the Athenian attitude to their guardian deities: "Lo, When the gods breathe gentle o'er the town, all runs to good."[25]

The guardian role of the goddess of Athens was not, however, confined to the Athenians and to their acropolis. In the earliest centuries of her worship as Pallas Athene, her primitive idols, Palladia, also guarded the heights of other cities. It was to this role of the guardian goddess that the Messenger refers in Aeschylus' drama, The Persians, when he reports to the mother of Xerxes: "Some power divine that swayed down the scale of fortune with unequal weight...destroyed our host." And then he expressed an attitude toward the goddess which was held throughout the world in which the influence of Athenian power was exerted: "The gods preserve the city of the goddess Pallas."[26] Something of the sense of her awesome power to guard and preserve a people, who trust her guardianship, is expressed in Aeschylus' Eumenides, when she herself claims that she "alone of all the gods holds the keyes to the armoury of Zeus in which his thunderbolts are sealed."[27] Euripides reaffirms a long established Athenian confidence in the guardian role of the Goddess, when a friend of Heracles addresses Demophon, King of Athens: "Nor are the gods who champion us weaker than the gods of Argos," even though, as he acknowledges, the people of the Argolid have "Hera, wife of Zeus (as) their leader." And then, with pride in the honor of Athens to have Athena as their guardian, he declares: "This I say as omen of success, that we have the stronger deity, for Pallas will not brook defeat."[28]

The guardian role of gods trusted by the Greeks is paralleled in other ancient civilizations. Amen or

110

Amon of Egypt was once a local deity of Thebes, but became one of the principal deities of the Egyptian pantheon during the Theban supremacy, when he became "the dynastic god of the New Kingdom".[29] Yet, Herodotus points out a basic fact that throughout Egyptian history "no gods (were) worshiped in common by the whole of Egypt save only Isis and Osiris,"[30] whose sovereignty over other deities persisted when the influence of others were subject to changes in dynastic policies.

Just as the Greek and Egyptian religions were polytheistic, so likewise were the religions of the ancient Babylonians, with whom the Israelites had cultural contacts, as they also had with the Egyptians. Although the Babylonian pantheon included many gods, it was Marduk, as guardian of Babylon, who held sovereignty over all the other deities, who were his subordinates. In this respect, his role was comparable to the role of Zeus in the history of Greek religions.

There is, of course, no basis for comparing features of any polytheistic religion with the religion of the Israelites, who acknowledged only one guardian god as worthy of their trust; but there is a parallel in the properties with which both the Babylonians interpreted the nature of Marduk and the Israelites interpreted the nature of their own sovereign god. The Israelites interpreted their god as "the Babylonian Epic of Creation" interpreted Marduk, when it declares that he is "the King of the gods of heaven and earth, the King of all the gods."[31] The Israelites acknowledged that the peoples with whom they had cultural contacts also had gods; and so they were aware of the plurality of deities to which other religions were oriented. But they oriented their religion to one god, whom they revered as their guardian, in relation to whom they believed the gods of other people were inferior.

Every ancient people acknowledged that other people worshiped gods other than they themselves did. Yet, each people trusted its own god or gods, as they did not trust the guardian deities of other people. Herodotus, for instance, records an address, attributed to Xerxes, leader of the Persians, when at the Hellespont, he began his invasion of Hellas: "Now let us cross over, having first prayed to the gods who hold Persia for their allotted realm.[32] From the point of view of the Persians, they were the special people of their gods, just as the Israelites regarded themselves as the "chosen people" of their guardian god. Lucian, for instance, described the "great sacrifices" which were celebrated by the ancient Syrians, "not far from the river Euphrates, which is called the Sacred City" because "it is sacred to the Assyrian Hera". It was at this religious occasion, as Lucian points out, everyone who attended brought "his own god and the images which each one has for this purpose."[33]

It is only when one understands the attachment of individuals and entire peoples to the gods which they trust, as they do not trust other gods, that it is possible to understand the full significance of the account given in the "apocryphal" Book of Judith, when "Holophernes, commander-in-chief of Nebuchadnezzar's Assyrian army, demolished all their sanctuaries and cut down their sacred groves, since he had been commissioned to destroy all the gods of the land, so that Nebuchadnezzar alone should be worshiped by every nation and invoked as a god by men of every tribe and tongue." This obviously was equivalent to destroying the religions in the vast regions over which the Babylonian ruler had political dominance; and it is, therefore, in light of this arrogance of the that one can understand their struggle to preserve their identity as a people, central to which was their religious tradition.

Herodotus can help one to understand the centrality of a people's god to their total life, whom they trust as having concern for them, and only for them, when he characterizes the Thracians as "believing in no other god but their own".[34] This characterization could be applied to an interpretation of the religious orientations of other ancient people, oriented in trust to guardian gods, to whom they appeal for help, such as they do not appeal to other peoples' guardian gods. The Old Testament preserves a record of the tenacity with which the Israelites were determined to retain the religious faith of their forefathers, oriented to the guardian god whom the Patriarchs trusted.

(ii) A guardian god's concern is for his own people

The god whom Abraham and Isaac trusted appeared to Jacob when he was on a journey, declaring to him: "I will be with you and I will protect you wherever you go"(Gen;2812). This assurance sums up the role of a guardian deity in relation to those who trust it for a guidance and a protection, such as they do not believe

112

would be accessible to them from any other reality. Others who also maintain a right to expect such providential help from the same guardian god are always related to each other, either in a family or in a community. The extent of such a community may vary from a tribe or a clan to a nation; yet, what is common to those who turn to a particular deity as their divine guardian is either a blood relationship or a broader ethnic relationship.

The Israelite's version of their guardian god stresses a contractual relation between them and their god, which in other religious cultures is less defined, although some reciprocity is always presumed between a divine guardian and those who trust its providence. When, and only when, they are faithful in acknowledging their total dependence upon their own god, do they also acknowledge that they have a right to look forward to their god's unfailing dependability. It is such a relationship that entails a reciprocity which is expressed in the characterization of Israel's god as "The guardian of Israel (who) never slumbers, never sleeps"(Ps.121:2). And it is this basic faith in the unfailing dependability of the guardian god, to whom the Patriarchs were dedicated in faithful worship, which is basic to Jacob's trust in the promises of the god whom his father also trusted, when his god assured him that he "will bring (him) back" to his home after his long journey. This assurance is itself implied in the fundamental creed of faith in the Patriarch's guardian god: "I will not leave you until I have done all that I have promised"(Gen.28:15).

Whereas this assurance fulfils an essential human need to trust a reality which does not disappoint one's confidence, the scope of those who come within the earliest version of the guardian god of the Patriarchs is restricted to their descendants. The blood relation in this case is basic to all subsequent ethnic qualifications for being a recipient of the providential guidance of the deity who was served by Abraham, Isaac, and Jacob. This sequence in the patriarchal tradition of a religion, as it is characterized in the Pentateuch, is a blood or family relationship. This is thoroughly unambiguous in the declaration in Numbers (6:1) that "Yahweh spoke to Moses", telling him to speak "to the sons of Israel"; and it is in light of this priestly version in Numbers that one can understand the intended scope of the account in Leviticus of "the Commandments that Yahweh laid down for Moses on Mount Sinai"(27:34). In this

113

text, it is declared that they were intended "for the sons of Israel".

The original intention of this text in Leviticus is that the god, worshiped in the religious tradition of the Patriarchs, entrusted the commandments to Moses, as leader of his people, consisting of the descendants of Abraham, Isaac, and Jacob, as this tradition is characterized in the Pentateuch. An extension of the denotative scope of "Israel" beyond the descendants who traced their blood relation, and therefore, their religious tradition, to Jacob, and in turn, to his father, and his father's father, is adapting this Old Testament text without respect for its original intention.

The scope of concern of the deity, who delivered the commandments to Moses, is again specified in a thoroughly unambiguous statement in Numbers (35:34): "I, Yahweh, live among the sons of Israel." The denotative range of this priestly version of "Israel" is the blood relation to the descendants of Jacob, who were likewise descendants of the Patriarchs who preceded him. This highly restricted version of "Israel", as the recipients of the Law, and specifically of the Decalogue, persisted throughout the centuries before the Christian era, and this is also unambiguously affirmed in the Qumran text of "The Document of the New Covenant in the Land of Damascus", commonly referred to as the "Damascus Document". This text of a Jewish Essene sect maintains that Abraham, as a "friend of God", did not live by "the will of his own spirit", but his fidelity to his god continued as the normative way of life in his son, and in his son's son, Jacob, whose name was changed to "Israel". The text declares that this guardian god of Abraham "handed down to Isaac and Jacob"(Israel), his requirements of them and of those who also followed in their religious tradition.35

Since the Book of Joshua is canonical in the traditional Hexateuch, its opening should likewise be respected as preserving the earliest priestly interpretation of the scope of the expression, "people of Israel". It declares that "after the death of Moses", Joshua was commanded by the god whom Moses served, to carry on the role of Moses, "servant" of his god; and this responsibility included the instruction "to cross the Jordan, you and this whole people of Israel,to the land which I am giving them"(1:1-2). "The people of Israel" referred to in this text are those whose blood relationship traced to the Hebrews, who journeyed from Ur of Chaldees in search of land, in total disregard of the fact that it was taken from those who owned it, is characteristic of guardian gods in antiquity. The god of the descendants of the Patriarchs was, as their tutelary deity, interested only in them as his people. His obligations, therefore, were limited to them, just as their obligations in worship were restricted to him as the one and only god whom they should worship. In other words, the god worshiped by the Patriarchs and their descendants was the god of a people whose blood relationship was basic to the tribal organization of all who were included in the "descendants" of the Patriarchs who entered Egypt as an identifiable people, distinguished from all other ethnically related people. It was to this people that Moses and Aaron referred in making their demands upon Pharaoh, doing so in the name of the "God of Israel": "Let my people go"(Ex.5:2).

The expression "my people" is critical in this scriptural text because it denotes those who had journeyed together in search of a new home, and who had endured, as one people, the adversities from which they trusted their god to liberate them.

The tribal character of the god on whose authority the leaders of the Israelites approached Pharaoh is unambiguous. The text in Exodus refers to "the god of the Hebrews"; and it was this guardian god of one ethnically related people, journeying to Egypt, who, according to Exodus, also identified his relation to his own people when he declared: "You shall know that I...am your god, the god who released you from your labours in Egypt"(8:7). And the identity of this god as tribal, not as universal, is stated as clearly as any language could affirm it when this deity of a people, wandering as a tribe or clan, declares: "I will remain with the sons of Israel, and I will be their god." The tribal or ethnic character of the god, to whom Exodus refers, affirms his concern for his own people alone when he declares: "It is I, Yahweh, their god, who brought them out of the land of Egypt to live among them"(29:45-46). The expression "to live among them" is of utmost critical significance for any ethnological study of ancient religions, the purpose of which is understanding ancient texts, as they were intended to be understood. This text specifically declares that the deliverance of the Israelites from Egyptian bondage was not only, or even primarily, for their benefit. It was also, and very likely, as acknowledged by the priestly authors, for the sake of the god who continued to have a people devoted to him as their sole benefactor. This text thus indicates the reciprocal relation basic to the ancient Israelites' version of their guardian god, as well as to parallel versions of the guardian gods of other ancient peoples.

A highly significant text of ethnological importance is a reference in Second Kings to the prophet Elisah, who maintains that, as spokesman for "the god of Israel", he is authorized to anoint the "King over Israel"; to which people he refers as "people of the Lord". The deity so referred to was regarded as guardian of this one people, whose religious orientation had remained the primary determinant of their cohesiveness as a people, searching for a homeland on which to become established as a nation, thereby terminating the trials of their years of adversities in this search for a permanent homeland to which they had been promised by their guardian god, to whom Jacob referred as his "shepherd" when he blessed his son Joseph (Gen.48:15). The eighth Psalm preserves this ancient version of the god worshiped by the early Israelites as "shepherd of Israel"(vs.1). Associating the properties of a shepherd, as guardian of his sheep, with the properties of Israel's guardian god, stresses their helplessness without his guidance, and therefore, their total dependence upon his care for them.

This version of the scope of concern of the god, worshiped by the early Israelites, is reaffirmed in later "apocryphal" writings, which are not included in the Palestinian canon, and therefore, are not a part of the Hebrew Scriptures, but nevertheless, are of utmost ethnological importance for the earlier canonical interpretation of "the heavenly Lord of Israel"(I Esdras 6:15). Second Maccabees is likewise important for pointing out that it is the "whole people Israel" who are the special people of their guardian god. And the exclusive claim to his sovereignty and to his concern is unambiguously declared in affirming: "Let the heathen know that thou are our god"(1:27). "Heathen is used in a specific sense in this reference for denoting all who do not worship the god in whom the Israelites trusted as their own guardian god. And the restricted scope of the concern of the god of the Israelites, as one people, is declared by Ezra in an apocryphal text in an interrogation which he addresses to the god of the Israelites: "Has any nation except Israel ever known you?" (II Esdras 3:32) The answer is obvious: Contemporaries of the Israelites among

restricting their providence to their own people, which certainly is not the property of a cosmic or universal god. Such a cosmic or universal character was remote from the primary concerns of a people who were subject to contingencies of weather, as well as of other people in relation to whom they lived and with whom they competed for limited resources, which each people regarded as essential for themselves, and therefore, turned to their own guardian god to help them preserve such available goods for themselves. A people confronted with their own survival were not oriented to cosmic dimensions and to a divine sovereignty over the totality of existing reality. They were rather concerned with their own survival in physical contexts of conditions often insufficient for themselves, let alone adequate for them and also for other people. Every shepherd, for instance, living in an arid country was concerned for the sheep over which he had responsibilities; and extending this responsibility to a guardian god, trusted as a shepherd of his people, enables one to understand what the earliest Israelites meant by believing that their god was their shepherd. If one cannot understand this, he then has no awareness of how the twenty-third psalm preserves the religious concerns of the earliest Israelites, as a migratory people. The guardian deity of such a people was believed by them to have concerns for them, and not for a world or a cosmos. The first verse of Genesis may well reflect the level of Babylonian civilization of the seventh century B.C., in its "Epic of Creation", but it has no relation whatever to the religious faith of the early patriarchs, who also as "shepherds" of their people, trusted a divine shepherd to provide a guidance and a security for them and for their people, which they themselves could not provide. This acknowledgment of such a radical contrast between their capacities and resources, and the capacities and resources of their guardian god, is the primary creed of their religious faith. No cosmological speculation entered into the religions of other people who lived in comparable physical and cultural contexts.

The ethnological significance of the greater part of the Old Testament is glossed over when what is attributed to the god, in whom the earliest patriarchs believed, is assumed to be formulated in this cosmological concept with which Genesis begins. This was introduced by scholars more than a thousand years later than the history of Abraham and his first descendants, if this is regarded as not later than 1800 B.C.

Some biblical scholarship, however, has little regard for the ethnological importance of the biblical text for preserving an early version of a religious faith, oriented to a guardian god of one people, who is concerned with them as his special scope of obligations, and is in no way committed, according to his own people's faith, to be considerate of the welfare of their neighbors, especially when they were also their foes. The suggestion, for example, in the scholarly studies, Documents from Old Testament Times, that it would be preferable to "reserve the term 'monotheism' for Hebrew religion and employ for the religion of Akhenaten a less restrictive term, such as monolatry, the worship of one god to the exclusion of others,"58 applies only to theological concepts, such as is affirmed in the first verse of Genesis, which affirms the culture of Hebrews who are removed by at least a thousand years from their earliest cultural origins in the tradition of Abraham, Isaac, and Jacob. It is a disservice, therefore, to anyone who seriously endeavors to understand the Old Testament, not to be aware of the cultural chasm between events recorded in the earliest history of the Israelites and the metaphysic or cosmology which is declared in the first verse of Genesis. When account is not taken of the characteristic properties of a tribal tutelary deity, but are predicted of a god worthy of universal worship, the spiritual level of such worship is reduced to the level of a primitive mentality, or the mentality of a tribal group, preoccupied with their survival, and not with spiritual enlightenment.

With very few exceptions, which will be acknowledged in a following chapter, the religion identified with the patriarchal tradition should be classified as monolatry, when this term is defined as it is suggested in the above quotation form Documents from Old Testament Times. Even a passage, such as in the forty-third chapter in Isaiah, is capable of being regarded both as an expression of a monolatrous version of religion, as well as of a monotheistic version of religion. If, however, the denotative meaning of the term "Israel" is regarded as the key to the meaning of the affirmation, "I am the Lord, your Holy One, your creator, Israel, and your king (vs.15), it is then an unequivocal affirmation of a monolatrous belief, since it would qualify as "worship of one god to the exclusion of others", whose "existence", however, is "not denied". The denotative range of "Israel" has one meaning in the religious tradition of the Patriarchs, and extending its denotative meaning beyond the descendants of the Patriarchs, is disregarding its historical meaning, as the historical books of the Bible are admirably careful to preserve.

A faith, such as is affirmed in Second Kings, that "there is no god anywhere on earth except in Israel"(5:15), is also characteristic of a monolatrous religion, such as the faith of a people in their own guardian god. This affirmation of faith declares a belief that among others gods of other people, there is no god who could have done what was credited to the providential help of the god worshiped by the Israelites. The collective term for this people is "Israel", and its meaning in the historical books of the Old Testament is respected only when its denotative scope is so restricted.

The eighty-first psalm preserves this historically early meaning of "Israel" when the god of the Israelites declares: "If Israel would only conform to my ways, I would soon bring their enemies to their knees"(vs.14). The assurance of military victory for one people is thus affirmed by their god, whose concern for them, is distinguished from all others in economic and political relations with whom they are forced to struggle for their well-being. The god of the early Israelites fought with them and for them, just as Chemosh, the tutelary deity of the Moabites fought for them. The ethnologically valuable ancient record, "The Moabite Stone", declares a Moabite faith in their god Chemosh, who commanded them: "Go, take Nebo against Israel". Following this instruction of Chemosh, he declared that whereas he "slew all", it was "Chemosh (who) drove out ("the king of Israel") before me".59 In other words, what Chemosh did for his own people, the Moabites, the guardian god of the Israelites did for them, and for no other people.

The Israelites, as a monolatrous people is clearly characterized in Exodus with the interrogation directed to their own guardian god: "Who among the gods is your like, Yahweh?...terrible in deeds of prowess"(15:11). The capacities of their god are directed on behalf of his own people, as the same reference declares when their god is credited with "stretch(ing) his right hand out," whereupon "the earth swallowed"(vs.12) the gods and the people devoted to them; and Yahweh did this on behalf of his own people.

The monolatrous type of religion of which Exodus gives an historical account is clearly stated in the command

137

which is attributed to the god of the Israelites:...do not repeat the name of other gods: let it not be heard from your lips"(23:13). Even the mention of the gods of other people would be a sacrilege for a people who should devote their unqualified trust and loyalty to their own god, and should not qualify it even so little as mentioning the names of other gods, since such names were regarded as identical with the gods themselves; and thus Israelites would admit into their lives, the gods of other people in the mere mentioning of their names.

The monolatrous, rather than monotheistic, character of the religion of Moses is declared in Deuteronomy when he spoke to his people, the Israelites, asking them: "What great nation is there that has its gods so near as Yahweh our god is to us whenever we call him?"(4:7). This text both attributes to Moses the belief that there are other gods of other people, and also the belief that the god whom he worshiped and served on behalf of his people, responded to their appeals for his providential help, which was not extended to other people, whose gods were depreciated in being contrasted with Yahweh, who was nearer to his own people than all other guardian gods were to their own people.

The priestly authors of Deuteronomy repeatedly praise the tutelary nature of Israel's god, such as again asking: "Did ever a god attempt to come and take a nation for himself away from another nation...with a strong hand"(4:34), such as was believed by the priests to be demonstrated when the Israelites defeated other people, and drove them from their land, adding it to their own spoils of military combat. The priestly acknowledgment that there are gods of other people is affirmed in the presumed tribute to their own god: "Bow down, all your gods, before him"(32:43).

The accuracy of historical reporting is to the credit of the authors of Second Kings when they point out that "each of the nations made its own god"(17:29), and it was the order of "the king of Assyria" that "one of the priests from Samaria should be sent back to...teach the people the usage of the god of the country"(vs.28). It would be ignoring the historical value of the Old Testament accounts of the history of the Israelites if the nature of the religion of their contemporaries were ignored, since a critical part of their history is their cultural contacts with peoples who had their own gods, which at times seemed to some of the Israelites as offering greater advantages than the guardian god to

138

such judgment was indiscriminate also for the "half of the city" which was taken by the Babylonians into exile, among whom were children, who were unaware of the reason cited by the Prophet for their suffering.

It is only a primitive version of what is just that so disregards the right of those who suffer punishment to understand why they are so punished. Whereas the people condemned by the prophetic tradition may well have been indifferent to obligations defined for them in the early years of their history, the prophetic tradition might have learned much from the spiritually profound question asked by Moses and Aaron: "If one man sins, wilt thou be angry with the whole community"(num.16:22).

Ezekiel also equalled this depth of understanding when he declared: "A man shall not die for his father's wrong doing"(18:17), but "It is the soul that sins, and no others, that shall die"(vs.20). Yet, the passionate zeal with which he indicted his people for what he, as a priest, regarded their religious obligations, accounts for much in his own prophecy against his people, to fall far below the spiritual level of his own wisdom, when it was not handicapped by the intensity of his indignation and anger.

A person interprets every reality from his own point of basic fact underlying all interpretations explains what John Locke maintains, which cannot be repeated to often when interpreting Scripture: "God does not unmake the man when he makes the prohet!" What one thinks about a divine reality is conditioned by what one himself is; and conversely, what one holds himself accountable for, as a moral being, is conditioned, or even in considerable part, is determined by what one regards as an ideal of what ought to be. A religious person is confronted by such an ideal in his interpretation of the nature of divine reality; and it is in this sense that one can acquire an inventory of a person's expectations of himself by knowing what he believes are true interpretations of a divine reality.

The struggle of the Israelites to survive as a people persisted for centuries after the dissolution of the Northern Kingdom in 722 B.C. In 197 B.C., Judaea became a province of the Seleucid Empire, ruled by Syrian successors of Alexander the Great. And it was pressed in its effort to persist as a religious tradition that the Pharisees, in 88 B.C., appealed to the Seleucid king, Demetrius III, to help overthrow the spurious priesthood of Alexander Jannaeus, referred to as "the Wicked Priest", for whom the Roman rulers were responsible. Since the Seleucid ruler was unaable to overthrow the well entrenched priest, he withdrew, and the Priest ordered the execution of eight hundred of the Pharisses.41 This is mentioned only to point out the life-and-death struggle of those who were dedicated to preserving a religious identity internal to a context which was antagonistic to it, and to the people who were devoted to it.

It is out of this political and cultural context that another determined effort arose to retain their religious tradition. This was undertaken by a sect which was identified as Zealots, who believed that the submissiveness of some, such as practiced by some of the Essenes, would eventually result in the extermination of their tradition as a people, the religious ideal of which was conforming to the ancient Law. Since the tyranny of Rome over the Jews respected no restraint for their rights, the Zealots undertook to appose the Romans, on the same principles as the Romans had tyranized over them. Their unrestricted opposition to the Romans was under the ancient motivation of the faithful among the Israelites to tolerate no master other than their divine sovereign.42 The banner under which they championed their cause of opposing the Roman rule was the ancient religious appeal for fidelity to their god. Since the Romans respected no rights of the Jews on behalf of their religious tradition, some among the Zealots, such as Sicarius, defended the retaliatory principle of doing to the Romans what they continued to do to them. This was the principle basic to a party identified as Sicarri, which defended assassination of Romans as an act of fidelity to their god. The sanction for this policy of disposing of those who were regarded as enemies of their god is, of course, scriptural. As the foregoing part of this section points out, the Old Testament repeatedly maintains that the guardian god of the Israelites destroyed entire peoples who were not obedient to his Laws and to his rule. Thus the most extreme principles of the Sicarii for opposing Roman rule were merely the policies of the theocracy which had been the religious ideal for centuries of the early Israelites.

There is, of course, no parallel in Greek religion for the theocratic concept of an entire people to live by laws which are regarded as conveyed to them as a totality, and which were to displace all ordinances which were sanctioned by human councils. The strong sense of Greek individualism could not have duplicated a religious tradition extending, as it did, for centuries among the Israelites. There are, however, scattered references in Greek literature, which seem to be parallels, such as the Homeric epigram that affirms the appeal to "observe the reverence due to Zeus who rules on high...for terrible is the vengeance of this god...for whosoever has sinned."43 This, however, cannot be compared with the life-and-death character of the Israelites' version of fidelity to their god, and the unrestrained penalty sanctioned by their god for infidelity to him.

The concept of an intolerance of a Greek deity to other Greek deities is likewise incidental, such as the jealousy of Artemis and Aphrodite for each other, which was expressed as vindictive behaviour in Euripides' Hippolytus, such as the decree of Aphrodite that she will punish Hippolytus for neglecting worship of her, and Artemis' vow that she will avenge her favorite's death, which was caused by Aphrodite. This characterization of intorerance of one goddess for another may have no more than dramatic significance in the Prologue to this play, and therefore, cannot be regarded as more than incidental in considering a parallel to the dominant role of divine intolerance and vindictiveness in the biblical version of the theocratic religion of the ancient Israelites.

The threat of Demeter, as interpreted in the Homeric Hymm, planning "an aweful deed to destroy the weakly tribes of earthborn men by keeping seed hidden beneath the earth"44 is, likewise, in no way comparabale to the threats of the guardian god of the Israelites, whose threat is his displeasure for a people's infidelity. Such a version of infidelity is basic to the biblical version of the nature of the deity worshiped by the Israelites, because it is a fundamental element in a theocratic interpretation of the total sovereignty over a people by one god who demands of them unqualified obedience to his Laws.

7. <u>There</u> <u>are</u> <u>no</u> <u>moral</u> <u>restraints</u> <u>in</u> <u>a</u> <u>god's</u> <u>expressions</u> <u>of</u> <u>his</u> <u>favoritism</u> <u>for</u> <u>his</u> <u>own</u> <u>people</u>

According to Genesis, when Abram reached Shechem, his god assured him: "I will give this land to your descendants"(12:6-7). Since this was territory occupied by the Canaanites, this presumed authorization, which was eventually to take away the land from them, introduces one of the most sobering aspects of a version of religion which is regarded in the Old Testament as based upon a divine sanction. Such a sanction, attributed to a guardian god, is a rationalized version of theft, under the gloss of a presumed divine authorization, which is expressed in a tribal god's assurance that "All the land you can see I will give to you and to your descendants"(vs.14-15).

There isn't the slightest consideration for what is just in this tribal god's presumption to give away land possessed by others because he has his own people to whom his concerns are confined; and what he does for them is without any moral consideration for its fairness or justice, such as is basic even in communities of primitive people, where some rights of property-possession are respected. This sanction for appropriating land which is possessed by another people is, however, compatible with a notion of a guardian deity, because his only concern is for the people for whom he has obligations, just as they have obligations only to him. The resticted relation of one people to their own guardian god, and his correspondingly resticted concern for them, is basic to the interpretation of such a deity, which is also affirmed in Exodus, when he assures his people: "...if you...hold fast to my covenant, you of all the nations shall be my very own"(19:5).

The covenant, of course, to which the tribal god refers is to his own people. Such favoritism of a tutelary deity for his own people is thus stressed when he assures them that the earth belongs to him, and therefore, as it were, he can do with any part of it as he chooses to do. This obviously is a gloss added by scribes and priests when this detail in the history of the Israelites was reconstructed to diminish, if possible, the immorality of taking possessions to which they otherwise had no rightful claim. Any moral censorship which a people would otherwise consider for such theft is thereby glossed over by the myth of a divine sanction.

The same type of gloss is again affirmed in Exodus in order to justify, if possible, what the Israelites did when they left Egypt. According to this account, the women among them, who were leaving Egypt, were instructed to ask "their neighbors", as well as other women, "for silver ornaments and gold", with which to "adorn" their own "sons and daughters". This obvious

182

instance of appropriating the property of others was defended in this scriptual account of their quardian god's way of retaliating for the injustices to them during their years of servitude to the Egyptians. According to the principle of "eye for an eye", this would be morally just; and it is on this principle that Scripture justifies "plunder (of) the Egyptians" as retaliatory justice, rather than an immorality, when judged by another moral principle, such as one which condemns retaliation. Retaliatory justice, however, is basic to most of the Old Testament's version of what the guardian god authorizes or sanctions for his people's acts in relation to other people, for whom their god has no concern, and consequently, no respect for their moral rights.

Another morally offensive religious interpretation which is admitted into Exodus in characterizing what the god of the Israelites did on behalf of his own people is that he made "Pharaoh obstinate", thereby destroying whatever intelligently enlightened acting he might otherwise have had in deciding what to do in preventing their exodus. Entirely disregarding this moral consideration, this account states, as clearly as possible, what constitutes the basic consideration of a guardian god: It is whatever he can do for his own advantage in strengthening his hold upon his own people's fidelity to him. This is declared when the god admits that he did this to discredit the intelligence of Paraoh "so that I may win glory for myself at the expense of Pharaoh and all his army". As the account in Exodus continues, it is explained not so much for the benefit of the Israelites, as for the glorification of their god, which their god admits when he says that thereby "the Egyptians shall know that I am the Lord"(14:3-4). In other words, he will thus demonstrate that the god of the Israelites is more powerful than the gods whom the Egyptians trust and worship.

The total disregard of the guardian god of the Israelites for any moral consideration is likewise affirmed in Deuteronomy, which stresses how the guardian god of the early Israelites "exterminates the nations whose land" he gives to his own people. And, as if clearly aware of the immorality of such a dispossessing of a people from their own "national" territories, refers to taking their "houses" when their "cities" are appropriated (19:1). The priestly acknowledgment that their god concerns himself in whatever he does to "avenge the blood of his people is

183

pointed out in maintaining that their god "take(s)
vengeance on his adversaries (who) hate him"(32:43).
This preoccupation of the Israelites' guardian god with
his intrenchment in the dependence of his people upon
him is a priestly way of stressing the imperative
necessity of their people to give unqualified fidelity
to their god, lest they be treated by him as he treats
"his adversaries".

Another aspect of a primitive version of a people's
tutelary deity is stressed in Numbers, which maintains
that the Israelites "made war on Midian as the Lord had
commanded...and slew all the men", but took "the
Midianite women...and carried off all their beasts,
their flocks, and their property". After "they took
all the spoil and plunder", they "burnt all their
cities"(31:8-10). Such "plunder" was the reward, as it
were, for the people whose fighting forces received
their god's reinforcement. But then the priestly
emphasis recurs in pointing out the anger of Moses with
the "officers of the army" who had "spared all the
men", since he had remembered how before, when they did
the same thing, it was such captured women who "set
about seducing the Israelites into disloyalty" to their
god.

Thinking only of the demands of their god upon them,
and not of the rights of their captives to be regarded
as human beings, Moses took both the god's wants into
consideration, and also the wants of the men in the
army, when he ordered that "every woman who has had
intercourse" shall be killed; but the life of others
shall be spared "for yourselves"(31:14-19), who
numbered, according to this account, "thirty-two
thousand"(vs.45).

The Book of Joshua continues an account of the early
Israelites "after the death of Moses"(1:1), and it
repeats the same presumption as had assured Abram of
"the land" which their god was "giving them": "Every
place where you set foot is yours"(vs.3) The god's
reinforcement of their military campaign is again
reassured: "No one will ever be able to stand against
you"(vs.6). In this entire book, there isn't so much as
one reference to a moral consideration for the rights
to life or property of any people whose territory the
Israelites desired to take for their own. The campaign
against Ai, for instance, ended with a "massacre" which
the text characterizes as "complete". Joshua, as
military leader, reinforced by his god, "did not draw
back his hand until he had put to death all who lived

in Ai". Thus their total destruction was not for any military advantage after the city had been defeated, any more than was its destruction by being "burnt...to the ground"(8:24-28). This destruction of an entire people, and everything for which they had worked, was "following the word of the Lord", which were his demands given to Joshua, including that "The Israelites kept for themselves the cattle and any other spoil that they took"(8:24-29).

The Book of Joshua, included in the Hexateuch as sacred scripture, continues with the repeated formula that the god of the Israelites "had delivered" every people who opposed their fighting forces "into (their) hands". Accounts of such campaigns conclude with the comment that when "Joshua and the Israelites...finished the work of slaughter", "all had been put to the sword", whereas by virtue of their god's role, "the Israelites suffered (not) so much as a scratch"(10:20).

The same formula is repeated: "The lord delivered Lachish into their hands", and the same type of commentary is added: "They...put every living thing in it to the sword"(32). The same description is given for the military campaigns against "the hill-country, the Negeb, the Shephelah, the watersheds": "Joshua massacred the population of the whole region." "He left no survivor, destroying everything that drew breath." And the same priestly comment is added that all this had been done "as the...god of Israel had commanded." Continuing to fulfil such a command of their god, "Joshua carried the slaughter from Kadesh-barnea to Gaza, over the whole land of Goshen." And again, the reaffirmation of the sanction for such merciless destruction of entire cities: "The god of Israel fought for Israel"(10:40-41).

The writers of the book of Joshua bend over backwards to argue the military successes of the Israelites as evidence for all that their god was able to do for them. The names of many kings and many people are enumerated to argue that no amount of military opposition to the Israelites, under the instructions of "the Lord to Joshua", could defeat the people whom their god championed. Their opponents, as the text maintains, was "a great horde, countless as the grains of sand on the sea-shore". Their god assured them, in the face of this massive opposition: "Do not be afraid of them, for...I shall deliver them to Israel all dead men."

The cruelty attributed to their militarily powerful
deity includes a total insensitivity in his command
that after destroying all the people, the army of the
Israelites "shall hamstring their horses", as if the
brutality to human beings was not enough, but needed an
additional cruelty to animals.

So successful were the fighting forces of the
Israelites, under their god's sanction for disregarding
the rights to life of every living thing, that the
account in this chapter closes with the priestly boast
on behalf of their god's behalf of their god's role
that the fighting forces "struck down" the armies of
those whose lands the god of the Israelites gave to
them, "until not a man was left alive"(11:1-8).

The eleventh chapter continues the enumeration of the
many cities and their entire populations they were
destroyed, in which "they did not leave alive any one
that drew breath". This merciless cruelty, as the text
declares, is attributed to the god of the Israelites,
who "laid his commands" on the leaders of their armies.
And the fidelity of Joshua to his god is indicated,
according to this scriptural account, by declaring:
"not one of the commands...by the (god) did(Joshua)
leave unfulfilled"(vs.14-15).

The account of Joshua's campaigns in "the hill-country"
is continued, with the same commentary of pride of
which the writers of the Book of Joshua had in the
military successes of the god to conduct these
campaigns of defeating and destroying entire cities and
their total populations, continued to take "their
kings" as prisoners, striking "them down and put(ting)
them to death".

The authors of this book attribute the same additional
immorality to their god as had been attributed to his
paralyzing of the intelligence of Pharaoh: "it was the
Lord's purpose that (these kings) should offer an
obstinate resistance to the Israelites in battle", so
that "they should be annihilated without mercy and
utterly destroyed, as the Lord had
commanded"(vs.16-20). This account implies, as is
evident, that if their god had not impaired the
intelligence or willing of the many kings, they may
have surrendered before their cities and their entire
populations had been destroyed.

The military successes under Joshua continued,
according to this account, until "all the hill-country

of Judah and all the hill-country of Israel" had been destroyed. In this destruction of "the whole country", Joshua "fulfilled the commands" of the god of the Israelites (11:22). Implied in such commands was the sanction of their god for the unrestrained "slaughter" of entire peoples, including their defenceless childred, as well as all the nonfighting population of aged and helpless. No record of sheer cruelty could eclipse what this book of scripture attributes to the sanction and commands of the tutelary deity of the Israelites under ths religious gloss of fulfulling the convenantal agreement which was first made to Abram: "I give this land to your descendants", approving thereby whatever they did to disposses those who inhabited it, in order to take it for themselves.

Among the diverse interpretations affirmed in Psalms, one is a continuation of the confidence affirmed in the preceding books of the Bible that it is at the "bidding" of the god of the Israelites that they are "victorious", and that it is by virtue of their god"s help that they "will throw back" their enemies. The same cruelty to others, and also the same low level of a nonspiritual religion, is affirmed by the Psalmist when he declares to his god: "in thy name we will trample down our adversaries"(44:4-5). In thus addressing himself to his god, he expresses no consideration for the rights of others to live, but only the military effectiveness of destroying those whom the Israelites regarded as their foes. The emphasis in this psalm is that it is their god who will "put all "(their) enemies to shame", indicates that it reaffirms the type of religion which is basic to the Book of Joshua, in which the principal orientation of a people to their guardian god is for his reinforcementof their military ventures.

Included in the Psalms is likewise the reaffirmation of a religious explanation for the dispossessing of people from their homes, in which the Israelites "drove out nations before them", and "allotted" to themselves "their lands...as a possession and settled...in their dwellings"(78:55). If the reflecting which is expressed in this psalm were done by a person with any moral sensitivity, this religious explanation might well be regarded as a gloss to lessen a distressing sense of guilt for a chapter in his people's history for which he has a deep sense of shame. But by attributing the dispossessing of other peope from "their dwellings" to the sanction of the god of his people, he removes completely any basis for such moral censuring, together with its accompanying guilt for what his people did in their military campaigns, of which the writers of the Book of Joshua took pride.

A part of the ease with which the psalmist removes the sense of shame and guilt from what was done by the Israelites, of which the priestly writers of Joshua approved and attributed to a sanction of their god, is thinking of all the people, who were so destroyed and robbed of their homes, as "heathen". Thus there is a double reason for absolving his people and himself from censure for destroying entire cities so that they could appropriate for themselves their cattle and other possessions: One is that these people were "heathens"; and the other is that it was the authorization by their god that they, as his people, should receive from their god the evidence of his superiority to the gods of "the lands of heathen nations".

A sting of conscience, however, is not totally concealed in the Psalmist"s rationalizing gloss, since he admits in the same verse, that what his people took from others were lands and homes for whose "possession...others had toiled"(105:44). This acknowledgment clearly reveals a basic moral sensitivity of what is wrong when one people take "possession" of goods for which "others had toiled"; and by such industry had a claim to them, such as "plundering" and "slaughtering" in warfare cannot morally defend or justify.

One of the lowest levels of both religion and morality is affirmed in Psalm 149, which combines in one verse the exhortation: "Let the high praises" of their god "be on their lips and a two-edged sword in their hand" with which "to wreak vengeance on the nations". Yet, this low level of spiritual and religious insensitivity is sanctioned by the purpose of doing so "to chastise the heathen"(vs.6-7). In other words, destroying people who are "heathen", because they trust gods which are others than the god regarded by the Israelites as their guardian god, is, according to the Psalmist, a way of demonstrating fidelity to the god of his people, and "load(ing) their kings with chains and put(ting) their nobles in iron", is what the Psalmist regards as "execut(ing) the judgment decreed against them" by the guardian god of the Israelites. And in so far as his people take part in this warfare against others, destroying them and plundering their possessions, they do "this" as an expression of "the glory of all his faithful servants"(vs.8-9).

The so-called "major prophets" reaffirm the same
religious faith that it was the guardian god of the
Israelites who reinforced their armies, making it
possible for them to defeat peoples with military
resources far in excess of theirs. Isaiah, for
instance, declares that it was "at the voice" of the
god of the Israelites that great "Assyria"s heart fails
her", and it was "the stroke of (the) rod"(30:31) of
the Israelites' god which accounted for their military
strength to engage the armies of so powerful a country.

Jeremiah repeats the version of the history of his
people, as this was affirmed in Joshua and in the
Pentateuch, when he declares that it was "The Lord
(who) opened his arsenal and brought out the weapons of
his wrath" "in the land of Chaldaeans". He repeats the
same challenge which is basic to the military campaigns
of which the Book of Joshua gives an account,
declaring: "Destroy her, let no survivor be left. Put
all her warriors to the sword; let them be led to
slaughter." The defeat of this people and the
destruction of their armies were regarded by Jeremiah
as "proclaim(ing)...the vengeance" of the god of the
Israelites (50:24-28).

Jeremiah reaffirms the long respected retaliatory
principle in previous biblical justifications for the
losses of the soldiers of the Israelites in their
encounters with their foes, when he declares: "Babylon
must fall for the sake of Israel's slain"(51:49). As
has been acknowledged, this justification for
retaliation is on the basis of one concept of justice,
and in this respect, therefore, Jeremiah's
interpretation that "the lord's designs against Babylon
are fulfilled"(vs.29), cannot be censured for the same
immorality as is basic to many other biblical defenses
by which the Israelites' warfare is justified.

Lamentations indicates its authorship by Jeremiah in
what it regards as compatible with a divine reality,
much of which is a repetition of the most primitive
version of a religion which is oriented to a tribal
deity. In his interpretation of such a reality, he
regards its moral level to be the same as his own, and
in this respect, Lamentations has more value for a
study of a psychology of religious beliefs than for a
theology which is worthy of being included in a
scripture. Addressing himself to the "Lord",
interpreted not as a universal or cosmic god, but
rather as a vindictive tribal god, he proposes that the
god show "how hard thy heart can be, how little concern

thou hast for" those whom he regards as having done "injustice" either to him or to his people. The retaliatory vindictiveness against his own people so thoroughly blends with whatever he may say in their defence, that is may well be one more instance of biased interpreting of scripture to try to reduce some of its offensiveness by maintaining that Lamentations is a consistent appeal to the god of the Israelites on behalf of avenging wrongs done to them as a people rather than his complaint against them for their disfavor of him. The author of Lamentations proposes that the tutelary deity of the Israelites "pursue" in anger those who have done "injustice" either to him or to others and "exterminate them". The tribute to this deity, as doing so "beneath thy heavens", in no way alters the restricted scope of his assumed sovereignty. The version of deity affirmed in this text has no property of a cosmic or universal god. The deity's properties rather are characters of a tribal god, whose scope of concern is for one people, and within this scope of concern, he considers it compatible with such a deity to propose that he "exterminate" whomever it is against whom he himself directs his diatribe.

The prophet Ezekiel has, in many respects, the same type of personality and insensitivity as the prophet Jeremiah. He too presumes to be a spokesman for the god of the Israelites when he assumes that this deity is addressing himself to the Edomites: "I will do to you as you did to Israel my own possession." In retaliation for effectively resisting the invasion of the Israelites into their territory, the Prophet continues to identify himself as spokesman for his god, declaring: "O hill-country of Seir, you will be desolate"; and when the Israelites bring this about, the Prophet assures them that then they and others also "will know that I am the Lord." In other words, such future military success will demonstrate that the guardian god of the Israelites is more powerful than the guardian gods of the "hill-country of Seir"(35"15).

The moral level of Ezekiel's theology is indicated in what he attributes to the nature of his god when he presumes to maintain that it is his god who challenges the enemies of the Israelites, declaring: "I will do to you what you have done in your hatred against them." And he assures them that when the armies of the Israelites are successful against them: "You shall know that I am the Lord"(35:11-12).

The prophet Joel continues, as both Jeremiah and

Ezekiel do, to anticipate "that time" when their god
will "reverse the fortunes of Judah and Jerusalem".
When the god of the Israelites enables his people again
to be victorious over their foes, he "will gather
(them) together" and "bring them to judgment on behalf
of Israel". And then again their god characterizes the
range his concern, not as a cosmic or universal god,
but rather as the guardian god of one people, referring
to Israel as "my own possession"(3:2-3).

The philosophy of history which is basic to the
prophecies of Joel, can be regarded as morally
defensible on the ancient principle of retaliation,
which linguistically and logically, is the clearest
possible formulation of a moral principle. When this
principle, however, is rejected on the grounds of mercy
or pity, then, of course, another appraisal of Joel's
theology would be implied. But the defensibility or
indefensibility of his theology, which regards deity as
respecting the retaliatory principle, is, after all,
contingent upon what is thought about the morality of
this principle. Since the nations which opposed the
Israelites, had "scattered" them, it would consistently
follow in formulating a theology of their god, that he
would "bring them to judgement", and "justly" impose
upon them a punishment commensurate with their cruelty
to his own people. This theology, however, cannot--as
it must again be argued--be criticized, without first
discrediting the retaliatory principle as "unjust".
And, of course, this cannot philosophically be done.
It can only be rejected out of respect for another
moral principle, such as pity, mercy, forgiveness,
irrespective of the gravity of an offence. When this
is done, it is replacing one moral criterion with
another, on the basis of which the very morality of
moral worthiness of a principle is defended as entitled
to supersede another. But this appeal cannot be
defended on the grounds of "justice", since the
retaliatory version of justice is incontrovertible as
an unambiguous formula for treating an offence on terms
of the offence itself, without disregarding its
conditions, and supplanting them with considerations,
such as pity, mercy, compassion. Such supplementing of
the retaliatory principle by another would be
"tempering" the most unequivocal version of justice
which is basic to so much of the Old Testament's
interpretation of what it is "right" for the god of the
Israelites to do in his judgment of others.

On the grounds of the retaliatory version of justice,
as the criterion of what is morally worthy, both for

human beings and also for a divine reality, the prophecy of Joel that "Egypt shall become a desert and Edom a deserted waste", would be worthy of being credited to divine judgment, since as Joel argues: "Because of the violence done to Judah and the innocent blood shed in her land"(3:19).

The same consideration may be maintained in defending the prophecy of Zephniah, which the Prophet acknowledges as "retribution", on the basis of the retaliatory principle. He argues that because those who were antagonistic to the Israelites "encroached upon their rights", their god "will appear against them" in a judgment which will include "all his terrors"(2:10-11).

The prophecy of Zechariah is of a different order than that of Joel's, although the prophecy that "The Lord will strike down all the nations who warred against Jerusalem" can be defended on the retaliatory principle of justice. Since Jerusalem was destroyed by people who were disrespectful of the moral rights of a people to practice a religion according to the customs and rituals of their ancient tradition, it would be "right" or "just", according to the retaliatory version of "justice", that such people should be punished, and such punishment could then defensibly be interpreted theologically as a divine judgment upon them. But the description of such punishment with divine sanction is of a different moral order, which the Prophet characterizes as a "plague" in which "their flesh shall rot in their sockets, and their tongues shall rot in their mouths"(14:12). Such a version of punishment would have no correspondence to the cause for the suffering of the people in Jerusalem when it was destroyed, and in this sense, could not be regarded as retaliatory in the strict sense of "an eye for an eye". Such a plague would be a version of penalty that was not determined by the type of suffering for which it would be imposed by divine sanction.

An argument in defense of the consistency of the retaliatory principle as a scriptural basis for a version of divine judgment is not necessarily expressing respect for it as a moral criterion. When any such qualified respect if entertained, the meaning itself of "justice" becomes entirely altered. A philosophy of morality then becomes subject to feelings, rather than to logic. Yet, such an inclination to suspend logic on behalf of feeling gains some credibility when one considers the prophet Nahum's

characaterization of the justice of a divinely
sanctioned judgment, according to the retaliatory
principle: "The Lord takes vengeance on his
adversaries; against his enemies he directs his wrath;
with skin scorched black, they are consumed like
stubble, that is parched and dry." The difference of
sentient beings, whether people or animals, and
"stubble that is parched and dry", is so radical that
their incommensurate characters make one cringe to
think of any type of life, capable of suffering, being
"burnt up like tangled briars"(1:9-11). It is,
therefore, such an application of the retaliatory
principle, cited as justifying revenge, without
restraint of charity or pity for those who are capable
of suffering, which brings the retaliatory principle
under a less charitable scrutiny. In spite of the
clarity with which the retaliatory principle of "an eye
for an eye" can be thought, its consistent application
as a criterion for determining a penalty which one can
approve, or even tolerate, tears one apart for reasons
other than logic. It is, as if, a minimum nature of
humanity could not, without shame, approve of itself
and what it does, if it were to sanction imposing
suffering without restraint upon other sentient beings,
even though it could be defended on the logically clear
retaliatory principle.

If the Iliad's characterization of the culture of the
Greeks describes not only Homer's times, but also an
era prior to them, which may even be as much as several
centuries; and if "the Israelite invasion of Canaan may
be placed within the last thirty years of the 13th
century,"45 then what is written in both of these
literatures may be considered for their cultural
parallels. What is of principal significance in such a
consideration is the version of religion of both the
early Greeks and the early Israelites of approximately
the same era.

Although the plurality of the Greek gods, of which the
Iliad is a record, differs radically from the monolatry
of the Israelites, both religions, nevertheless,
include the favoritism of a god for one, and only one,
people, and corresponding antagonism to other people
who trust and worship other gods. The Iliad stresses
the conflict of favoritisms of gods which are expressed
in the life-and-death struggle of two foes in the
Trojan war. Whereas both Hera and Athene "took pity"
on the Danaans "in their uttermost hour of
destruction"(VIII:350-54) by the Trojans, their desires
to help their favorites were thwarted by Zeus,

sovereign of the gods, whose favorite was the Trojan Hektor, referred to in the Iliad as the "the loved of Zeus"(492-94). So devoted was Zeus to the Trojans by virtue of his favoritism for their principal prince, Hektor, that Athene declared if it were not for Zeus, "great Hector, Priam's son", would, in spite of his great fighting skills and massive strength, have been killed by the Argives (356-359).

Notwithstanding the customary pride of Zeus in his daughter, he opposed her, refusing to quality his opposition to her "grim wrath"(449) toward the people whom he favored, and whom she wanted to destroy. Thus internal to the family of Greek gods was the same favoritism for different people as is basic to the Old Testament's interpretation of the guardian god of the Israelites, whose concern was only for the Israelites, with a corresponding disfavor for all other gods who were trusted by other people as their divine guardians.

Both Hera and Athene were in bitter conflict with Zeus, and "sought to divis(e) evil for the Trojans (457-58), even though by so doing, they were opposing the sovereign of the gods. The final book of the Iliad reaffirms their loyalty to the Argives and their continued "hatred for sacred Ilion"(XXIV:25-27). The conflict, therefore internal to the three deities who were most closely related in Greek polytheism, no more decreased throughout the nine or ten years of the Trojan War than the antipathy of the god of the Israelites changed toward other gods during the history of the Israelites which is recorded in the Old Testament. So loyal were both Hera and Athene to the Argives or Danaans that they continued to be sorrowful" for them to a degree that their allegiance to them was unqualified by their family relationships to Zeus, who would "not let (them) stand by the Argives"(VIII:414). Although forbidden by their sovereign to take an active role on behalf of their favorites, they nevertheless, were determined to "put good counsel in the Argives, if it may help them; so that not all of them will die because of (Zeus') anger"(467-68). Hera finally acknowledged to Athene that she "can no longer...fight in the face of Zeus for the sake of mortals: (425-28), and she admits that she will not contest him in "work(ing) out whatever decrees he will" on both his favorites, the Danaans, and their foes, the Trojans (430-31).

As both Athene and Hera, so also Apollo, had no respect for the affinity of Zeus for the Argives after their principal warrior, Achilleus, had ruthlessly abused the corpse of Hektor, the Trojan, and in doing so, brought "dishonour to the dumb earth in his fury"(XXXIV:54).

Notwithstanding Zeus' allegiance for the Argives, whose final victory was achieved by Achilleus' defeat of Hektor, Apollo disparged the victor as "this cursed Achilleus"(39).

The characterization in the Iliad of the several deites as having favorite peoples, which favoritism includes their antagomisms for the foes of their favorites, is a parallel in every respect of the Old Testament version of the god of the Israelites, whose antipathy for the foes of the Israelites equaled the hatred which the Israelites themselves had for their enemies. The radical difference, therefore, of a Greek polytheism and the monolatry, so consistent throughout the biblical version of the history of the Israelites, should not eclipse the parallel feature of the two versions of guardian gods, and all that is characteristic of their favoritisms and their antagonisms, which are anthropomorphic projections of the antagonisms and hatreds which determine human histories.

8. A guardian god's relation to a people is regarded by them as his choice

One of the first chapters in Genesis introduced the idea that the guardian god of the Israelites has favorites, who are his choice among others. This is affirmed in declaring that he "looked with favour on Abel and his offering, but he did not look with favour on Cain and his offering"(4:5). A following account in Genesis maintains that whereas their guardian god was so dissatisfied with mankind that he decided to "rid the earth's face of man", there was, on the other had, one among them who "had found favour" with him. This was Noah (6:7-8). So fond was the god of this one man among the entire creation that, when he entered the ark, as his god had instructed him to do, his god himself "closed the door behind" him (7:16). Thus no detail which would be helpful for the god's favorite would be ignored; and it was as if every event in the life of his favorite was his god's concern.

The god's favor for Noah extended to Noah's three sons and their families; and this detail accounts for the population of "the whole earth"(9:19), including people whom the god did not favor. Exodus stressed the favoritism of this god for one people only, who were descendants of Noah. When Moses and Aaron were leading them, the god gave special instructions for them, who had "heard that the Lord had shown his concern for (them) the Israelites", and had become aware of "their misery". In gratitude for the god's awareness of their plight, "they bowed themselves to the ground in worship: (4:31)

Exodus makes it clear that it was not the Israelites who had selected the god whom they wanted to be their guardian, but it was the god who had chosen them as "the people whom" he had made his "own"(15:16). It was, therefore, by virtue of their god's preference for them to the Egytians, as well as later, to every other people whom they encountered in their struggles to become established in a homeland.

The so-called "miracle" of the way by which the "chosen people" escaped the far more powerful Egyptian military forces is paralleled in an account which Herodotus gives when the Persians under Artabazus "had besieged Potidaea for three months". He describes the occurrence of "a great ebb-tide in the sea", saying that when the persian commander "saw that the sea was turned to a marsh", decided "to pass over it into Pallene". But before the soldiers could complete the crossing, "there came a great flood-tide, higher, as the people of the place say, than any one of the many that had been before". The Persians who did "not know how to swim were drowned, and those that knew were slain by the Potidaeans". What is of religious significance, and therefore, a parallel of the Israelites' interpretation of their escape from the Egyptians, is that "the Potidaeans (interpreted) the cause of the high sea and flood, and the ensuing Persian disaster", as punishment of the Persians for their "profan(ing) the temple and the image of Poseidon", who for the people living near and on the sea, was their guardian god. What is of special interest for anyone who is sympathetic with religious interpretations of events, that many other people regard as "natural", is the acknowledgment by Herodotus-who presumes to narrate events as an historian-that he agreed with the Potidaeans in believing that "this was the cause" for the Persians' destruction.46

One may, therefore, venture the surmise that if Herodotus had given the same account as Exodus gives of the Israelites' crossing "the sea", he might have acknowledged that it was a divine intervention which "drove the sea away all night with a strong east wind and turned the sea-bed into dry land"(14:21).

"A doctrine" which Deuteronomy "never tires of repeating" is that "of all the nations, Israel has been chosen" by their god as "an act of...divine favour.47 The Deuteronomic text declares that it was the god of the Israelites who had "chosen (them) to be his very own people out of all the peoples on the earth"(7:6). Their god, addressing them, assures them that he "has chosen (them) out of all peoples on earth to be his special possession"(14:2). In another instance of addressing the Israelites, their god declares that he "has named (them) as his very own"(28:10). And to make this promise perfectly clear to them, states it in a figure which even the least spiritual among them could understand, when he declares that he "will make (them) the head and not the tail", and they "shall be always at the top and never at the bottom" among all other nations (vs.13).

Psalms recalls "the covenant made with Abraham"; and also the "oath given to Isaac"; as well as "the decree by which the god of the Israelites "bound himself for Jacob", from whom they received their name, expressive of their god's special favor for them. It is this to which the Psalmist refers as the "everlasting covenant with Israel", for whose "sake he admonished kings: 'Touch not my anointed servants'"(105:9-15). Psalms repeats the Deuteronomic doctrine that the god of the Israelites "has chosen Jacob to be his own and Israel as his special treasure"(135:4).

Jeremiah likewise repeats the same doctrine that "Israel is the people" whom their god "claims as his own"(51:19). The initiative, in other words, for the divine guardianship, which the Old Testament regards as the basic premise in narrating the history of the Israelites, is the god's, who has chosen them as his own people from among all others. It is not their choice or their initiative. Their choice consists of their acceptance of his choice of them which is expressed in their worship of him as their sovereign, and as their guardian in all that they do which affects their future as his "chosen people". This interpretation of their relation to their divine guardian dominates the philosophy of history which is affirmed throughout the Old Testament; and it continues to be affirmed by the Jewish Essenes, whose "Scroll of the War Rule" addresses their god with the interrogation: "And who is like Thy people Israel whom Thou hast chosen for Thyself from among all the peoples of the lands."48

The preface to the Trojan War is the disfavor of the goddess Artemis for Agamemnon, and in consequence of this, for his brother, Menelaus, to both of whom Aeschylus refers as "the kings" with whom the goddess was angered, and by stopping the winds, immobilized the entire fleet of a "thousand ships by Argives manned, a warrior force to champion their cause."49

The Iliad cites the disfavor of Zeus with the entire "Achaian people" because of the unfairness with which their leader, Agamemnon, had treated Achilleus--"that man whom Zeus in his heart loves".50 It was the sovereign deity, Zeus, who had chosen Achilleus as his favorite, and therefore, showed his disfavor for anyone who had done an injustice to him. Thus the same immorality is expressed in Homer's interpretation of Zeus as is expressed in the Old Testament's interpretation of the god of the Israelites, when an entire people is made to suffer for the act of their leader. The act of a god, in other words, is showing his preference for one whom he regards as his favorite from among all others, is likewise without any moral respect for others' rights.

The influence upon a god, whether Zeus or the guardian god of the Israelites, is without moral limits when his "chosen" or his favorite is offended by others. Such was the case with Zeus, according to the Iliad, who once declared that "For all the cities beneath the sun...there has never been one...nearer to my heart than sacred Ilion...and the people of Priam,"51 and yet, he was confronted with his divided loyalties between them, as an entire people, and Achilleus, the "man whom (he) in his heart loves". An entire people, therefore, was rejected by Zeus, when he favored Archilleus, and permitted him to kill Hektor, which then brought about the destruction of "sacred Ilion", even though the Trojans had never gone withouth fair sacrifice" on the altars to Zeus.52 The favoritism of Zeus for one person, leader of the Myrmidons, who was an ally of the forces under Agamemnon, made him decide who meant more to him, the entire kingdom of Priam or the heroic Achilleus, who fought against them, defeating them when he killed their field commander and their most powerful warrior.

The one warrior whom Zeus admired and chose to champion thus rated higher in his affection than an entire people who had honored him in their worship. There is no basis, therefore, in rationality or morality for defending the choice which Zeus made to champion one man, any more that there is in all that the guardian god of the Israelites did when he championed his "chosen people", and destroyed many nations and entire peoples whom the Israelites apposed in their military campaigns.

Athene had favorites, whom she chose to prefer to other people, such as Menelaus, whom she helped to defeat the Trojan prince Paris.53 She also "did not forget" Menelaus when he was attacked by Pandaros, leader of the Trojans from Zeleia. She stood "in front" of him, and turned aside arrows that otherwise would have killed him.54 Whereas Athene rescued Menelaus, whom she chose to defend in his encounter with Trojan warriors, Aphrodite defended the Trojan prince Paris, who would have been defeated in an encounter with Menelaus.55 Athene's guardian role is prominent in the Odyssey, in which she assures Odysseus before he returns to his palace: "I myself shall no be long absent from you in my eagerness for the fighting"56 which was to occur when he avenged himself on the young nobles who had occupied his home during his absence. And when he was already in the hall of his palace, he continued to be mindful that it would only by "with the help of Athene" that he could accomplish what he most wanted to do.57

Apollo's favor for the Trojans was intensified when Agamemnon "dishonoured Chryses, priest of Apollo".58 Although Diomedes from Argos, one of the most noteworthy among the Achaian forces, was clearly aware of Apollo's guardian protection of Aineias, yet he "forward drove to kill Aineias", repeating this attack "three times, and every time the god saved him.59

Taking account of an ancient Greek version of deities' guardian roles, both of entire peoples and also of particular individuals among them, is instructive for showing the parallel to this same notion of guardianship of a god which is recorded in the Old Testament of the ancient Israelites, who also believed that their guardian god chose them as his favorites of all people, as well as having special favorites among them to whom he entrusted responsibilities which he could not entrust to others. Their fulfilment of such assignments, which expressed their god's trust, was their response to the initiative of their god to select them for the honor of being his chosen ones.

9. A people's guardian god depends upon their fidelity for his own prestige among other gods

As has already been pointed out, the guardian god of the Israelites was as dependent upon them as they were dependent upon him. His prestige among gods of other peoples rested upon the Israelites' witness to his loyalty to them in satisfying their needs, which included their successful opposition to other people, as they invaded their territories with the objective of securing a homeland for themselves.

Although the Israelites' successes in their military campaigns against other people were attributed by the Faithful to their god, who was their protector, biblical accounts also acknowledge that the reason for their god's support of them was not one-sided or nonreciprocal. Whatever he did for them, to enable them to be feared by those whom they apposed, was also for his own advantage: It enabled him to be feared by other people as a god who was more powerful than the gods of the people whom the Israelites defeated. Military conflicts between the Israelites and their foes were also contests between their guardian gods. The victory of the side which won an encounter was to the credit of their god; and hence, the god of a people was as concerned for his won prestige in a successful military encounter as were the people whom he was believed to have helped win the battle with their foes.

Exodus makes this concern of the god of the Israelites for himself perfectly clear when it maintains: "These are the words of the...god of the Hebrews: 'I have let you live only to show you my power and to spread my fame "throughout the land".'(9:13-16) This is as unambiguous a statement as can be made that the primary concern of the guardian god of the Israelites was not for them as a people, but it was rather for his own prestige, and for the achievement of his "fame throughout the land". The Israelites were his instrument or means to achieve this, and it was their successes in their relations to their neighbors which demonstrated the superiority of their god to the gods of the people over whom they became militarily victorious. This self-centered concern of their god with his prestige or honor among his own people, and also among other people, is again clearly declared in Exodus, which attributes to their god the acknowledgment: "I acted for the honour of my name that it might not be profaned in the sight of the nations who had seen (him) bring (his people) out" from their bondage to the Egyptians (20:22-23). In other words, after having demonstrated his power over the Egyptians, and thus over their gods, he would not want anything to occur among his people whom he had so befriended that would bring discredit upon himself for his failure to continue to help them, which would also include being the superior of the gods of other people whom the Israelites would encounter in their efforts to become established in a homeland.

Ezekiel repeats the point of view, which Exodus had already made perfectly clear, that what the Israelites' god had done for them was not primarily for their sake, but rather for his own sake. The Prophet declares: "Tell the Israelites that these are the words" of their god: "It is not for your sake, you Israelites, that I am acting, but for the sake of my holy name."

The occasion for this stern reminder to the Israelites was that their guardian god was not their possession to use at their convenience, but rather, they were dependent upon his providence for everything they occomplished. Therefore, when they failed to give him the credit to which he was due, by virtue of their dependence upon him, he asserted his rights to their unqualified fidelity. According to this text, the Israelites had disregarded the acknowledgment of their total dependence upon their god, and failed to revere him as they ought to have done. They had even been respectful of their neighbors' gods, and this was the intolerable offence of breaking his commandment that they should honor no other god but him. It likewise was disregarding every covenant which their forefathers had made with their god, and for these reasons he accused them of having "profaned" his "holy name". What the Israelites had failed to do to honor the name of their god, he decreed that he himseld would do. Hence the sobering accusation of his people: "I will hallow my great name, which has been profaned among those nations"(36:22-23).

Isaiah also reminded the Israelites of their subordinate status in relation to their god, maintaining that it was their god who had entrusted to him, as his prophet, to remind them: "You are my servant, Israel, through whom I shall win glory"(49:3). The glory or distinction which their god would thus gain as his superiority to the gods of other people would, of course, be contingent upon their successes, which he himself would have secured for them. But, as is a common human trait, after achieving a desired good, made possible by another's help, the Israelites promptly forgot the source of help, without which they could not have accomplished what they did. It was, therefore, their ingratitude which was basic to their infidelity that was the occasion for being reminded of their unworthiness as a people, whose status as his servant was ignored in their pride for their own achievements, credit for which they took for themselves, instead of acknowledging it as due entirely to the providence of their god. Isaiah reaffirms the same acknowledgment, that whatever shall take place when benefits accrue to the earth and its people, "shall win...a great name" for the god of the Israelites (55:12-13), and its occurrence shall thereby testify to the divine source which was responsible for them. Whenever such an awareness was consistently dominant in the life of the Israelites, they were faithful to their god; and their acknowledgment of their gratitude for his providence was their fidelity to him. Whenever there was a failure of the Israelites to acknowledge their total dependence upon the providence of their god, they were under his judgment for their infidelity.

The twofold aspect of the relation of the Israelites to their guardian god persisted throughout the history of the faithful Israelites, and this was reaffirmed in the apocryphal "Song of the Three", which was an addition in the Greek version of Daniel, but which, nevertheless, expressed the same awareness of the mutual dependence of the Israelites upon their god, and his dependence upon them. This mutuality of dependence in a reciprocal relationship is expressed in the twofold appeal: "Grant us again thy marvellous deliverance and win glory for thy name, O Lord"(vs.20).

The success of a people, which they acknowledge as contingent upon the providence of their god, reflects upon his capacities to make such successes possible for them. One of the boastful claims of military successes is credited to the Israelites by the authors of First Kings, who describe an inactivity for several days between the two opposing armies, when "on the seventh day, battle was joined, and the Israelites destroyed a hundred thousand of the Aramaean infantry in one day" (20:29-30). This most improbable number of the defeated, nevertheless, was intended to confirm a prophecy to "Ahab king of Israel" that the god of the

Israelites would give the vast multitude "into (their) hands", and this would coerce their acknowledgment "that (he is) the Lord"(vs.14). That is, it would demonstrate to the Iaraelites that their god could do for them what the god or gods of their enemies could not do for their people.

Isaiah repeats another boast of the unequaled power of the god of the Israelites, when, addressing them, he declared: "All who take up arms against you shall be as nothing, nothing at all"(41:12). He adds, of course, the explanation for the improbable record, declaring, as a spokesman for their god: "For I, the Lord your god, take you by the right hand." Then to express the sole reason for this prophetic claim, he quotes the god as declaring: "It is I who help you." Then again, to teach them that their successes will not be due to their resources and capacities, he depreciated such capacities, apart from his providence to them, as the capacities of a "worm" or a "louse" (vs.14).

The god of the Israelites is the principal beneficiary in the disproportionate advantages of successes of the Israelites in their encounters with other people, and not the Israelites, who are totally dependent upon him for such successes; and the Prophet lets them know their god's estimate of his own role in whatever they accomplish: "The Lord himself has done it." That is, "the Holy One of Israel has performed it", and not the Israelites, apart from this dominant role in their successes, which those who are not among the Faithful, will claim for themselves. And the Prophet points out the underlying motive for all that their god had done for them: It is "that men may see and know"(vs.20)

There are neither religiously nor morally sensitive restraints with which Ezekiel undertakes to characterize the "glory among the nations" which the god of the Israelites will endeavor to demonstrate so that "the Israelites shall know that (he is the Lord their god"(39:21-23). The Prophet describes the banquet, referred to as the "sacrifice", which the god of the Israelites will provide for all who come to celebrate his superiority as their god, when he himself gives the invitation to "gather from every side of my sacrifice" to "eat the flesh of warriors and drink the blood of princes of the earth", who did not acknowledge him as the one god, supreme above all other gods. They are depreciated for their having failed to acknowledge his superiority to the gods of other people, by referring to them as having the significance in the great "sacrifice" and banquet as "rams and sheep, he-goats and bulls". This demonstration of the god's contempt for other gods, and for the people who worshiped them, includes the god's invitation "to drink yourself drunk on blood at the sacrifice", to which he refers as one that "I am preparing for you." Ezekiel certifies that it "is the very word of the lord god that "at (his) table" people "shall eat (their) fill of horses and riders, of warriors and all manner of fighting men." This perverse "sacrifice" conceived by Ezekiel, and attributed to the plan of the god, for whom he presumes to be a spokesman, is for the purpose that this god "will show (his) glory among the nations". And its primary purpose, according to the Prophet, speaking for his god, is that "the Israelites shall know that I am the Lord their god."

Sacrifices of cattle often reached enormous dimensions among the Greeks in their sacrifices to their gods, regarded as appropriate for acknowledging the seovereignty of some of their deities, but there is nothing in their literature which parallels what Ezekiel attributes to the god of the Israelites, who invites his guests to "eat your fill of horses and riders, of warriors and all manner of fighting men" (39:23).

Even the Athenian Greeks of an era some centuries later than the time of Ezekial were capable of a bewildering notion of how to express respect and reverence for Athene, the guardian goddess of their city-state. A member of the Boule persuaded the membership of this body to accept his proposal, and to "put it before the Ekklesia" to authorize as an Athenian verdict that the admirals or generals, who were accused of failure to rescue the sailors in the fleet at Arginusae, were to be condemned to death, and "one-tenth" of their confiscated property was "to belong to the Goddess".60 What is repugnant in this judgment is that it had been condemned as contrary to Athenian law to try Athenian citizens as a group, rather than as individuals. Yet, only Socrates and Euryptolemos had the courage to oppose the illegal practice, even though one-tenth of the confiscated property of the illegally condemned was to be given to the goddess Athene, guardian of the justice of Athens!

Chapter Six

SACRIFICES TO A GOD

1. Sacrifices to a god are, according to the Bible, as old as humanity

Genesis maintains that sacrifices to a god began with human history. According to this explanation for the origin of sacrifices as integral to a reverence for divine reality, it characterizes Abel, one of the sons of Adam and Eve, as "a shepherd", who "kept flocks", and who "brought the first-born of his flock" as a sacrificial offering to the god whom he acknowledged as the providence responsible for the earth and all that it supports, such as his flocks. His brother, Cain, also according to Genesis, "tilled the soil", and he "brought some of the produce of the soil as an offering"(4:2-4) to the god, who, like his brother, he acknowledged as the ultimate cause for the fertility of the earth.

The subsequent history of human beings was not respectful of the divine cause for all upon which they were dependent for their life; and according to Genesis, they were not even regarded by the divine reality as entitled to live. This is the biblical explanation for the universal flood, the only human survivors of which were Noah and his family. The first expression of Noah's acknowledgment of his gratitude to the god who had spared him and his family was constructing "an altar" on which "he offered burnt offerings"(8:20). Thus according to the biblical account, the first human beings who were born on the earth, and the only human beings to continue to live after all others had been destroyed, acknowledged their gratitude to the divine reality by offering sacrifices of either cattle or grain.

When the Israelites were about to be liberated from Egypt by their god's intervention, their leader, Moses, informed the Egyptian Pharaoh that they would "need animals from (their) own flocks to worship" their god (Ex.10:26). According to this account, the god of the Israelites instructed Moses "to make...an altar of earth" on which to offer sacrifices from the people's "flocks or herds"(20:24).

205

Moses, in turn, "directed certain young Israelites" to prepare "bullocks" for "sacrifices"(24:5) to their god, who had been their guardian and protector in liberating them from their servitude to the Egyptians. These "young men of Israel" respected their leader's instructions and "sacrificed bulls" to their god (vs.6). The Israelites were later commanded by their god "to offer a bull as a sacrifice" for an atonement of their sin (29:36), which was their failure to do all that their god had expected them to do to show their fidelity. Another daily sacrifice which they were commanded by their god to make on "the altar", dedicated to him, was "two yearling lambs", and this daily sacrifice was to be done "in perpetuity"(vs.38).

In the course of making such sacrifices, the priests of the Israelites were aware that a specified procedure was necessary to insure a fulfilment of such divine commands; and they instituted a ritualistic schedule, such as directing that "the first lamb" must be "offer(ed) in the morning", and the second, between "the two evenings"(vs.39).

The third book in the Pentateuch indicates the increasing role of "the Aaronite priests" in conducting the sacrifices, as a precaution that they conform to divinely ordained requirements. Such requirements became more complicated, thereby making the priests indispensable in the religious life of the Israelites. Priests "slaughtered" the sacrificial animals as their god "had commanded Moses"(9:11). This explanation for the source of such priestly procedures entrenched the priests as indispensable in the scrupulous fulfilment of their god's instructions of exactly how animal sacrifices to him were to be conducted.

The priestly authors of Leviticus specify that the priests "shall slaughter the bull" and then "the Aaronite priests shall present the blood and fling it against the altar and around at the entrance of the Tent of the Presence"(1:5-6). For the scrupulously exact performance of this entire procedure, a well trained priesthood was obviously necessary.

The fourth book in the Pentateuch indicates the increasing complexity of sacrifices which, in turn, entrenched the priesthood as essential to the religion of the Israelites. A sample of such complexity of prescribed animal sacrifices is sufficient to enable one to understand that a priesthood was necessary in this religion as it developed under the progressively increasing supervision of its priesthood. Every day of the week, there were specific sacrifices which the priests explained as requirements of their god that were obligatory upon the Faithful. "On the first day of every month" it was obligatory "for the Israelites, through the office of their priests, to sacrifice "two young bulls". "On the second day: twelve young bulls." "On the third day: eleven bulls." "On the fourth day: ten bulls." "On the fifth day: nine bulls." "On the sixth day: eight bulls." "On the seventh day: seven bulls." This detailed schedule, which includes specified numbers of animals for the sacrifices on each day, is certified by the priestly account in Numbers as being transmitted to "the Israelites" from Moses, who, in turn, told them "exactly what the Lord had commanded him" (29:11-40).

As the prosperity and correlated wealth of the Israelites increased under their rich ruler Solomon, the numbers of the animals which were sacrificed also increased. The account in First Kings is that "Solomon offered...to the Lord twenty-two thousand oxen and a hundred and twenty thousand sheep." This massive number of animals were killed on the occasion of "dedicating the house of the Lord" in Jerusalem (8:63-64). Although the biblical account of this dedication of the temple took the life of these many tens of thousands of animals, the account also points out that they were "shared-offerings to the Lord", that is, shared with the thousands of Israelites who, like the Greeks, ate the roasted or cooked cattle.

This extravaganza which was sponsored by the wealthy Solomon made such an impression upon both the people and their priests that the same account is recorded in Second Chronicles, which reaffirms the number of animals that "the king and all the people offered (in) sacrifice before the Lord" (7:4-6).

Although Ezekiel is included in the Bible among the prophets, he was, nevertheless, a priest, and therefore, thought as a priest. Hence he repeats priestly instructions, as previous books in Scripture narrate, such as stipulating: "When you have completely purified the altar, you shall present a young bull without blemish, and a ram without blemish", and these "you shall present...before the Lord" (43:23). His detailed stipulation of what constitutes acceptable sacrifice for their god includes for "a daily sin-offering, a goat, a young bull, and a ram". The priestly stipulation is again affirmed that "all of them shall be...free from blemish(vs.24-27).

Even though the First and Second Books of Esdras are not included in the Hebrew Scriptures, but were written for the Greek-speaking Jews in Egypt, they nevertheless, stress what their priestly author regards as of utmost significance in the history of both the northern and the southern kingdoms. It reaffirms the biblical accounts of the reign of Josiah as the king of Judah, who reigned for thirty-one years, during which time he was remembered for the notable solemnity with which the sacred celebrations were conducted, such as one in which he "made a gift of thirty thousand lambs and kids and three thousand calves" to be shared with the priests and Levites. "The priests and the Levites" then "stood in all their splendour before the people...to make offerings to the Lord"(1:7-11). Then "they roasted the passover victims over the fire in the prescribed way" and "carried portions round to the whole assembly"(12-13).

2. Sacrifices of animals to a god are prehistoric practices among the Greeks

The term "hekatombe"(hecatomb), which literally means "hundred-ox", occurs in accounts of Greek religions to designate one of the notable sacrifices to a god. There is, however, according to Kerenyi, "no evidence from Minoan and Mycenaean times of the sacrifice of a hundred animals at once." There is, on the other hand, historical evidence that "the sacrifice of the hundred cattle was offered...at Athens, to Apollo." A name by which he was then identified was "Hekatombaios", being named after the sacrifice, rather than the sacrifice being named after the god in whose honor it was performed. This "priority of the sacrifice"[1] to the identified deity to whom it was dedicated indicates something of the antiquity of the sacrifice of the number of cattle at one time.

There are many evidences among the Greeks for sacrificial offerings of animals which are prior to any historical dating of the particular deities to whom such sacrifices were dedicated. The places on which sacrifices had been made, before any historical identification records to which particular deity they were oriented, were as it seemed, "waiting for the advent of the deity"[2] in whose honor they were to be acknowledged. In other words, there are instances in which the practice of making sacrifices predate an historical record of the deity to whom they were offered. Two such "primitive cult practices" were later identified as "the Pyanepsi and the Eiresione, both having occurred among the early Greeks at "seed-time". According to Parke, they were included in early versions of Athenian religions, "for many centuries without any very specific deity or patron"[3] as the recipient of the acknowledgment by the Athenians of their dependence upon a named deity for the fertility of their crops. During the sixth century, when these cult practices continued to take place, they were incorporated into a religious festival that was dedicated to Apollo, and thereafter, became associated with this deity.

The Iliad, of course, is a most valuable literary record for religious practices of considerable antiquity, which possibly are centuries prior to its author's time. There is a reference in the second book of the Iliad to the Athenian acropolis "where bulls and rams" were sacrificed annually by the Athenian youths.[4] Another reference occurs in the same book to a sacrifice made by each man before he left for a military campaign, addressing "his offerings to his favourite among the everlasting gods", praying that "he might come through the ordeal with his life". It was on such an occasion that a specific reference is made to Agamemnon who "sacrificed a fatted five-year old ox" to Zeus.[5]

The third book of the Iliad describes a proposal which Menelaus, brother of Agamemnon, made. It was to "bring a couple of sheep, a white ram and a black" one, to be offered to the "Earth and Sun", and another one to be offered to Zeus.[6] Lattimore interprets the reference to "the Sun, God"[7] rather than to the Sun such as Rieu interprets it. What is significant in this section, however, is the animal sacrifice which was directed to some realities that were esteemed as divine, and therefore, as capable of helping men engage in the perils of warfare.

The sixth book of the Iliad narrates the instructions given by Helenos, prince of Troy, to his bother Hector, greatest of the Trojan fighters, to go to their mother, and ask her to go with other older women to the temple of Athene on the acropolis of Ilium, to appeal to her for her protective help in their encounter with their enemy, and to promise "to sacrifice in her temple" "twelve yearling heifers", "if only she would have pity on the town and on the Trojans' wives and little children."8

The twenty-second book describes the conflict of affection which Zeus experienced as he grieved for the Trojan Hector, who was being pursued by Achilles, anticipating his death by Achilles, also a favorite of Zeus. What is significant in this section is the acknowledgment by Zeus that the Trojan prince had always been loyal to him in sacrificing "the thigh of many oxen in (his) honour, both on the rugged heights of Ida and in the lofty citadel of Troy".9

Animals were sacrificed to Zeus over a very considerable area of the ancient world, extending from Phrygia to Crete, and of course, as has been pointed out, in the Peloponnese. Kerenyi describes "a mound of ash with bones of sacrificial animals on one of the peaks of Mount Lykaion in Arcadia, on which there was "an altar dedicated to Zeus".10

The Odyssey refers to "a sacrifice of bulls and rams" made to Poseidon by the Ethiopians, whose "distant land" the god visited, where "he enjoyed the pleasures of the feast".11 The third book describes the generous preparations which Nestor of Pylos made for the return of Odysseus. He told Telemachus, son of Odysseus, of the "many thigh bones of bulls"12 which had been sacrificed to Poseidon, god of the sea, appealing to him to be helpful to Odysseus on his long journey home. The preparations for his return included nine companies of men, each sacrificing nine bulls.13

In 425/4 B.C., during the Peloponnesian War, Athens decreed that each community under obligation to her and her guardian goddess, Athena, should send a cow for a sacrifice to the goddess. Since, as Parke points out, there were "officially some four hundred communities...assessed for tribute", the number of cattle would have been considerable for the "sacrifice to the goddess...on the great altar of Athena."14

Whereas the altar to the goddess was on the highest elevation of the Acropolis, another massive animal sacrifice was performed on the side of the Acropolis at the altar which was near the Dionysiac theater. The procession of animals to this altar, dedicated to Dionysius, included two hundred and forty bulls. The sacrificial animals, however, were not only for the god, but primarily for the Athenians, and for all who took part in the ceremony. This type of animal

210

sacrifice was referred to in the Old Testament as "shared", meaning that the edible parts of the sacrificial animals were eaten by the people. And since this ceremony was dedicated to Dionysius, Parke comments that after the "dinner of beef that night", those who attended "probably washed it down with abundant wine", after which was "a revel". And all of this "formalized licence" was under the gloss of a sacrifice to a god! 15

The often massive slaughters of animals under the gloss of religion were as integral to the corporate life of the Greeks as they were to the community life of the Israelites, since both peoples were obviously carnivorous. It is, therefore, understandable that a dramatist, such as Euripides, could not recreate Greek life for the theater, without also including references to animal sacrifices. In his Hippolytus, the Chorus refers to the "heaps (of) the slaughtered steers" both at Olympia, "by the streams of Alpheus", and at Delphi, 16 "The Pythian shrine of Phoebus". And the Chorus prefaces this reference with a commentary which expresses Euripides' attitude toward this bizarre version of religion: "Idly, idly!" Or another translation refers to all this as "In vain, O in vain." 17

In The Suppliants, Euripides refers to "the Pythian shrine" at Delphi in which there was "a tripod" that Heracles brought from Troy, and it was over this that "the throats of three sheep" 18 were to be cut. This was to be a witness before Apollo that Adrastus, king of Argos, had made a solemn oath to Theseus, king of Athens. Whereas the purpose of this slaughter of animals was to confirm an oath of one man to another, it was made sacred and inviolable by its witness of the god Apollo.

Another purpose for slaughtering animals is referred to by Euripides in his Heracleidae, in which Demophon, king of Athens, declares: "My seers have filled the town with sacrifices, to turn the foe to flight and keep our country safe." 19 In the same drama, Iolaus, an old friend of Heracles asks: "What god's altar have we left uncrowned?" 20 And another translation states this question: "What gods rest unimplored? What refuge upon earth have we not sought?" 21

There are no essential differences in the reasons or motives which underlie the animal sacrifices of the ancient Israelites and Greeks. There is, however, a very great difference in the preoccupation of the Israelites with the scrupulous ritualistic procedures that included the sacrifices of animals. It was their intense concern, reinforced by the highly entrenched priesthood, that no detail was to be omitted in the ritualistic sacrifices. It is this difference to which Kerenyi likely refers when he points out that "express commands...were never an essential part of Greek religion",22 such as they were among the Israelites, when the priesthood maintained that every detail of a complicated animal sacrifice was specified or commanded by their god.

3. A religious gloss rationalizes animal sacrifices

Every aspect of what is done, either by a community as its religion, or by individuals apart from a community, expresses a moral conditioning. The character of human beings, either in a group or apart from others, is revealed in whatever they do. This character foundation, therefore, is an indisputable aspect of religion, and is exemplified in the religions of both the Israelites and the Greeks.

The cultivation and preservation of a consistent orientation of human life to a reality revered as divine is difficult, and consequently, is rare. This fact is explained by the moral principle: "All things excellent are as difficult as they are rare."23 And their difficulty of cultivating and preserving accounts for their rarity among human beings.

The characterization which is given in Leviticus of the motivation for animal sacrifice is genuinely religious: "Aaron presented the breasts and the right leg as a special gift before the Lord"(9:21). The very acknowledgment of its "special" character may be interpreted as a frequently occurring wish of some people that such desirable food could have been used for a purpose entirely apart from such a religious act. And a very considerable part of the history of animal sacrifices, both of the Israelites and the Greeks, supports this analysis.

Pinsent maintains that ancient Greeks regarded the ritual sacrifice of animals as one part of "a sacred meal at which men either ate the god in the form of his sacred animal, or shared a meal with the god who was believed to be present" with them during such an occasion. In either case, this interpretation of an animal sacrifice could be regarded as a genuine religious acknowledgment of a distinction between human beings and a reality of a different order, revered as divine. Although there is no dating of the specific period in which this religious acknowledgment underwent a radical change, nevertheless, what was once dedicated to a divine reality in such a sacrifice became less and less generous or more and more meager. As Pinsent also points out, it became a common practice in such rituals that "fat and bones were burnt" as the offering to a god, whereas the people who took part in the ritualistic performance "consumed or used all the useful parts of the animal". And a religious rationalizing of this thoroughly nonreligious economy was expressed in classifying the unusable refuse or remainder as "holy".24

Parke takes account of the same phenomenon in the history of Greek religions when "the worshiper drank the wine at a festival", and then as a "sacrificial act", "presented the god with a small quantity as his share".25 The proportion of whatever was "given" to a god in a ritualistic act of so-called animal "sacrifice" tended to become less and less substantial, until the god's share was the smoke ascending upward, regarded as "the sweet savour of a burnt offering", and rationalized even further when people believed that the gods on high were satisfied "to live off the smoke".26

Both the Iliad and the Odyssey substantiate this analysis which Pinsent and Parke affirm about the progressive reduction of a genuine religious motivation in animal sacrifices among the Greeks, and a corresponding increase in their preoccupation with themselves and the satisfaction of their own appetites.

The first book of the Iliad refers to a plague which the Greeks believed had been imposed upon them by Apollo; and they wondered if "he might accept a savoury offering of sheep or full grown goats"27 as a sufficient condition for terminating the plague. Lattimore's translation removes the slightest question about what the Greeks considered to be the god's share in this animal sacrifice. They wondered "if given the fragrant smoke of lambs, or of he goats",28 the god would be satisfied enough to stop his punishment of them with the plague.

The fourth book of the Iliad indicates that Zeus also was satisfied with the "savour" from burning fat as his

share of a ritual which was dedicated to him. He
acknowledged his complete satisfaction with the
Trojan's version of their dedication of animal
sacrifices, declaring: "Never...did my altar go
without its proper share of wine and fat."29

The eleventh book makes it perfectly clear that it was
the "burning fat from an ox's thigh" which was regarded
as dedicated "in honour of Zeus".30 And the
twenty-fourth book reaffirms the satisfaction of Zeus
with the Trojan's practice of giving him his "proper
share of wine and fat".31 Lattimore's translation again
points out that it was "the smoke and savour" of the
burning animals which Zeus was satisfied to accept as
his "portion of honour".32

A reference in the fourteenth book of the Odyssey may
in no way indicate an actually later date of
composition than the foregoing references in the Iliad,
but it does at least illustrate the tendency in
perfunctory rites to become more and more meager in
what is considered adequate for a god's share in a
ritual sacrifice of an animal. This part of the
Odyssey describes what the servant of Odysseus did to
prepare for the return of his master. He "dragged in a
fatted five-year old hog and brought it up to the
hearth". As "a man of sound principles", "he did not
forget the immortals, but began the ritual by throwing
a tuft of hair from the white-tusked victim into the
fire...praying to all the gods that...Odysseus might
come back to his home".33 Lattimore's translation again
makes it even more clear what was regarded as a
sufficient part for the gods to receive of a
sacrificial animal: It was the "hairs from the head of
the...pig" which were thrown "into the fire as
dedication...to all the gods", while the old servant
prayed to them.34

Biblical interpretations of rituals in which animals
were burned, under the gloss of "sacrifices" to the god
of the Israelites, parallel those which are given in
the early Greek accounts in the Iliad and Odyssey.

The priestly writing of Leviticus refers to "a
food-offering of soothing odour to the Lord"(1:9;13).
Numbers describes the requirement imposed by the god of
the Israelites upon them: They must make "an offering
of soothing odour from herd or flock to the
Lord"(15:4). And the same chapter repeats that they
must "make an offering of soothing odour to the
Lord"(vs.7). This requirement is again reaffirmed in

the following verse: "When you offer to the Lord a young bull" it will be "a food-offering of soothing odour to the Lord"(vs.8-11). The same characterization of "a food-offering" as a "soothing odour to the Lord" is once more repeated in this chapter(vs.13). In a subsequent chapter, Numbers repeats that the "fat" of an animal burned on an altar is the "food-offering of soothing odour to the Lord", and an unambiguous comment is added: "Their flesh shall be yours"(18:18). A later chapter in Numbers refers to the commands which the god of the Israelites gave to Moses, that "the Israelites...present the food for the food-offering of soothing odour"(28:1-2), and the requirement of them is repeated that it must be "a food-offering of soothing odour to the Lord"(vs.8).

Psalm 66 mentions offering the god of the Israelites "fat beasts as sacrifices and burnt rams as savoury offering"(vs.15). Rituals which included animals, burned on an altar, may, however, be anything but a religious orientation to a divine reality. This is acknowledged by both Greeks and Israelites when people are preoccupied with themselves, such as when they consume "the main edible parts of the animal". Classifying this aspect of a community practice as "worship" is, therefore, reducing religion to a level which is restricted to human appetite, and has no orientation to a divine reality of an order beyond or transcendent of human beings themselves. Parke admits this when he maintains that "a sacrifice" of this type "brought with it the compensation on most occasions of a large meal" for the male participant and for "his family".35 This was, in fact, an anticipation of relief performed by governments without a religious sanction of worshiping a divine reality in so doing. This generalization is supported by a reference in the first book of the Iliad to a sacrificial ritual in which a prayer was addressed to Apollo, and after "All had made prayer...they drew back the victims' heads and slaughtered them and skinned them, and cut away the meat and wrapped them in fat." These were then "burned...on a cleft stick", over which wine was poured, "while the young men with forks in their hands stood" ready to eat the euphemistically yet misnamed, "sacrificial" offering to the god.36

This so-called "offering", under the gloss of a religious act of "sacrifice" is, of course, an accommodation to the type of want which is uppermost in the hierarchy of people's values. Herodotus clarifies what constitutes the most highly valued good in such a hierarchy of values when he says: "The day which every man most honours is his own birthday. On this day he thinks it right to serve a more abundant meal than on other days; before the rich are set oxen or horses or camels or asses, roasted whole in ovens; the poorer serve up the lesser kinds of cattle."[37]

In light of Herodotus' honesty to acknowledge the dominance of the carnivorous hunger in the life of many people, even under the gloss of a "sacrifice" to a god, one can appreciate the absurdity of the explanation for slaughtering animals as a religious act of honouring a god, as also honouring the animals, such as Scully proposes in maintaining: A "sacrifice" of an animal to a deity was "an act of reverence to the animal, since it dignified with ceremony and hallowed with gratitude the everyday deaths of his kind."[38]

An explanation which is given in Numbers for the dominance of animal sacrifices in the religion of the early Israelites is, on the other hand, honest, and therefore, is a credit to the authors of this biblical book, who refer to the time in the early history of the Israelites when they "wept...and cried": "Will no one give us meat?"(11:4). And this same text refers again to "their wailing": "Give us meat to eat"(vs.14).

The carnivorous appetite of this ancient people thus was not glossed over in at least this honest account of the reason for a religion which was dominated by ritual practices that included slaughtering animals, incidentally for the ordour directed upward, but primarily for satisfying the hunger of a carnivorous people. Another honest explanation for this aspect of the religion of the early Israelites is given in Deuteronomy, which refers to the time when their "boundaries" will be extended and they then can have the food for which they hunger. Aware of their hunger for meat, the authors of Deuteronomy declared: "Because you have a craving for it, then you may freely eat it...then you may slaughter a beast from the herds or flocks...and freely eat"(12:20-21). Rather than misapplying a religious interpretation to the motive for wanting to satisfy their carnivorous hunger under the gloss of a pious act of sacrifice, these biblical writers explain that it is their god's providence to provide people with "herds or flocks", which is a religious interpretation of the source of life's sustenance, without rationalizing a ritualistic religion that provides meat for carnivorous hungers, under the gloss of "worship".

Notwithstanding the severity of nonbiblical criticisms of the priestly version of ritualistic worship, as this type of worship is characterized in the Old Testament, they cannot equal the severity of its criticism by the Old Testament prophets. A brief mention of this is being given in the following, but an extended consideration of it will constitute the following chapter.

The type of criticism of animal sacrifices, which is basic to a critique of them in the biblical books of the Prophets, is anticipated in Psalms, such as in the fiftieth, which in affirming the appraisal by the god of the Israelites, asks: "Shall I not find fault with your sacrifices, though your offerings are before me always?"(vs.8). Their god then declares: "I need take no young bull from your house, no he-goat from your folds"(vs.9). And the reason, which would be cogent to every Israelite, is that their god is the ultimate providence from whose charity everything that lives flourishes. It is this providence to which their god refers when he reminds them: "All the beasts of the forest are mine and the cattle in thousands on my hills"(vs.10).

The primary premise of a creed of religious faith, of which every reflective Israelite was clearly aware, is affirmed by their god, in order to help them understand pretending that they are their generous gifts to their god, when everything on the earth is his possession. It is this profound religious understanding which is basic to regarding their god as declaring: "The world and all that is in it are mine"(vs.12). And one of the most incisive of criticisms of anthropomorphic interpretations, which are basic to the entire procedure of ritualistic animal sacrifice as offerings to a divine reality, is affirmed in attributing to their god an interrogation of those who engage in such practices, even though they may do it in the sincerity of naive beliefs: "Shall I eat the flesh of your bulls or drink the blood of he-goats?"(vs.13).

It would certainly seem that if this single Psalm, when understood, would have been the death-blow to the priestly practices of animal sacrifice. Yet, in spite of it, the practices continued, without so much as the alteration of one daily schedule of slaughtering animals, under the pretext of offering to the divine reality what already exists by virtue of its providence. Hence this profound admonition: "Offer to

God the sacrifice of thanksgiving"(vs.14), fell on ears which did not hear it, or at least did not take it to heart. It is this single admonition, attributed by the Psalmist to their god, which became the thesis of the entire prophetic tradition, as this is recorded in the Bible.

The fifty-first psalm is an address by the Psalmist to his god, which acknowledges: "Thou hast no delight in sacrifice;" and which then states the clearest of religious awareness: "If I brought thee an offering, thou would not accept it"(vs.16). This penetrating scrutiny of a long established practice of the Psalmist's forefathers, as well as of his contemporaries, is a preface to his affirmation of one of the most lucid and convincing of spiritual insights into a type of worship which alone is worthy of being directed to the ultimate determiner of human destiny: "My sacrifice, O God, is a broken spirit"; and aware of the indispensable self-censure which removes handicaps to an enlightened moving beyond oneself, is then declared: "A wounded heart"--painfully sensitive to its deficiencies--"thou wilt not despise"(vs.17), when it acknowledges its gratitude for the divine generosity in all the good that flourishes on the earth.

The prophet Isaiah is one among his people on whose ears these two profound psalms did not fall without determining his entire reappraisal of the ritualistic religion of his people. His stern censuring is directed to them in a question which he regards as coming to them from their god: "Your countless sacrifices, what are they to me?" And then, as if their god were remembering the centuries of the ritualistic animal sacrifices, conducted by the priests, emphatically declares: "I am sated with whole-offerings of rams and the fat of buffaloes; I have no desire for the blood of bulls, of sheep and of he-goats." No appraisal or comment could be more stern about practices of the priests than the declaration which Isaiah attributes to the god of his people: "The offer of your gifts is useless, the reek of sacrifice is abhorrent to me"(1:11-13).

It is this same censuring of all forms of ritualistic worship which is reaffirmed by the prophet Jeremiah, whose basic ministry to his people can be summed up in the declaration of the futility of the priestly paraphernalia, which dazzled unreflective people, who were impressed by a show that had no relation whatever to a change in their characters, and hence in the quality of their lives.

This severe censuring of their ritualistic version of worship is directed to them by the Prophet who, speaking for his god, asks them: "What good is it to me if frankincense is brought from Sheba and fragrant spices from distant lands?" And in one all-inclusive disparagement of this priestly version of ritualistic worship, the divine judgment is affirmed: "I will not accept your whole-offerings, your sacrifices do not please me"(6:20-21).

The type of prophetic condemnation of ritualistic worship which has developed and had become increasingly complex in the course of centuries, by virtue of the institutionally entrenched priesthood, was directed by both Euripides and Aristophanes against comparable ritualistic practices of their contemporaries, who continued the same version of religion as their forefathers who, for centuries, had subscribed to such ritualistic animal-slaughter on altars. Euripides sums up his reaction to the entire practice included by the Greeks under the gloss of worship, when the Chorus in Hippolytus declares: "In vain, O in vain...the blood of her oxen outpoured."39

Aristophanes has the genius to lift his criticism of Greek religious practices out of the immediate context of long established rituals, which consumed much of their time and resources. Transplanting the drama from land into "the air" in The Birds, he has Prometheus express his own reflecting on Greek religious festivals and rites, when Prometheus, pitying the forsaken gods, declares: "There is not a man now who sacrifices to the gods," and speaking for them, laments: "The smoke of the victims no longer reach us." Being denied all the customary slaughter of animals on altars, he declares that the "gods"...are dying of hunger", and therefore, "threaten to make an armed descent upon Zeus, if he does not open markets where joints of the victims are sold."40

The Greeks who attended the performances of this drama understood very well what the reference meant to the "joints" of slaughtered animals, which were offered in the sacrifices to the gods, while the Greeks used whatever was edible for themselves. A ritualistic version of religions could not have become less spiritual than the type he criticized, and less oriented in a worthy way to divine reality, but more centered upon human beings themselves, especially for satisfying their carnivorous appetites.

Aristophanes thus is a historian of the low level to which Greek religion deteriorated, with its preoccupation of people for themselves and the least spiritualized of their wants, among which, therefore, there was no longer even a residue of genuine religious motivation.

Greek philosophers, such as Phaedo, Plato, Cleanthes, became witnesses to a spiritual version of religious orientation to a reality transcendent of human beings; and in this respect, their contribution to a refinement of human life parallels the role of the prophets in the Bible, who likewise witness to a quality of life of which a human being is capable when he orients himself to a wider world than the limited restrictive interests of his most assertive wants.

4. Human sacrifice is of great antiquity

Human sacrifice is a prehistoric phenomenon. It was, for instance, a customary part of funerals in the late Shang dynasty in China, the date of which varies among scholars, but it is approximately the period identified with Abraham, which is the beginning of the history of the Israelites. Human beings of the lowest stratum in the highly stratified Shang society in ancient China were "sacrificed at burials"; and something of the extent of this practice may be inferred from the fact that "In one excavation at only one cemetery site, the skeletons of about two thousand slaves were discovered."41 This practice of human sacrifice was a customary "part of funerals" in the ancient Shang capital of Anyan. A motive underlying this practice, however, was not its orientation to gods, but rather to ancestors, who were believed to derive strength from the blood of such victims.42

A converse motive accounts for a practice of eating human flesh as a way of deriving strength from the deceased for the survivors. Herodotus describes a "custom of the Issedones" that "the nearest of kin" of a dead man would combine his flesh with the flesh of animals "for a feast". Herodotus generalizes that "Every son does so by his father, even as the Greeks in their festivals in honour of the dead."43

A remembrance of this ancient custom among the Greeks

is retained in their mythology of Kronos, the father of
Zeus, who ate his children as soon as they were born,
until the mother of Zeus saved him by means of a trick
on the canabalistic Kronos. This myth may well be more
than a mere fanciful creation of a practice of eating
human flesh. As kerenyi maintains, "the Kronos myths
show evidence of remoteness from the Zeus era",
providing an indication of a practice of very
considerable antiquity.44

The practice of sacrificing human beings as a religious
rite developed in early centuries in Greece from the
evidence on Mount Lykaion in central Arcadia in the
Peloponnese.45 Kerenyi interprets the practice of "the
human firstborn sacrifice", such as took place in
Arcadia "in the Zeus religion" as the god's
"requirement of total submission", to which he refers
as a religious concept "in its crudest form".46

The Iliad, as has been acknowledged, is a most valuable
history of early Greek religion, and therefore, its
account of Achilles' preparation for the funeral of his
friend, Patroclus, is important for understanding the
custom of sacrificing human beings. He declares that
at the pyre of his friend: "I am going to cut the
throats of a dozen of the highborn youths of Troy."47
There is no mention in this account, however, that this
is motivated by any religious consideration, such as a
sacrifice to a god. It is merely one more expression
of the violent anger of Achilles, as he himself
acknowledges. It is revenging the death of Patroclus,
who was killed by the Trojan Hector. But it,
nevertheless, has significance in understanding Greek
religion, since a practice of human sacrifice was
accepted in their mores, and thus, could also be
regarded as acceptable in their religion. The
acceptability in Greek mores of sacrificing a human
being to a deity to appease the anger of a deity, was
not a very considerable extension of the same reason
that Achilles slaughtered the twelve young nobles of
the Trojans. Just as he regarded this act as lessening
his anger, so the oracle assured that the anger of
Artemis for the Greeks would be satisfied "if someone
sacrificed his daughter"48 to the goddess in making
atonement for the offence of having killed a she-bear
in the shrine which was dedicated by the Greeks to
Artemis.

Much of this offence, and the proposed solution by
oracle or prophet, became popular in Greek drama of
both Aeschylus and Euripides. It was the anger of

Artemis which the prophet Calchas believed would be appeased if Agamemnon were to sacrifice his daughter Iphigeneia.49

The expedition of the Greeks to Troy and their return from Troy, after its defeat were marked by a human sacrifice. The intended sacrifice of the royal daughter of Agamemnon began the Greek departure from Aulis, and their sacrifice of the Trojan princess, Polyxena, began their return home from Troy.50

In his Heracleidae, Euripides also had Demophon, King of Athens, acknowledge that his seer proposed he must command the "sacrifice to Demeter's daughter (of) some maiden from a noble father sprung".51 This was regarded as an appeal for divine help to reinforce the Athenians against an imminent attack by the King of Argos. Also in his The Phoenissae, Euripides has the seer Teiresias deliver the oracle to Creon, the ruler of Thebes, of the necessity to "sacrifice Meneoceus, thy son", as a means to save his city.52

According to Genesis, the god whom Abraham worshiped, instructed him: "Take you son Isaac, your only son, whom you love, and...offer him as a sacrifice"(22:2). This biblical interpretation of Abraham's consent to sacrifice his own son may be a moralizing refinement of a long established practice among Western Semites, in proximity to whom Abraham and his descendants came in endeavoring to become established in their homeland. Hence this stroy of Abraham's sad willingness to part with his son, as a demonstration of his unrestricted fidelity to the god whom he revered as ultimate sovereign is, notwithstanding its merit of fidelity, an instance of the tragic extreme to which otherwise worthy religious motivation can be expressed.

One can understand some aspects of the religion of the early Israelites by taking account of the religious practices of the peoples with whom they had cultural contacts. Among these were the Moabites, and an incident about them, as described in Second Kings, is significant in this analysis of human sacrifice. The Moabites were engaged in a war with the Israelites, when their king "saw that the war had gone against him". He thereupon "took...his eldest son...and offered him as a whole-offering"(3:26-27). Although the biblical text is variously interpreted, there is no textual uncertainty about the account of what the Moabites' king did. There likewise has long been a misunderstanding, as Kerenyi points out, about the

Semitic practice of sacrificing children, the "Semitic name for which is molek." "Molock" was not the name of a Semitic god, "as was long believed," as Kerenyi explains.53

A less direct cultural influence upon the earliest of the Israelites may have been Phoenicia, among whose people was a practice of sacrificing their sons on certain occasions, and when the Phoenicians colonized Carthage, this practice continued among them. The Carthaginians not only included Kronos in their mythology, as did the Greeks, but also in their religion, one practice of which was a "sacrifice (of) a man to Kronos".54 In light of cultures in the Mediterranean area and in Asia Minor, which included human sacrifice, it is not surprising, therefore, that this practice also occurred among the Israelites as they became more and more interrelated with other peoples.

The Book of Judges records the vow which Jepthah, a judge of Israel, made to his god, that he would offer to him the first creature to come out of the door of his house on his return from fighting the Ammonites. He made this promise provided his god would "deliver the Ammonites into (his) hands". After defeating them, he returned home, and to his intense sorrow, he was met by his daughter, "his only child". Yet, he recalled his vow, which he explained to his daughter; and trained in the Faith, she willingly accepted the necessity of her sacrifice to their god. "It became a tradition that the daughters of Israel should...year by year commemorate the fate of Jepthah's daughter"(11:30-40).

This biblical account is especially significant because it indicates the respect which the Israelites had both for the Judge who could not break his vow to his god, and also for his daughter, who revered the integrity of her father's vow to their god. Thus this account is important for understanding the biblical narrative of Abraham's acceptance of the sacrifice of his son as compatible with fidelity to his god.

But later Israelites, centuries after Abraham, accommodated themselves so much to their neighbors' culture that they conformed to their religious practices, which included human sacrifice. Psalm 106 laments the deterioration of the religion of the Israelites, when it declares: "They worshiped" the idols of their neighbors "and were ensnared by them".

So thoroughgoing was their adaptation to foreign religions that "they sacrificed...their sons and their daughters" to the gods of their neighbors, offering "the blood of sons and daughters...to the gods of Canaan"(vs.36-38).

Jeremiah condemns his people for "defiling" the places of worship which their forefathers had dedicated to the worship of their god, when they "built a shrine...at which to burn their sons and daughters"(7:31). The Prophet reaffirms this condemnation of the Faithless for having "built shrines to Baal, where they burn their sons as whole-offerings to Baal"(19:5).

Ezekiel reaffirms the same accusation of his people for their "loathesome" practices of taking their "sons and daughters", who were intended for the service of the god of "their fathers", and instead, "sacrificed them to the images" of foreign gods. Ezekiel speaks for his god when he declares to these faithless people: "You slaughtered my children...you surrendered them to your images"(16:20-21). The Prophet reaffirms this sacrilege of the Israelites who accommodated themselves so entirely to the cultures of their neighbors that, speaking for his god, he declares: "They came into my sanctuary and desecrated it by slaughtering their sons as an offering to their idols." And the total perversity of this faithlessness to their god is repeated by the Prophet as the sorrow of his god, declaring: "They have...offered my children to (idols) for food"(23:37).

5. Types of ritual worship changed radically in later centuries

In later centuries, both Greeks and Hebrews looked back with such a sense of repugnance at the earlier practice of human sacrifice among their ancestors that the literatures of their two cultures attempt to argue that intended sacrifices of human beings were not completed: They were instead replaced by animals. In both cultures, however, the change of victims was brought about by divine intervention, and not by an actual change of the attitudes of the people themselves in earlier times.

The ancient Greek legend that the wrath of Artemis would be appeased--and the plague which she imposed would end--was already altered in antiquity by the account of Embaros dressing a "she-goat...like his daughter" and sacrificing the animal instead of his daughter.55 Possibly even earlier than this, the so-called "Cyprian histories" maintain that there was a comparable change in the more ancient tale of the intended sacrifice of Iphigenia by her father, Agamemnon, since the goddess herself prevented this by taking her from the altar before she could be killed; and the goddess put a stag in her place.56 This is the sequence which is also affirmed in Euripides' drama, Iphigenia in Tauris, when Iphigenia narrates what took place:57

> "The blow would have struck. I saw
> The Knife. But Artemis deceived their eyes
> With a deer to bleed for me and stole me through
> The Azure sky."

A parallel alteration is made in the account in Genesis of Abraham's intended sacrifice of Isaac. This biblical narrative is that as Abraham "stretched out his hand and took the knife to kill his son...the angel of the Lord called to him...Do not raise your hand against the boy...Abraham looked up, and there he saw a ram...and took the ram and offered it as a sacrifice instead of his son"(22:10-12).

A distaste for the sacrifice even of animals was expressed among many people, such as among the Magi, who, as members of the Persian priestly caste, used only inanimate materials in their sacrifices.58 The same distaste for "bloody sacrifices" was expressed in the cults of the Egyptian Isis, whose offerings were incense.59

A comparable distaste for animal sacrifice was expressed in some Greek cults which offered "fruits, vegetables, cereals, fish" to the deities whom they worshiped in their festivals.60 The use of animals for sacrifices, however, was not universally displaced in other Greek festivals. But the fact that some cults eliminated such sacrifices is a significant cultural phenomenon in the history of Greek religions, expressive of a refinement in the aesthetic, as well as in the moral, sensitivities of some Greeks.

The ancient practice continued of offering their gods wine, and in some instances of sacrifice, milk also was offered in the ritual celebrations of religious festivities. As was consistent with the role of

Demeter, cereal grains were included in her worship. Such an offering of cereal was the principal feature of the Pelanos festival in her honor.

There may, of course, have been more than religious considerations underlying the Greek's use of incense in rituals, since this accompanied their sacrifices of animals and fish, and would, therefore, have helped to make the surroundings less offensive for some people.

Oil offerings in some rituals among the Greeks may also be mentioned,61 and the parallel to rituals among the Israelites is evident (Ex.29:2;23, Ex.30:25, Lev.2:2;4,etc.). Another element in religious celebrations of both Greeks and Israelites was singing. The Iliad includes a reference to singing as one of the means regarded by the ancient Greeks as having a propitiatory function: "Young Achaians", according to the narrative in the first book, "all day long...propitiated the god with singing, chanting, a splendid hymn to Apollo."62 Euripides refers in The Heracleidae to the "song the young and light of foot can dance and chant"63 in religious festival activities. Parke maintains that "the all-night service of such Pannychides were a common feature in Greek worship".64 The "legend of Orpheus as the founder of a religion" was "firmly established in the sixth century", and one of "the essential elements" in this legend, is a "sacred song".65

There is an unmistakable parallel of song in the religion of the Israelites. Exodus refers to Miriam, "the prophetess, Aaron's sister" leading "the women" in the refrain: "'Sing of (our god): he has covered himself in glory'"(15:20-21). The parallel of sacred song in the worship of the Israelites certainly accounts for the considerable number of psalms in the Bible. And what is especially significant in these is their preservation of a very great part of this people.

The artistic enrichment of Greek religious celebrations with theatrical performances is without parallel among the Israelites; and this is not an indication of less aesthetic sensitivities or requirements, but as a disfavor for any tendency to compromise a religious orientation to divine reality by a concession primarily oriented to human delight or entertainment.

The religious role of drama was not regarded as primarily for its entertainment value, but was regarded as specifically sacred, and therefore, was included in cultic activities which were dedicated to divinities. The fact, on the other hand, that it was the cult principally of Dionysus in which drama became such an integral element is itself diagnostic of a shift of orientation from a god to the Greeks themselves. Yet, the theater was integral to more religious celebrations than those dedicated to Dionysus. "A vast theatre", for example, was included in the "ancient sanctuary" of Dodona, which was dedicated to Zeus.66 And a comparable theater at Epidaurus was included in the cult of Asklepios. The theater at Delphi, to mention only one, was integral to the honor accorded Apollo.

The fact that "the developed tragedy" among the Greeks was not a theatrical equivalent of discourse about any deity, such as Dionysus, indicates as much as do the athletic contests that they were for a mixed purpose, even though under the gloss of religion. The Olympian games were founded in the eighth century B.C.; the Pythian games, which became integral to the Delphic religious festivals, were founded in 582 B.C.; and in 566/5, athletic contests were included in the Panathenaia.67

The admiration of the Greeks for athletic contests accounts for their inclusion in all their festivals of importance. Since these had a religious function in earlier centuries, the athletic contests were incidental in such orientation, even though sometimes anthropopathically explained as for the delight of deities. But a far more realistic explanation is the frequent phenomenon that genuine religious devotion does not indefinitely continue among any people, and there is no more eloquent commentary on this fact than the Old Testament.

6. Mixed motives underlie behaviors regarded as religious

A desire to revere a reality to which human beings regard themselves as subordinate motivated the earliest expressions of religion among the ancient Greeks and Israelites. As has been pointed out in the preceding discussion, sites set apart for sacrifices to such a reality, regarded as a different order from human beings, preceded an identification of the specific reality which was so acknowledged. It is in this sense, therefore, that places designated for such sacrifice, as an early expression of worship, were, as if, "waiting for the advent of the deity, unless he or she was already present".68

If such collective efforts of people were regarded as an historical beginning of worship, and some such corporate worship is a primary expression of religion, then an interpretation of religion as "acts and experiences of individual men in their solitude", such as William James and A.N. Whitehead characterized it, is not very helpful for understanding a worship that includes a community of people. Nevertheless, what is helpful in James' definition of "religion" for uderstanding its earliest expressions among the Greeks in particular, is his acknowledgment that such a religious orientation is "in relation to whatever they consider the divine".69

This nonspecific referent of worship is the aspect of the earliest uses of altars among the Greeks. Such a use has been identified "as early as the beginning of the first millenium". and the feature of this early form of worship, which is significant for considering in this section, is that the altar was "a simple stone". This stone of approximately eight feet by four feet was, as Kerenyi points out, "the germ cell of more and more imposing altars". By contrast to this simple altar, from which the ancient Greeks directed their homage to a reality that they revered as a higher order then the earth itself, are complex altars that were included in corporate worship in following centuries. One such structure was the "Rhoikos altar erected about 550 B.C.", whose "immense size", "covered two hundred times the area" of the earlier altar.70

The question which one cannot help asking himself is whether there is any correlation between an increase in immensity and elegance of equipment for expressing religious reverence and the quality or sincerity of it. The history of Greek religion is a record of the increasing artistic enrichment of such structures associated with corporate worship, such as the altar at Pergamon, known throughout the Mediterranean World during the Hellenistic era as one of the splendors of art. Whereas there can be no question of the architectural advance in arts of this character, in contrast to the simple stone altar centuries before, a question, nevertheless, does arise about the relation of such achievements in art and the integrity of a religious motive. Such a religious motivation is incompatible with an emphasis upon human intelligence and skills, and is mindful only of a human dependence upon a reality whose acknowledged sovereignty over human life underlies all earnest religious orientation beyond it and its own resources.

Whereas altars in the history of Greek religion preceded other structures, such as temples, the same motive which accounted for the enlargement and embellishment of altars accounts also for constructing temples in such sanctuary areas in which an altar was once regarded as adequate for establishing a sacred site. Such a simple site was, nevertheless, dedicated with a reverent desire to refer to a reality regarded as transcendent of those who collectively acknowledged their subordination to a sovereign more ultimate than anyone among them.

It may even be an expression of an awareness of the danger entailed in qualifying a religious motive for worship by an increase of sanctuary structure that accounted for delaying the building of a temple dedicated to Zeus on the sanctuary site at Dodona, which before "the middle of the fifth century", was "the most used in the ancient world". And it was not until this later time that a temple to Zeus enriched the temenos site of Dodona. The sovereign of gods had previously been worshiped at an "altar in the open air".[71] A temple to Hera, however, preceded the one dedicated to Zeus, and it may be that an acknowledgment of his universal domain explains the profound religious propriety of not restricting his worship to a temple, but rather worshiping him under the vault of the heavens. This hypethral type of Greek religious structure may well have expressed a religious integrity which became impaired as the construction of temples dominated the concerns of the Greeks in following centuries.

The fact that "the most essential structure in a Greek cult"[72] was the altar, which preceded other structures in the sacred area, may be more a worthy tribute to the profoundity of the ancient Greek religious sensitivities than the later proliferation of temples, each, as it were, undertaking to surpass the other as architectural accomplishments.

The history of Greek architecture and sculpture would certainly have been very different if the earliest version of Greek religion, with an altar as the sole structure in a sacred site, had continued. But what the relation of such awesome art had to the integrity of the religious motivation expressed in the earliest

229

versions of an altar as sufficient for worship will, of course, never be clarified beyond the vaguest sort of surmise. The fact, however, that both altars and temples "grew to enormous size", such as was the case in "the Samian sanctuary",73 makes one at least wonder which motive was dominant in such projects, the religious, as an acknowledgment of the subordinate status of human beings, or their marvel and admiration for their engineering and artistic achievements. Something of the mixed motivation underlying altar and temple constructions, as artefacts expressing religious or essentially nonreligious intentions, is a bewildering question when one takes account of the competition of the cults of Zeus and Hera at Olympia, when the "sacrificial altar for Hera" was surpassed by "another larger one for Zeus".74

Something of the mixed religious and nonreligious motivations are certainly evident in the constructions of temples, such as in Agrigento and in other cities of Sicily, where tyrants vied with each other in demonstrating both their wealth and their power. As Pinsent soundly points out, "National pride and the desire to impress visitors with the power and wealth of the city was a powerful motive for temple building in the ancient world."75 Kerenyi points out the same motivation as dominant in the contest of ancient cities for building temples which eclipsed in elegance the temples of neighboring cities, when he maintains that "building of temples may have been intensified by the pride of state", under the religious gloss that gods "seemed worthy of such costly forms of worship."76

If there should be any uncertainy about making an appraisal of the motivation which was dominant in temple construction, there surely need not be such hesitancy when one thinks of the dimensions of the Olympieion, which the Peisistratids undertook in Athens, but which was not completed until several centuries later by Hadrian.

One may surely be thankful for all that the Greeks did to demonstrate their extraordinary genius for architecture and sculpture, and yet entertain a question about what relation this genius had to religion as an acknowledgment of the final dependence of human beings, not upon human genius, but upon a reality transcendent of even the most awesome expressions of such human endowments.

It seems only a sensible appraisal of the incredible

temple constructions in Greece to recognize that for them "religion was spectacle".77 Taking account of the total cost for constructing the Parthenon alone is staggering, even though it was justified as "the Virgin's Palace". The question of just how genuine such a costly project was for a religious consideration is certinly intensified when the Propylaea, or entrance to the Acropolis, crowned by the Parthenon, cost more than the Republic's annual revenue, eliciting the complaint of many that it was "destroying the treasury".

The same question about the relation of spectacle to the integrity of religious reverence for divine reality continues likewise when one takes account of the Panathenaia, the professed motivation for which was "to do honour to the great goddess of the city". Yet, the fact that "it became a most elaborate institution" in which "all the inhabitants of Attica and even the Athenian empire combined" makes one question the primary motivation as religious, rather than as political.

Such a political advantage, however, under the gloss of "honor to the great goddess of the city",78 would not necessarily be incompatible with a religious motivation to acknowledge gratitude for a divine source of protection, but the contest of spectacles in pagentry and every imaginable version of celebration, tends to fare unfavorably for a sincere acknowledgment of human helplessness apart from a divine source of help. The sponsoring of the "Great Panathenaia" by the appointment of public officials, such as the ten Agonothetai,79 who were responsible for organizing it, indicates its political importance, entirely apart from whatever religious significance such a festival may have had for intensifying an awareness of a people's dependence upon their guardian goddess whom they presumably sought to honor.

The procession in religious festivals was regarded by the Greeks as an essential part of a ceremony designated as honoring a deity. The term pompe for designating such a procession meant to them "a sending", and specifically "sending an offering to the deity".80 The intention underlying this particulr interpretation would certainly qualify as genuinely religious, just as would the Proerosia, which was included in the worship of Demeter, and was regarded as "an offering" to her, with the religious intention of invoking "her blessing" at the time of ploughing the land and sowing seeds.[81] An acknowledgment of a people's dependence upon a divine reality for the growth of grains, which were basic to their livelihood, was a religious interpretation of their life in relation to a reality other than their resources or their abilities. And when this genuinely religious purpose for a ritual or a celebration was dominant, and was not diluted by its subordination to other motives or purposes, its religious nature would certainly be unquestioned. The same respect may be accorded a festival such as was dedicated to Artemis, during the tenth Attic month when girls "carried boughs of the sacred Athenian olive bound with white wool",[82] and made a supplication to the goddess "on behalf of the community". The very fact of its character, unemcumbered with costly equipment, may well express the genuineness of the supplication, which was not threatened by being overshadowed with lavish pagentry.

A different estimate can hardly be avoided for the Athenian _leitourgiai_ , popularly regarded religious "services for the people", since this public activity was possible only by the support of "the richest men in Athens". Something of the character of this type of liturgy as a "public service" can be appreciated by the fact that its endowment required the support of a very considerable number of its wealthiest citizens. Even though there is no essential incompatibility of religious motivation in a ceremony, a liturgy, or a festival, and the wealth which alone can make its splendor or elegance possible, it is evident that any competition of their aspects with the primary character of an acknowledgment of dependence upon a divine reality is an impairment of the primary religious role of such activities, notwithstanding their inclusion in a well-established religious calendar.

The same respectful appraisal may be made of festivals in a religious calendar, whether of the Greeks or of the Israelites, in which people took part in some sort of meal. In such a community event, regarded by those taking part as celebrating "a divine presence", the food may certainly be considered an element in a religious practice. Such an occasion was regarded by the Greeks, at least in theory, as "man and god (being) present to one another". If this awareness were dominant, rather than being diluted by many other possible responses of those taking part, the "festive meal"[83] would be worthy of respect as genuinely religious. But the sociability of one human being with another, together with the assertive role of appetite for food, would give the religious purpose for such an occasion a competition so vigorous that only people of rare natures could keep the religious meaning of such a meal as a genuine "sacrificial" occasion.

Since "In ancient Greece...cattle and sheep were never plentiful",[84] their relative scarcity could well be the basis for a genuine sacrifice, when given to a deity or used in a ceremony in which the motive of sacrifice to a divine reality was uppermost. But in so far as the cattle sacrificed were food for the human participants in the celebration, the "sacrificial" aspect could be more a gloss for a nonreligious aspect of human life than for a genuinely religious one.

A thoroughly unequivocal version of religious sacrifice, because directed to a divine reality as a gift, was the "tithes of the land", which Leviticus characterizes as "levied on the produce of the earth or the fruits of the trees", which were regarded by the Faithful as belonging to their god, and therefore, were "consecrated" to him(27:30).

The three principal feasts which are specified in the Pentateuch were occasions in which the Israelites were made aware of their dependence upon their god for the fruitfulness of the earth, which expressed his providence. Exodus specifies one such religious event as "the pilgrim-feast of Weeks", the occasion for which was "the first fruits of the wheat harvest". Another was the feast of "Ingathering of grapes and olives" in the autumn, called the feast of Tabernacles (or shelters)(34:22-23). The Deuteronomic injunction to the Israelties is: "You shall keep the pilgrim-feast of Tabernacles...when you bring in the produce from your threshing-floor and winepress"(16:13). Another such injunction is for their celebration of "Unleavened Bread"(vs.16). The practice of eating "unfermented cakes" is referred to in Genesis as the food which Lot served the two guests at his home before Sodom was destroyed by divine judgment upon it(19:3). The second occasion which is mentioned for eating "unleavened cakes" is in Exodus, which is also associated with divine judgment. This time it was upon the Egyptians, and since this judgment was "kill(ing) the first born of man and beast" of the Egyptians, but sparing, or passing-over, the Israelites, it was known as Passover. This event was commanded by their god "as a day of remembrance", which was to be a "pilgrim feast" or "a festival of the Lord"(12:12-14), and was to be celebrated "for generation after generation for all

time"(Lev.6:18). The genuineness of the religious
motivation for the occasion of "the pilgrim-feasts of
Unleavened Bread, of Weeks, and of Taberncles"(vs.16),
is expressed in the command: "No one shall come into
the presence of the Lord empty-handed. Each of you
shall bring such a gift as he can in proportion to the
blessing which the Lord your God has given
you"(Deut.16:16-17).

7. Obedience to the commands of a god is very
different from attempts to coerce a deity to conform to
a human being's demands

The tutor and companion of Achilles, as characterized
in the Iliad, showed his awareness of the conditions
for revering a divine reality, when he counseled
Achilles to control his pride and to acknowledge his
subordination to the gods who, in response to human
swayed". Such a response, however, of divine realities
is to "humble prayers", when the one who sincerely
makes appeals, "bends the knee in supplication".[85] This
characterization of a religious attitude contrasts with
a defiance of divine beings that is associated with
unbending demands, affirmed in the insolence of anger
toward whatever annoys or displeases an individual.
The attitude of an individual which alone is compatible
with a religious desire to be obedient to a god's
expectations or requirements is a willing subordination
of one's wishes, and certainly of his demands.

A far wiser Achilles, and one demonstrating his
capacity to subordinate his insistent demands to have
what he wants, is characterized in the Iliad when he
accepts the proposal of the seer to appease Apollo,
whose displeasure with the Achaeans was destroying
them.[86]

This same type of counsel of a way which is appropriate
for human beings to relate themselves to divine
realities is given by Athene to Pandarus, leader of the
Trojans from Zeleia, when she proposes that he
subordinate himself in acknowledging his need of
Apollo, for which he will promise to make the god a
sacrifice after his return to his home in "the city of
sacred Zeleia".[87]

The Odyssey's characterization of Telemachus expresses
his awareness of an attitude of human beings, in hours

of great distress, that is consistent with a religious acknowledgment of their need for divine help, when they are honestly aware of their own limits. The youth counsels his mother to "vow to all the gods the service of complete" sacrifice, provided "Zeus grants" his help to restore their home to its former order, after the inroads of those who trespassed upon their rights.[88]

The borderline between a devout religious subordination to the decisions of a god for whatever he wills for human beings, and what they propose he should will, is so precarious that there is no trustworthy way for one who is not actually internal to another's experiences to distinguish what is compatible in his attitude with a religious attitude, and what is not compatible with it. The presumption, however, which anyone makes that a god could be persuaded by a human being's promise of some reward, such as is included in a so-called "sacrifice", is antithetical to the basic religious awareness of the subordinate status of human beings in relation to divine reality. The presumption that a human being has the resources to make a proposal which can persuade a god to act as the human being desires the god to act, is a negation of the nature of a religious acknowledgment of total dependence upon a divine reality for its help. Such an acknowledgment is twofold: It is an awareness of the limits with which a human being is faced in achieving what he sincerely wants or really needs; and it is also an acknowledgment that a reality which is transcendent of all human resources is alone capable of fulfilling such needs.

It seems most questionable, for instance, that a genuine acknowledgment of total dependence upon a divine reality is expressed in the procedure by which the Greeks negotiated with the goddess Artemis before the battle of Marathon. Although aware of their desperate inferiority of numbers in contrast to the Persians, the Greeks, nevertheless, presumed a leverage over the goddess when they promised to sacrifice a goat to her from every Persian whom she gave the support to kill. The attitude itself of bargaining for any advantage, which a human being has, negates the sense of absolute dependence in a time of need for which all human resources are actually inadequate. Any such notion of a leverage of bargaining with a god destroys the basic admission that one is totally unable of himself to do what he appeals to a divine reality to enable him to do.

The precarious borderline between an attitude which is

basic to a religious response of human awareness of
total helplessness, apart from a divine reality, and an
attitude which does not acknowledge such total
helplessness, is expressed in any type of proposed
bargaining or stipulating of terms for a presumed
negotiating between human beings and a divine reality.
Such bargaining dominates Achilles's presumption that
Apollo could be persuaded to give his help in combat
"if given the fragrant smoke of lambs (and) of
he-goats".89 The same bargaining, which a leverage made
possible by what a human being can do with resources
over which he has final control, is expressed by
Chryses, priest of Apollo, when he proposes that he
could have a temple dedicated to the god if the god
were persuaded to help him regain his daughter from her
captivity to Agamemnon.90

The leverage of human beings over divine realities is
affirmed, for example, in the most offensive of
irreligious arrogance in both the characterizations of
Orestes and Electra in _The Libation-Bearers_ by
Aeschylus. Orestes makes the threat to deities of the
underworld that human beings could withhold "the wonted
funeral feasts", and thereby maintain they would "be
porportionless of honour" without "the rich and savoury
banquet of burnt offerings".91 And Electra follows her
brother in reaffirming such a threat of denying to the
gods what is within her control, because her own
possessions. Addressing herself to Persephone, she
declares that "of the fulness of my inheritance will
from my father's house at my bridal, offer libations
unto thee".92 Such libations, of course, can be
withheld, with a correlated refusal to worship a deity.

The same uncertain borderline between an acknowledged
human dependence upon a god for help, and a presumption
that a human being has leverage over a god is expressed
in Exodus, when the god of the Israelites appeals to
them: "Build me a sanctuary so that I may dwell among
them"(25:8).

The prophet Haggai characterizes the dependence of the
god of the Israelites upon his people, when he
declares: "The words of the Lord" are that his people
should "build a house acceptable to me where I can show
my glory"(1:8-9). As if the heavens and the earth were
not sufficient manifestations of divine glory, the
naivete in this biblical text characterizes the
leverage which the Israelites presumed to have over
their god. And this is expressed in the Prophet's
contrast between what people have, which they can

provide for themselves, and what their god wants for himself, but cannot also provide for himself. This biblical text maintains that the harvests of the Israelites were destroyed by their god, who complained: "Because my house lies in ruins, while each of you has a house he can run to"(vs.9-10). What may well be noticed in this text is not its anthropopathic naivete, but its way of negating the basic creed of religious faith that the ultimate divine reality is not contingent upon anything which is not already under its final control. Hence considering that human beings have what is desirable, which they can acquire for themselves without their dependence upon a divine providence, is a disregard for the basic element in a religious attitude that underlies all genuine religious expressions of it. The characterization of the helplessness of a god to acquire what is within the resources of human beings, and is contingent upon their generosity, is an extreme naivete, which is a thoroughgoing incompatibility with even the minimum conditions for a religious acknowledgment of a human being's subordinate status in relation to a divine reality upon which all human life is finally dependent. This naive version of theology is embellished by shifting the leverage from divine reality to human beings, when the text maintains, presuming to speak for the god of the Israelites: "It is your fault that the heavens withhold their dew and the earth its produce"(vs.11).

It is this particular biblical version of the way human disobedience to their god can obstruct his providence, and can impair his sovereignty over the world, which constitutes a grave qualification in biblical theology. This, in fact, is a frequently recurring emphasis in Scripture which constitutes a serious qualification of the essential nature of religion itself. Any qualifications of the final sovereignty of divine reality over human life, with a corresponding lessening of an acknowledgment of the absolute dependence of human life upon the final divine sovereignty, is an impairment of essential conditions for religious life.

8. Religious motivations readily pass into magical practice

There isn't one motive which is expressed in unquestioned religious integrity which is not also subject to becoming a nonreligious behavior. Whereas

237

"purity", as a religious concept means being unmixed or unqualified by any element which is foreign to a relation to divine reality, it, nevertheless, commonly acquires a meaning that denotes a property of objects, such as cult statues or cult procedures. Thus instead of denoting a quality of dedication to a divine reality which is unqualified by any aspect of life other than total devotion to such a reality, it often acquires a meaning of "uncontaminated cult statues" and "mysterious cult procedures"[93], thus losing its religious connotation as a thoroughgoing dedication of one's life to a divine reality, such as is affirmed in the religious ideal of loving one's god with _all_ one's heart and _all_ one's mind.

The unconditioned character of such devotion is its religious purity, which is lost when properties employed in religious practices, such as "cult statues", are considered to be "pure" provided they have not been subjected to some treatment which is forbidden in cultic disciplines.

The normative role of purification in a ritualistic version of religion is preparing a person to make himself worthy of his relation to a divine reality, which is brought about by a ritual in a definitely prescribed manner, according to the requirements of a particular religion. A celebration, for example, which was dedicated to Apollo was the Thargelion. The first day of this celebration was devoted to becoming prepared for entering into the awesome relation with the god. It was, in other words, "devoted to purification",[94] in order to prepare a participant for the following day, which entailed a relation beyond himself, in distinction to the purificatory procedures that were preoccupied with eliminating a residue of some offence which would otherwise impair his worthiness to relate himself to his god.

Another concern in Greek culture for purification was expressed in an Athenian law which required that on the day an individual died, his body was to be removed, and the deme or related families were to be "cleansed". This entire procedure was regarded as "religious" rather than "hygienic".[95] If, however, this practice did not impress the members of the deme with the stern fact that they, as well as all human beings, have no final control over their life, and therefore, are impotent in averting its inevitable ending, the confrontation with the death of one of its members might well have not had the slightest association with a religious interpretation of human life and its total helplessness in at least one event which is inescapable for every living creature. If the "cleansing", therefore, were an operation confined to the part of a dwelling in relation to which the dead person had been in contact, such cleansing, even if according to a prescribed ritual of the cult, may have had no more than a surface association with religion. It may, in fact, have had no more religious meaning for the members of a family of the deceased than any number of other superstitious practices, performed because they had always been performed, or at least had been remembered as having been. But a motivation for acting which is merely conforming to a superstition is a far cry from an awareness of one's relation to a divine reality that imposes upon him an obligation to make himself worthy of such a reality, by removing from his life whatever would dishonor it, and thereby discredit the integrity of a religious motive to make himself acceptable to the reality upon which he acknowledges his final dependence.

One meaning of "purification" among early Greeks, which obviously was entirely superstitious, or a mystery without being understood, was "pollution", as a type of infection, referred to as miasma. Anyone who was believed to be so contaminated was then believed to be especially vulnerable to accidents, such as shipwreck. If, however, the cause for such an occurrence that brought about an individual's suffering or death was not ascribed to a punishment by a god, it would have no property justifying an association with religion. The unintended killing of Laius by his son was regarded as the cause of a plague among the Thebans, and its control was believed to be contingent upon bringing the guilty person to justice. If the version of such justice were legal, and did not entail appeasing an offended god, it would have had no uniquely religious significance. A fear of the threat to a community by such a plague could be based entirely upon an ignorance of its nature, and therefore, a superstition about what would possibly be an effective means for its control.

A peripheral association with religion of such a homicide may be no more than a legal prohibition against such a guilty person coming into the sacred site of a temple or taking part in any "public religious ceremonies"96. When, however, there is an explicit reference of some act relating an individual to divine reality, as was the intended attempt of Orestes to atone for killing his mother, by "appeasing the powers below"97, there is then every reason to regard it as religious.

The uncertain demarcation, on the other hand, between religious and nonreligious attempts to effect a "purification", as a removal of an offence to a divine reality, is evident in atoning rites in which the literal "washing away" of an offence by bathing is often performed under the gloss of religion, but without any sense of contrition for an act which is regretted as an impairment of one's relation to his god. Pausanias, for instance, records an annual rite performed in Nauplion, in the spring, when the statue of Hera was bathed for the purpose of restoring her virginity.98 Presuming to accomplish this in her case, as the wife of Zeus and mother of children, would have a meaning too subtle to be understood by most participants in the rite; and their unclarified mystification of what was ritualistically attempted would have little bearing upon their own remorse for having changed the general scheme of their own life.

Some possible religious association, on the other hand, can be understood with Orestes' endeavor to be purified, in the sense of being washed clean of the offence of matricide, when in the Eumenides, he expresses his belief that he has been "purified (by)...flowing streams".99 But since the practice of taking part in "a bath in (a) river" became purely "the symbolic bath" of being cleansed, its religious significance became more and more vague and undefined as the practice attracted more and more people.100 Its religious meaning then became so indistinct that the entire ritualistic act progressively had less and less of a relgious residue in its significance. This becomes perfectly explicit in the so-called "purification" rites in the Eleusinian Mysteries, which consisted of "two methods--a sea-bath and a sprinkling with pig's blood". The second method is historically significant, even if having no religious significance for the participants, since a sacrifice of pigs was a more ancient rite for effecting atonement. Since this misunderstood rite continued in the celebrations dedicated to Demeter, it was an easy rationalization to explain the purpose of a sacrificial pig's blood as having fertilty effectiveness. But even if not a farfetched gloss, it would have no relation to purifying, in the sense of removing an offence in an individual's life that would impair its presumed relation to a divinity, in relation to whom a human being should not be encumbered by whatever would

handicap the ingression of a divine reality's help into
his life as a suppliant for a god's role in restoring
him to a less censurable life.

The entire procedure included in the Eleusinian rites
of purification became less and less related to any
spiritual change in an initiate's life when the
initiates went by cart or carriage either to the port
of Peiraeus or the beach of Phaleron, where they walked
"into the water carrying a piglet".101 The fact that
the sea water was construed as being effective for such
purifying should remove the last inclination of any
interpreter of this procedure to regard it as having
any spiritual significance, other than an understood
association somehow with the goddess Demeter. And one
of the unexplained mysteries is how the goddess was
honoured when the Mystai returned to Athens, and after
slaughtering a pig, sprinkled himself or herself with
its blood.

This procedure illustrates how practices, which once
had some clearly defined meaning as a religiously
motivated act, degenerated in time into a practice
without the slightest awareness on the part of its
participants of its relation to a divine reality, for
the purpose of making a participant more worthy of such
a relationship. The superstitious or magical role of a
pig's blood in the ritualistic procedure of purifying a
human being, in the sense of removing from him a grave
offence, is clearly illustrated in the _Eumenides_ when
Orestes reveals his superstitious version of a
religious rite by claiming: "The pollution wrought by
my mother's slaying is washed away...by purification of
slaughtered swine."102

Whatever suggestions have been made in the foregoing
about the ill-defined borderline between some
practices, under the gloss of religion, and their
purely magical intentions, are as applicable in
analysis of some priestly practices recorded in the
Bible as they are to ancient Greek practices. The
unqualified magical function of a rite, recorded in
Leviticus, is obvious, as this is characterized in this
ancient priestly writing: "The priest shall burn the
pieces of fat at the altar on top of the food-offerings
to the Lord, and shall make expiation for the sin that
man has committed, and it shall be forgiven him"(4:35).
This presumption made in this priestly interpretation
of the relation of "the pieces of fat at the altar" and
"the sin that the man has committed" is in every
respect the same arrogance of magic as Orestes

expressed in maintaining that the offence of killing his mother was cancelled by the blood of "slaughtered swine".

The downright immorality of dismissing the gravity of any moral offence, even to the extent of an outrage against a sensitive conscience, is further expressed in the priestly book of Leviticus. After prescribing that "The ram for the guilt-offering shall...be slaughtered", it is declared that "the priest shall take some of the blood of the guilt-offering, and put it on the lobe of the right ear of the man to be cleansed and on his right thumb and on the big toe of his right foot"(14:25-26). With every additional specified procedure in this priestly performance, the offensiveness of its purely magical character intensifies to an extent that one finds himself faced with an insurmountable handicap even to be respectful of the ignorance underlying the antiquity of this rite. It is this type of practice, under the gloss of religion, which is basic to the most violent criticisms of religion, often becoming a disparagement of religion as the last entrenchment against an enlightenment by science and the arts. But, as has been acknowledged, no criticism of this perverse version of religion, whether under the name of science or philosophy, can match the unequalled disparagement of it which is so eloquently affirmed by the Old Testament prophets, whose version of religion is considered in the next chapter.

Chapter Seven

DISCLOSURE OF DIVINE REALITIES

**1. Religious celebrations and sacred days of both
ancient Greeks and Israelites express their belief that
divine reality is attentive to their homage and moves
toward them with favor as its response to their worship**

An important aspect of Greek culture in a study of its
religion is the fact that the names of most of the
months in the Attic year were derived from festivals
which were dedicated to their gods. The name of the
first Attic month, "Hecatombaion", was derived from the
Hecatombaia, a festival, which from early centuries,
was dedicated to Apollo. The meaning of the term for
this festival is itself a record of the nature of its
occasion, which was a sacrifice of "hundreds of
victims" to the god.[1] This sacrifice expressed a belief
that the god took notice of it, and was aware of the
motive or the intended purpose for it. This
interpretation thus indicates not only what the
participants thought about their need for divine help,
but also what they believed was the god's awareness of
their need. What is furthermore expressed in such a
sacrifice, after which a month is named, is the
people's belief that what they did in reverently
relating themselves to their god conditioned his
attitude of concern for them, and therefore, what he
would consider doing in response to their appeal,
oriented to him in the sacrifice.

The fact that the festival, which included the
sacrifice, marked the beginning of the Attic year,
expresses an ancient religious belief of the dependence
of corporate well-being upon the initiative of a divine
reality toward a community. Such a presumed initiative
of Providence, in conferring a benefaction upon human
beings, expresses a religious faith that there is a
reciprocal relation between them and the divine reality
to which they orient themselves in worship. The divine
reality is thus believed to disclose its concern for
them when they reverently acknowledge their dependence
upon it for its help.

The second month in the Attic calendar, Metageitnion,
was named from a title, "Metageitnios", with which

Apollo was referred in a cult, whose festival was celebrated "as a holy day in various Ionian centres", such as Delos, Ephesus, Miletus, and Samos.2 The religious significance of this festival, therefore, was not merely local, but, by virtue of the considerable area in which the god was worshiped, it was a feature of Greek culture.

The derivation of the name of one more month may be mentioned merely to point out the dominance of a religious belief of the ancient Greeks that their orientation to a divine reality expressed their trust in its providence for them, as its response to their acknowledgment of their need for its blessings. This third month in the Attic calendar is the Boedromion, whose name is derived from a festival that was dedicated to Apollo, which took place on the seventh day of this month.

Other months were named according to the same principle of acknowledging an established festival that was oriented to some deity, such as the fourth month, which was named after a festival dedicated to Demeter,3 and the name of the ninth month was derived from a festival dedicated to the goddess Artemis.4

The Greeks' religious acknowledgment of their dependence upon divine reality for their corporate well-being, which acknowledgment continued from early centuries, was reaffirmed by the Athenians after the end of the Peloponnesian War. In 403/2, an "official religious calendar of sacrifices" was "inscribed on the back of the same stone walls of the Stoa Basileios which had 'the laws of Solon' on the front".5 Although it was not included in the legal code, it nevertheless, expressed a civic acknowledgment that religious reverence for divine reality is not a local or individual option, but rather is one of primary significance for the Athenian Empire, and therefore, for all of its people. This acknowledgment has a special importance in a history of religion, since it affirms a belief of considerable antiquity that there are guardian gods of nations, upon whom the welfare of a nation depends. In this ancient religious acknowledgment of the civic significance of a people's religion is expressed a belief that divine reality is a sovereignty which is more ultimate than human rulers, and therefore, the effectiveness of their reigns depends upon the favor of such a reality toward them and their people.

Sacred days for the Greeks, as well as for the Israelites, were determined by phases of the moon. The religious importance of the lunar calendar traces to prehistoric times for the Greeks, since the earliest beginnings of the worship of Hera have associations with such lunar phases.6 Eleusinian Mysteries likewise were related to phases of the moon. Preparations for the Mysteries began at full moon, and rites of purification took place during the period of the waning moon.7 In his Heraclidae, Euripides refers to the birth of the goddess Pallas Athena as taking place "with the new moon".8

Since the religious orientation of both Greeks and Israelites expressed their beliefs that whatever they did on holy days and in their festivals, which were dedicated to divine realities, made a difference to such realities in relation to them, it is appropriate in this analysis to take account of the lunar calendar of such sacred days.

Kerenyi points out that although there is no word in the ancient Greek vocabulary for "religious experience as a special experience", the term "religio", on the other hand, once meant "scrupulous carefulness".9 If this is an early connotation of this general term, it then stresses an attitude which is basic to the manner in which both ancient Greeks and Israelites respected sacred days. They were so regarded as being sacred by virtue of how both peoples avoided doing anything on those days to incur the disfavor of divine reality. And the converse of this concern is that by doing nothing to offend a deity, they believed that they were related to the deity in a way which was favorable for them, in a religious sense of receiving divine approval, which was basic to every expression of providential blessing.

The seventh day of the third Attic month was a festival which was dedicated to Apollo; and the seventh day of the fourth Attic month likewise was dedicated to him. This festival especially expresses the religious meaning which is being considered in this chapter, since the rites which were included in it were explained as celebrating the return of the legendary Theseus from Crete, after having been successful in destroying the Minotaur, which had annually demanded the lives of Athenian youth. The specific religious character of this celebration was acknowledging Apollo's providence in the undertaking, and acknowledging also the gratitude of Theseus and his companions to the god to whom they had vowed offerings on the occasion of their safe return from this mission. The public nature of this religious celebration, the Pyanepsia,10 meant to all Athenian participants, who understood the intention or motivation underlying the festival, that this mission carried out by Theseus and his companions was not only to their credit, but also primarily to the credit of the god who remembered their vow, which acknowledged their dependence upon his providential help.

The religious (religio) meaning of sacred days and sacred events in the calendar of both Greeks and Israelites is that their sacredness consists of "warnings not to deviate from the way...prescribed in the Festival Calendar".11 The sacred character of a period in the calendar is its supreme seriousness in the relation of human beings to divine reality. Its seriousness, therefore, is the reason for the taboos and prohibitions which became integral to the customs of both people, even when respect for such sacred days did not have specific religious significance for some among both peoples. Plato, for example, did not take account of this particular aspect of the religious nature of holy days when, in his Laws, he explains their origin as the "pity" of "the gods (for) the toils which our race is born to undergo", and therefore, "have appointed holy festivals, wherein men alternate rest with labors".12 This explanation considers the initiative of divine reality toward human beings in their pity for their "toils", from which the gods, as considerate of human beings, justified the religious festivals. The explanation, so given, does not, however, take account of the human motive for establishing such religious festivals as occasions for making special appeals for divine pity or charity; and it is this aspect which is primary in a consideration of a history of the origins of religious celebrations as what human beings do to appeal to divine Providence for its help. Such appeal is motivated by a belief that there is a divine source of help which human beings may enlist by what they do. Considering the initiative of divine reality, such as Plato does, apart from the initiative of human beings, would more appropriately come within the scope of a theology, instead of a history of religions, when such a history takes account of what human beings do to become worthy of such divine consideration.

Athenian laws took account of the sacredness of days, as well as of places which were dedicated to deities,

246

thereby indicating an awareness that prohibitions, which are primarily religious in their origin, often acquire utmost importance in civil legislation. The Athenian festival Plyteria was sacred to all who worshiped Athena as the guardian goddess of their city-state and empire, and was devoted to the ritualistic purifications of the statue of the goddess, which included its washing at the Peiraeus. According to Athenian law, "no Athenian would dare to touch any serious business on that day."13

Any behavior in a temple or on the sacred area surrounding it was not only an infraction of a cult prohibition, but it was also an offence for which civil laws prescribed punishment. Solon, for example, made it a legal offence to speak ill of anyone in a temple; and the laws which he instituted for such offences remained "in force in the fourth century".14 As late as the last quarter of that century (376/5), several citizens of Delos were "convicted of impiety", and were "condemned to exile and heavy fines"15 because they were disrespectful of Athenian administrators (Amphiktyones) in the temple of Apollo and Delos. What is especially significant in the imposition of this severe penalty is the classification of the offence to these officials as "impiety", which connotes offence to a deity. It was, in other words, the Athenians' primary concern for the offence to the god by what was done in his temple, rather than to any insult or injury to the officials. Any desecration of a temple and its sacred area was extremely grave because regarded as offending a deity, and thereby, impairing his favor for an entire people. Penalizing an offender, therefore, was showing a god that his people were aware of their dependence on his favor, and would not tolerate irreverence or disrespect for anything, time or place, which was dedicated to his worship.

So serious was any disrespect for the sacred, such as the area surrounding a temple, that even an unintended trespass on it, could incur the death penalty, as was imposed upon two children, who unaware of such prohibitions, entered the sacred area at Eleusis. According to Athenian law, and according also to the priestly jurisdiction among the Israelites, "an act would be regarded as impious even if the doer did not know that it was so when he committed it."16

A judgment of guilt in such a case would ordinarily be regarded as morally unjust. But by virtue of the extreme gravity for an entire people of a desecration

of a sacred place or a holy day, no latitude could be
ventured in a consideration of an individual's acting
without intention. Incurring the disfavor of a divine
reality was regarded by Greeks and Israelites alike as
so grave that the divine reality took precedence over
any consideration for a human offender, since a god
could impair the well-being of an entire people for the
unpunished offence of a single human being.

If no other consideration indicates a people's
awareness of a divine initiative toward them, such an
initiative certainly is indicated in a divine judgment
upon anyone for his desecration of a sacred site or
holy day.

One of the frequently repeated emphases in the Old
Testament is the unqualified necessity to revere the
holiness of the Sabbath. Exodus, for example, declares
this injunction: "Remember the sabbath day and keep it
holy"(20.8). The religious explanation for this is
affirmed in the following verse, which might well be
regarded as the basic motive for every genuine
religious act: "The seventh day is a sabbath
for...your god." And this is affirmed after
acknowledging the rights of human beings to consider
themselves for a part of the week. But no schedule of
life is sound which only takes account of such rights,
without also acknowledging the obligations of human
beings to the Providence which enables them to have the
benefits of their industry. Their health, and the
fertility of the earth by which they live, are made
possible for them by their god. The uncompromising
demand, therefore, is made: "You shall do no work that
day," including the specific prohibition of no work for
a man's children, his servants, his animals, as well as
for any "stranger who lives" in his household(vs.10).

The explanation, however, which is added for the
cogency of this injunction weakens the strength of the
foregoing characterization of the religious motive for
revering the sabbath, which motive is that after human
beings have preoccupied themselves with working for
their own benefits, they should take account of the
ultimate condition which sustains their life. This is
not their labors, which express their skills,
intelligence, and industry, but is rather the
underguerding of all that they do by the Providence,
without whose benefactions there would be no life.
Since human welfare is contingent upon the divine
source from which every good is derived, it is,
therefore, their obligation to acknowledge their

dependence upon it. But this should be done not only on the seventh day of a week. It should be done every day. Yet, as a concession to the pressure of human work, the seventh part of a week is set aside for this essential acknowledgment of life's dependence upon its divine source, and the providence which sustains it. In light of this genuinely religious justification for an unqualified dedication of the seventh day to a worship, which acknowledges the human debt to its creator, the appended myth of a creation which took place in six days, with the seventh day for the creator's rest, is indeed extremely weak. The religious reason for the sacredness of the Sabbath is not the opportunity it provides for a human being to rest, but rather to be free from all distractions from an unconditioned acknowledgment of his dependence upon a divine providence, which makes possible his life, its support, and its well-being.

The "scrupulous warning" which has been referred to in the foregoing discussion as an original meaning of "religio" was taken without qualification by the Israelites in conforming to what was regarded as a divine injunction to do no work whatsoever on the sacred sabbath. The Book of Numbers records an incident which took place "During the time that the Israelites were in the wilderness: A man was found gathering sticks on the sabbath day." As a way of stressing the divine sanction for the prohibition of all work on the sabbath, this biblical text maintains that their god "said to Moses: 'The man must be put to death; he must be stoned by all the community outside the camp.'" The priestly reason for attributing this judgment of death upon the man who disregarded the absoluteness of the sacredness of the sabbath--with the prohibition against any activity that would impair its dedication to their god--is to stress the injunction as imposed by their god, indicating his expectation of their acknowledgment of their total dependence upon him. Thus work, apart from such devout acknowledgment of dependence upon their god, would impair this sacredness of the day, just as any trespassing upon a sacred site would impair the absolute right of a divine claim to it as sanctified to the worship of a deity, and so sanctified that no qualification of its absoluteness was tolerable. Hence, the rationale for the death-penalty for an offender, rather than for any relaxing of a prohibition which could so readily eventuate in a progressive disrespect for the absolute sacredness of the temple which is dedicated to a god. Such sacredness includes no provisions for its compromising by any human being--even though his trespass be unintentional. According to the same principle, an infraction of the absoluteness of the sacredness of the sabbath would justify the severest of penalites, carried out by a community in order to avoid a penalty that it might suffer for neglecting the prosecution of a single offender against a right reserved only for divine reality.

There are, of course, consequences which may be entailed in scrupulously conforming to any uncompromising principle. This is made evident in the account which is given in First Maccabees about the inability of the king of Judaea to withstand a siege by "the people of Bethsura", because the people of "the town (had) no more food to withstand a siege, (since) it was a sabbatical year when the land was left fallow"(6:48-50). The tragic consequence of a practice of leaving the land without cultivating, as an implication of a religious principle, is undeniable. Its tragic character is misapplying the principle of respecting the sacredness of a sabbath as a human obligation, and extending its application to the land. Yet, what is instructive in this thoroughgoing application of a principle, regarded as a divine command, is its actual irrelevance to the religious motive for human beings dedicating the seventh part of a week as a special occasion to be mindful of their debt of total dependence upon the divine sovereignty over human life.

2. Both Israelites and Greeks believed there are intermediaries between divine reality and themselves

By virtue of intermediaries between an ultimate divine reality and human beings, the distance, as it were, is reduced which separates their radically different natures.

Realities referred to as "angels" constituted one such type of order which mediated the god of the Israelites to his people, and thereby, made his presence tangible to them in a being which may have had the appearance of a human individual, and yet, was not limited to human capacities. It was such a messenger of the guardian god of the Israelites that "called to Abraham from heaven", when he was in the act of sacrificing his son Isaac on the altar. Calling "Abraham, Abraham", the angel drew the Patriarch's attention away from the intended act of sacrificing his son, and made him attentive to "the angel of the Lord" who gave the command: "Do not raise your hand against the boy"(Gen.22:10-12). The angel thus was an agent of the god whose plan included that Isaac should succeed his father in the role of the second of the patriarchs, both to direct them in their search for a homeland, and also to instruct them in the appropriate worship of their god. For these reasons, the angel performed the role of executing the plan of the guardian god of the Israelites to have Isaac become the next in the succession of patriarchs.

A second account in Genesis includes the role of the angel in carrying out the god's plan to have Isaac become the father of descendants who would be devoted to their god. According to this text, Abraham instructed his servant to go to Abraham's "own country and to (his) own kindred to find a wife for...Isaac"(24:2-4). Aware of the necessity to preserve the purity of blood for retaining the purity of faith, and therefore, of worship, Abraham assured the servant that he would not be alone in discharging this responsibility; telling him that his god "will send his angel" to lead him (vs.7).

The role of the angel in this case was critical to the entire history of the Israelites' fidelity to the god whom Abraham worshiped. Had there been a marriage of Isaac to a person with a foreign religion, the entire plan of the god to have a "chosen people" who were dedicated to worship, would have been impaired, or even completely curtailed. Abraham was clearly aware of the critical nature of the appropriate marriage for his son when he declared: "The Lord...swore to me that he would give this land to my descendants". Such "descendants", however, would continue the religious tradition begun by Abraham only upon the condition of the fidelity of his son to their god.

The mere mention, therefore, by Abraham of the "land" which his god had promised to his "descendants" was the occasion for another intermediary of the god to assure the Israelites that they would be successful in acquiring a homeland. Exodus describes this occasion when the guardian god declared to his people that "If you listen carefully" to the angel he will send, they will acquire the promised land. The guardian god assured them: "My angel will go before you and lead you"(23:23-24).

Thus another critical occasion in the history of the Israelites prompted their god to send an intermediary to perform a mission which could not depend upon human untrustworthiness to effect. Joshua, who succeeded Moses as the leader of his people, was clearly aware of the critical character of his responsibility to secure the homeland which had been promised to his people in the covenant made by their god with Abraham. Hence, he was prepared to believe that a divine help would come to him as he led the Israelites; and so he was conditioned to accept such an intermediary of his god, when, in the form of a man, the emissary announced: "I am here as captain of the army of the Lord." And as a certification of his authority as delegated by the divine sovereign, he commanded Joshua: "Take off your sandals: the place where you are standing is holy"(Josh.5:14-15). The holiness or sacredness of the place was conferred by the angel, even though he appeared to Joshua as a man.

Psalm 91 sums up the ministry of such angelic intermediaries of the divine reality when it declares: "He has charged his angels to guard you wherever you go"(vs.11-12). And even though there is no identification of a specific representative, messenger, or intermediary of the divine reality to human beings, the Faithful believed that in the wisdom of their god there is always his guardianship and guidance, which on some occasions of utmost importance are performed by a representative who has the benefit of a wisdom which is of an order higher than human intelligence.

A remarkable parallel of the Old Testament characterization of angels is expressed in literature of the ancient Greeks. In the case of the Greek version of angels, however, they are not intermediaries of a divine reality, but are themselves gods or goddesses, who are disguised in forms which often are not detected by human beings, although there are occasions when their identity is recognized, notwithstanding their disguise. The goddess Aphrodite, for instance, appeared to Helen as an old woman in the form of a "wool dresser".17 The goddess Athena "disguised herself as a man, and slipped into the Trojan ranks in the likeness of a sturdy spearman called Laodocus."18

Since Poseidon did not want to be recognized as helping the Argives, "He took the form of a man; and in that disguise kept moving to and fro, stirring up the troops."19 In another instance, both Poseidon and

Athena when together, disguised themselves in "human form" and appeared before Achilles, taking "his hands in theirs, and giving him their encouragement."20

Apollo, who favored the Trojans, disguised himself as one of the sons of the king of Troy, and spoke to Aeneas.21 A second time, Apollo appeared to him; but this time, "the god took the form of a herald".22 Another time the god went to Hector in the disguise of a man called Mentes, a leader of the Cicones.23 And once more, "he went up to Hector, disguised as Phaenops, son of Asius".24

A role of divine beings, who assume human form in various disguises, is explained in the Odyssey. It maintains that "the gods disguise themselves as strangers from abroad, and wander round our towns". A mission which is thereby performed is likewise explained: They do so "to see whether people are behaving themselves or getting out of hand".25 There are, as has been pointed out, other roles which they also perform, as is illustrated by Athena, who is the principal deity to assume various disguises in the Odyssey's narrative, since she is the guardian goddess of Odysseus during his ten-year long journies.

In the first book of the Odyssey, she appears on the threshold of Odysseus' court during his absence, assuming "the appearance of a Taphian chieftan".26 After some time, when she disappeared, the son of Odysseus, "felt the change" which had taken place in his discouraged attitude toward the future. And sensing a renewed courage, attributed the change to the visit of a divine being, being certain that "it was a divinity".27 When he again was dejected, not knowing the whereabouts of his father, the goddess "assumed the apearance" of a trusted friend of his father; and later in her way of helping him, assumed the appearance of this friend and went into the city to instruct its men to assemble in the evening as a preliminary to helping the distraught Telemachus.28

When Odysseus was among the Phaiakians, the goddess "came to meet him, disguised as a young girl carrying a pitcher".29 She later went to the city, "disguised as a herald" from the king of the Phaiakians, who wanted to help Odysseus and his son.30 Finally, when Odysseus landed on the shore of his island home, he was met by the goddess, disguised as a young shepherd.31 At this time, Odysseus recognized her, and admitted to her that it was difficult even "for a man of good understanding to recognize" her, since she "take(s) every shape".[32]

Odysseus evidently was aware of the various forms she assumed, since in the third book, he refers to her appearing as "a vulture" (or a "sea-eagle"), and in this form was responsible for an "amazement (which) seized on all the Achaians".[33] Toward the end of the Odyssey in Book XXII, which describes Odysseus' attacking the suitors who had occupied his palace during his absence, the goddess watched the fighting from a beam in the great hall in the form of a swallow.[34]

3. Both ancient peoples believed that human prophets disclose divine will to human beings

The Homeric Hymn to the Delian Apollo characterizes one of the first acts of the god after his birth, as making a promise about his future prophecies: "I will declare to men the unfailing will of Zeus."[35] So interpreted, the primray role of Apollo is prophetic of the will of the ultimate sovereign of the gods. Since it is his prophecies which are declared by human prophets, he is thus the intermediary between the ultimate sovereign of gods and human beings. In the first book of the Iliad, Achilles requests the prophet Calchas to "Speak...in the name of Apollo, beloved of Zeus", and "interpret the gods' will to the Danaans."[36] Distraught by the punishment which Apollo imposed upon them, Achilles accepted the judgment of the seer, "knowing well the truth", he understood the god's will, which he in turn explained to the leaders of the assembled forces.[37]

The Odyssey also identifies Polyphaides as "a seer of Apollo", who at time, was "the leading prophet in the world".[38]

The chorus in Sophocles' Oedipus the King characterizes Teiresias, "our prophet", as "he of all men best might guide a searcher...to the light", because there is no other "man (who) sees eye to eye with Lord Phoebus (Apollo)".[39] Oedipus, in acknowledging the chorus' tribute to the Prophet, as "the god-inspired seer in whom above all other men is truth inborn," admits that Teiresias (is a) seer who comprehendest all,/Lord of the wise and hidden mysteries,/ High things of heaven and low things of the earth."[40] This characterization of a prophet by the Greek dramatist may be regarded as an appropriate characterization of the Old Testament's interpretation of the qualifications of prophets, who addressed themselves to the Israelites, as spokesmen for their god.

The total confidence in Teiresias, as a spokesman for Apollo, who in turn, was the voice of Zeus, is also affirmed in Euripides' The Phoenisae, when Eteocles, prince of Thebes, admits: "One thing only have we still to do, to ask Teiresias, the seer, if he has aught to tell of heaven's will."[41] Although the Old Testament prophets interpreted themselves as Eteocles interprets Teiresias, as declaring "heaven's will", many of the Israelites did not have the confidence in their prophets that the prince Eteocles had in the prophet whom he trusted for disclosing the judgment of divine reality upon human affairs.

Those among the Israelites who respected their prophets' presumptions as being spokesmen for their god, regarded them as intermediaries of their god to his people, declaring as their god's representative, his divine judgment upon them.

According to the Old Testament, the tradition of prophets begins with Moses, as "a providential instrument of God for the guidance of his chosen people".[42] Deuteronomy characterizes Moses as the one "whom the Lord", the god of the Israelites, "chose from all (their) tribes to attend on the Lord and to minister in (his) name"(18:5). Moses, in turn, assured his people that their god "will raise up a prophet" among them to whom they "shall listen"(vs.15). And he supported his own assurance to them by declaring that it was their own god who had made the promise: "I will raise up for them a prophet...and I will put my words into his mouth"(vs.18).

What is especially important in understanding the nature of prophecy, as it is interpreted in this text, is that what is declared by a prophet, as a spokesman for his god, are "words" which are put "into his mouth" by the god for whom he speaks. This was the claim also of the infant Apollo that he "will declare to men the unfailing will" of the sovereign gods.

The directness of the mediation of a genuine prophet, such as Moses, is described in Deuteronomy as one "whom the Lord knew face to face"(34:10). In other words, there is no intermediary between such a prophet and the god for whom he is a spokesman. Rather, what he declares to his people is the mind or will of the god with whom he has direct contact, unqualified by any likelihood of fallacy of an interpreter's role. A prophet so characterized, is not an interpreter of the god's will, but is rather the human medium for conveying that divine will directly to his people. This analysis of the nature of genuine prophecy thus makes no allowance for the human peculiarities of a prophet. He is rather a transparent vehicle of the judgment or will of the god whom he represents. Whereas no philosophical version of prophecy could accept this analysis of any mediation of the thought of one by another, this, nevertheless, is the basic confidence of Scripture that what a true prophet attributes to his god as his will or judgment is that will or judgment, and it is not his analysis of it, which would then be conditioned by his intelligence and his personal perspective.

This biblical criterion of the genuineness of prophecy, as a direct affirmation of divine judgment, is intended as a challenge to competing claims of prophecies by any number of so-called "prophets" among other people. Yet, the claim to be a prophet, speaking for a god, is not an authentication of the genuineness or validity of the claim. The priestly authors of Numbers, therefore, maintain that a genuine prophet is one whom the god himself certifies as a chosen one to whom he speaks "face to face, openly and not in riddles"(12:8). By virtue of this directness, the claim for its authenticity is that the prophet "shall see the very form of the Lord"(12:8).

Although there obviously are insurmountable problems in any philosophical acceptance of this belief, what is, nevertheless, important is understanding the biblical awareness of the necessity for a criterion to determine the genuineness of prophecy, which is the correspondence of what a prophet affirms with the divine judgment for which he certifies its genuineness. The circularity of this is, of course, evident, and it is for this reason that prophets themselves reject prophecies, even though they are affirmed with this claim of conveying the will or judgment of the god for this special role in conveying his will to his people.

The Book of Numbers proposes a criterion of the genuineness of prophecy when it cites the qualification of Joshua as a worthy successor of Moses for conveying the will of the god of the Israelites to them. His qualification so interpreted is that he is "a man endowed with spirit"(27:18), by which is meant, that it is the nonhuman endowment within him which is the condition that accounts for the trustworthiness of his judgments, since they actually are judgments of his god.

The Israelites believed that when they had exhausted their own resources in doing what was beneficial for themselves, they could justifiably depend upon their god to send them a prophet or prophetess, who would instruct them with their god's wisdom for what they should do that would be trustworthy, such as their own judgments were not consistently capable of being. Hence, after being "oppressed...harshly for twenty years" by the overwhelming military might of the Canaanites, they turned to Deborah, "a prophetess" whom they trusted "for justice"(Judg.4:5). In the tradition of prophecy among the Israelites, she offered to them the certification of her judgments, by declaring "These are the commands of the Lord, the God of Israel." This claim, however, is not accompanied with any presumed certification for the genuineness of her judgments, which she attributed to their god, whereas such a criterion is proposed in the characterization of Samuel as given in First Samuel, which declares that "as Samuel grew up, the Lord was with him, and none of his words went unfulfilled"(3:19). According to this text, it was this empirical verification by which "All Israel recognized that Samuel was confirmed as a prophet of the Lord"(vs.20). It evidently was this correspondence of what he prophesied with what confirmed his prophecies that accounted for the Israelites' confidence that their god "had revealed himself...to Samuel"(vs.21).

4. The discrediting of one prophet by another bewildered the Israelites about which prophet actually discloses the will of their god

A feature of the Old Testament history of prophets which helps to account for the scepticism of the Israelites toward the claims of prophets to speak for their god is the conflict between the prophets themselves. Even before the two centuries during which prophets were numerous, and their role had become a dominant feature of the religious history of the Israelites, the Book of Nehemiah records the emergence of a conflict between the claims of prophets themselves, each affirming credentials to disclose the will of their god.

Nehemiah describes the scheming of a contemporary prophet who attempted to discredit him; but after thinking about the scheme which he proposed, Nehemiah declared: "It dawned on me; God had not sent him." Nehemiah then points out that the motive of the presumed prophet was to harm him, rather than to disclose to the Israelites a revelation of their god. Nehemiah furthermore maintains that he was being opposed by more than the one who schemed to "intimidate" him, and thereby to silence him, declaring that "also the prophetess Noadiah and all the other prophets...have tried to intimidate me(6:10-14).

The competition of self-proclaimed prophets among the Hebrews evidently was so widespread at the time of Job, that his friend, Eliphaz the Temanite, declared: "If God puts no trust in his holy ones", how much less could human beings trust them(15:15-16).

According to a traditional interpretation of the Old Testament, the tradition of the major prophets began with Isaiah, who declared to the Israelites: "Your guides led you astray and confused the path that you should take"(3:12). Among such "guides", of course, were those who claimed to disclose to their people, the intentions of their god. So resentful, however, the Israelites must have become by the competing claims of all those who presumed to have qualifications to be spokesman for their god, that at least many of them became intolerant of all who claimed to be prophets. So biased were they against the rash of those declaring contradictory prophecies--and all in the name of their god--that they did not even distinguish between their merits, and in consequence, rejected Isaiah and his prophecies, just as they rejected all the others. Isaiah describes their intolerance of him as expressive of their contempt for prophecies and prophets of all sorts. In opposition to those who rejected him, he declared: "I offered my back to the lash...I did not hide my face from spitting and insult." So confident was he in his credentials as a spokesman for his god that he was supported in affirming prophecies by his assurance that his god "stands by to help" him, and "therefore no insult can wound"(50:6-7). But such confidence, of course, which the Prophet had in his role as disclosing the will of his god is no criterion by which his contemporaries could assess the genuineness of his claims as a prophet.

Jeremiah's presumed role as a prophet, disclosing the will of god, met with the same contempt of his contemporaries as Isaiah encountered. That there was an increasing number of self-styled prophets during the troubled times in which he lived is evident in his own reference to the plurality of "prophets", whom he, in turn, disparaged as "frauds"(6:13). He believed that he had a criterion by which the competing prophecies which he disparaged could be rejected, declaring: "The Lord answered me. The prophets are prophesying lies in my name. I have not sent them"(14:14). The prophet himself, of course, was the only one who was convinced of the truth of the presumed disclosure which he cites as certification for his own credentials as a genuine prophet. In other words, his claim to be a prophet of his god, disclosing his god's judgment upon his people, did not convince other self-styled prophets any more than their claims to genuineness convinced him. And the conflict of such competing claims left the Israelites convinced that no one of the many claims had a sounder basis than another to be respected as "revelation" of the will of their god, rather than the biased ideas of human beings, each presuming that he had credentials which no one else had to make pronouncements in the name of god.

Jeremiah referred to prophecies which competed with his "deluding fancies"(vs.15). But what he thought of them, is what the Israelites thought of his prophecies, notwithstanding his own conviction that they were certified as genuine by the god for whom he presumed to be a spokesman. The conflict of competing claims to the genuineness of each claim persuaded the Israelites that all of the claims had equal value, which in their estimate, was of no value, other than the ideas of "deluded" men, declaring "deluded fancies".

The animosity generated in a competition of conflicting claims for the genuineness of prophecies, made by self-styled prophets themselves, is indicated in the contempt which Jeremiah had for his contemporaries, who, like himself, regarded themselves as prophets. He pronounced them as "godless"(23:11). But since the nature of being "godless", according to a prophet's own judgment, was affirming a belief which was attributed to a revelation of a god that differed from what he himself claimed, the meaning of Jeremiah's denunciation of others as "godless" had, from the point of view of the Israelites, only emotive significance, expressing his antagonism for other prophets, rather than constituting an informed estimate of their untrustworthiness.

The intensity of Jeremiah's own contempt for those who opposed him, and discredited his prophecies, is evident in his disparagement of them as speaking "lies" in what they attribute to him. Hence he sought to discredit their trustworthiness by declaring: "I have heard what the prophets say...who speak lies in my name", which he maintains are only "their inventions"(vs.25-27), declaring for his god: "I am against the prophets...who concoct words of their own and then say, 'This is his very word.'". But again, Jeremiah's argument to discredit the prophecies of others, is an argument to which others appeal for discrediting his claims to genuine prophecy.

In this debate between prophets, the Israelites, as witnesses of the contest, dismissed all of the prophets and their prophecies likewise as disclosing nothing genuine about divine judgment, but only about the prophets' own ideas about what such a divine reality would pronounce, provided the divine reality were in their place, speaking from their perspectives. Obviously any critical Israelite would, apart from his own preference, have no basis internal to such competing prophecies, to regard one as more genuine than another. And the upshot of this dilemma is that they rejected all such prophecies, seeming to be most annoyed with the prophets who, like Jeremiah, were most assertive in insisting that they alone affirmed true revelations. When, therefore, he maintained that his contemporaries should "put every madman who sets up as a prophet into the stocks and the pillory"(29:27), he prescribed what they themselves regarded appropriate treatment for him, who depreciated every other self-styled prophet, such as "the prophets of Samaria" as "men of no sense".

The eagerness of the contemporaries of Jeremiah to want some prophecy about a future is indicated in the number of prophets who were active during his own prophetic mission, since he refers to "prophets of Samaria", and to "prophets of Jerusalem", as if there were self-styled prophets everywhere among his people. It is, therefore, not surprising that, with the competing number of prophets, each claiming some way of acting as having a divine sanction, that whatever they did, acting on such prophetic proposals, would seem to Jeremiah as leading his "people Israel astray". And it is also understandable that he should believe there was "a godless spirit (which)...spread over all the land" when people consulted "the prophets of Jerusalem"(vs.15), rather than listening to him. Since his contemporaries regarded him as only one among those making conflicting assertions in the name of their god, he was angered with them for not acknowledging him as the only genuine prophet at the time, and consequently, he appealed to those who would listen to him: "Do not listen to what the prophets say", disparaging their prophecies as "visions which spring from their own imagination". Such competing claims thus clarified no criterion for the genuineness or the truth of what any prophet declared as a disclosure of a divine reality.

Whereas Jeremiah's prophecies, in light of what took place to confirm them, had a validity which prophecies that contradicted them did not have, yet, at the time, without having the benefit of such confirmations, his contemporaries could not recognize the truth of his prophecies, and in their impatience with the competing voices of prophets, "imprisioned Jeremiah in the court of the guard-house attached to the royal palace." Thereby removing him and his considerations of their unsound policies, which if they had listened to him, and seriously respected his judgments about them, might have saved themselves from the tragic disaster which he predicted, when Jerusalem and Zedekiah, its ruler, would fall "into the hands of the king of Babylon"(32:2-5).

Ezekiel continues the depreciation of "the wicked folly of the prophets" who were contemporary with him and competed with him for their credibility among the Israelites. He disparages them, as Jeremiah had done, for "inspirations (which) come from themselves", and therefore, without authority as revealing the will of their god, such as many claimed for his own pronouncements. As is characteristic of the prophets among the Israelites, those whom he accused of "lying divination", also prefaced their pronouncements with the identification which is presumed to certify the genuineness of prophecies: "It is the very word of the Lord." Yet, in response to them, Ezekiel declared that "it is not the Lord who has sent them"(13:3-6), comparing their prophecies to "whitewash instead of plaster", thereby maintaining that they were without substance, which genuine revelations would have. Although such prophets claim that what they declare to the Israelites "is the word of the Lord", their god, yet, Ezekiel declared that "the Lord has not spoken" anything that they attributed to the divine reality, but instead, what they attribute to the divine source, is "false" and "a lie"(22:28).

Amos was not one of the so-called "professional" prophets, presuming to have a status of authority comparable to those of an established reputation. He was instead, a shepherd, living on the edge of the desert of Judah(1:1); but in reflecting on the conditions of his people, and recalling the consequences which previously followed such similar conditions, he believed that he had a responsiblity to point out to them the correlation of what once took place under similar circumstances, and what could, therefore, realistically be assumed to occur again.

As devoutly religious, he regarded his obligation to his people, not as a moral duty, but rather as a divinely sanctioned mission, such as genuine prophets, who believe they are called by their god to perform. He, therefore, left his home "to prophesy to Israel"(7:14). This was during the tragically corrupt reign of Jeroboam II (783-743), and he presumed to depreciate the surface character of rituals, under the gloss of religious devotion, without either sanctity or morality. Identifying himself as a spokesman for his god, he declared: "I hate, I spurn your pilgrim-feasts; I will not delight in your sacred ceremonies." His disparagment of their irreverent character continued, as if declared by his god: "When you present your sacrifices and offerings, I will not accept them." Since this depreciation of established public forms of worship was a disparagement of the entire priestly system, it was inevitable that Amos, like Jeremiah and Isaiah, were opposed by the priesthood, which was so entrenched in Hebrew culture.

Rather then protesting his expulsion from Israel, as Jeremiah would have done, he accepted his rejection, and returned to his home, convinced that the corruption of the kingdom could be corrected by a moral rebirth of justice and righteousness, and not by the "shared-offerings", "the sound of (the people's) songs", and "the music of (their) lutes". His pronouncement, having spiritual authority, and therefore, worthy of being attributed to a judgment of a universal sovereign, was: "Let justice roll on like a river and righteousness like an ever-flowing stream"(5:21-14).

The prophet Micah, as other prophets before him, prefaced his prophetic role with the same credentials: "These are the words of the Lord"; and their specific purpose, according to him, was "concerning the prophets who lead (his) people astray", promising genuine "prosperity in return for a morsel of food"(3:5). In other words, for a surface proposal, without substance, fraudulent prophets deceived people by underestimating the gravity of their social and political conditions, which could be altered only by a radical reform, and not by glossing over their surface with a pseudo-solution, offering a specious type of help, but without realistic relevance to the existing conditions that threatened an entire people's welfare.

His pointed critique of the ills of their culture has the authority of moral substance, and an understanding of the basic spiritual conditions for human well-being, when he accuses the people's rulers of "selling justice"; and accuses "priests of giving direction in return for a bribe"; and declares that "prophets take money for their divination". And in spite of the continued low moral level of their society, they yet superficially "rely on the Lord", as if by magic, he can do for them what they have a moral duty to do for themselves, in "dealing justly, in loving tenderly, and in walking humbly with God"(6:8).

The sheer integrity of Zechariah's condemnation of spurious prophecies is expressed in the powerful characterization of eventual divine judgment upon all human dishonesty and perversity, even when under the gloss of religious practices, including the fraudulent claims of prophets. His prophecy, by virtue of its moral honesty, carries its own credentials of authenticity, when he anticipates the inevitable judgment upon a perverse culture: "On that day every prophet shall be ashamed of his (fraudulent) vision when he (dishonestly) prophecies, nor shall he (deceptively) conceal his real nature). He will be forced to declare that he is "no prophet", but a fake, "schooled in (dishonesty) from boyhood"(13:5-6).

5. Emphases of the prophets among the Israelites were conditioned by social and political contexts in which they lived

As has been pointed out, Amos lived during the reigns of Jeroboam II (783-943). The conditions of the culture of the Israelites at that time determined what he regarded as having utmost importance for them, which consequently became central to his prophetic addresses to them. The powerful military equipment of Assyria was being directed toward the west, and the anxiety of the Israelites was being expressed in the type of despair which reaches out for whatever offers a momentary good, no matter how deceptive it may be in terms of a genuine well-being, both individually and collectively. Hence, Amos addressed himself to the profound mistake of his people to grasp for any and every specious good, when their entire future was in jeopardy. From his more enlightened understanding of what constitutes both individual and corporate health and security, he attacked the injustices of his people, the origin of which he regarded as entailed in their faithlessness to their god, whose wisdom, as expressed in the commandments given to their ancestors, could alone save them in their difficulties. He, therefore, directed his condemnation to their isolatrous worship at Bethel, in which the purity of the Patriarchs' worship of their guardian god was adulterated by trust in foreign gods, such as Baal and Astarte. Having lost their trustworthy orientation to their god, trusted by the Patriarchs, they floundered from one licence to another, thereby destroying the character of an entire people, which is the only social foundation for political strength.

A prophetic contemporary of Amos, who had essentially the same emphasis, was Hosea, a native of the Northern Kingdom. The parallel emphases of these two prophets is understandable, since they were internal to the same social and political contexts, and therefore, were aware of the same chaotic pattern of life of their people, bewildered and distrought by the imminent threat of the Assyrians. He may have continued his prophetic ministry among his people until the fall of Samaria in 721.

A principle basic to prophecy, as recorded in the Old Testament, is that it is conditioned by the contexts internal to which the prophets lived; and so essential is this conditioning for an understanding of the prophets that the Book of the Prophet Isaiah opens with an identification of the kings during whose reigns he lived and prophesied, mentioning "the reigns of Uzziah, Jotham, Ahaz, and Hezekiah, kings of Judah". He was born about 765 B.C., and therefore, was internal to the same social and political disorder which conditioned the prophecies of Amos and Hosea. He too believed that an orientation to the guardian god of the Patriarchs was the only sound way to avert national disaster. This religious analysis implied his disparagement of all political entanglements with other countries, irreverent to his god, which, in turn, was his disparagement of all trust in a military method to secure a national defense. According to him, his people had abandoned trust in the guidance of their destinies by Providence. The one conviction which underlies his entire prophecy to his people is that trust in their god would be manifested in conforming to the commandments entrusted to them as the way for living worthily of a people oriented to the guardianship of the god of their forefathers.

The Judaean prophet Micah was also active during the reigns of the kings Ahaz and Hezekiah, such as was Isaiah. Since he also was aware of the inevitable dominance of Assyria, as the threat to the survival of his people, he made no attempt to conceal their hatred, due to their fear of this massive challenge to their future.

Judging from the Old Testament's preservation of the prophetic ministry of Jeremiah, he may well be regarded as the second most prominent of the prophets in the tradition. But, as the prophets before him, he too lived in times which were tragic for his people, both preceding and following the ruin of the Southern Kingdom. The expanding military dominance of the Chaldaean empire was the dominating concern and terror of his people, and in light of their military threatening them, he was convinced of the futility for his people to trust a military method for their defence. And as a religiously devout person, he believed there was only one trustworthy help for his troubled people, which was the providence of their god that would be inevitable, provided they became worthy to receive it by virtue of their fidelity.

Rather than accepting his proposal to trust the providence of the god who had been the guardian of their ancestors, their leaders entered into military alliances with Egypt, their ancient enemy, and did so because, under the threat of Nebuchadnezzar's invasion of Palestine, they were caught in a dilemma of enlisting one traditional enemy against another, which at the time seemed the greater threat. The Holy City of Jerusalem did not withstand the siege of Nebuchadnezzar, and when it surrendered to him, many of their people were deported. Still not respecting what the Prophet regarded as the only sound security, his people continued to trust the principle of using force against force, and revolted against the Chaldeans, whose armies, a few years later, in 587, burnt the

Temple, and deported more of the inhabitants of the city. Since Jeremiah lived throughout these tragic times for his people, he had only one concern: It was the preservation of the sacred religious tradition of his ancestors, since this alone, as he believed, witnessed to the only true faith, and therefore, the only sound orientation for human life. But the leaders of his people continued to trust military resources to combat a military threat, and his prophecy of the inevitable disaster entailed in this was confirmed by what took place.

The leaders of Jerusalem had the benefit also of Ezekiel's prophecies of the inescapable disaster that would be entailed if they continued to trust military means to defend themselves. The counsels which he affirmed as warnings to them by the god, whose prophet he claimed to be, were, of course, ignored, just as were the counsels affirmed by Jeremiah, as prophet for their god.

Since Jeremiah may have fled to Egypt after the fall of Jerusalem, he was no longer able to minister to his people, whereas Ezekiel continued his ministry in a way which was adapated to the new chapter in the life of his people. This was a ministry to them as exiles in Babylon. Although the historical accuracy of this twofold ministry, both before and after the Fall, is not entirely dependable, what is most important in his ministry is that his appeal to his people for a spiritual reordering of their lives, made no effective difference in what took place among them.

Other prophets who were active during these turbulent times, before the fall of Jerusalem, were Habakkuk, Nahum, and Zehaniah. This critical era in the history of the Israelites was interpreted in essentially the same way by these several prophets. The core of their analysis of the weakness and defeat of their people is the same: When their forefathers were oriented to their god as a faithful people, they were guided and defended by his providence. When, however, the Prophet's contemporaries trusted other types of help and other sources of security, they suffered the tragic consequences of their mistaken folly. They turned entirely to human resources, disregarding the faith of the Patriarchs that superior to the sovereignty of human rulers is one supreme and eternal sovereign, whose wisdom alone is the source for trustworthy direction in all that human beings endeavor to do. Disregarding this wisdom is, therefore, itself the judgment which was the tragic occurrence of their loss of the Holy City, its temple, and the servitude of its people.

The "great age of prophecy" lasted less than two centuries, from the mid-eighth century to the Exile after the fall of Jerusalem in 587. The prophets active in this period, and whose emphases are preserved in the Old Testament are, as has been already mentioned, Amos, Hosea, Isaiah, Micah, Jeremiah, Ezekiel, Habakkuk, Nahum, Zephaniah--dominated by the two great prophets, Isaiah and Jeremiah. After their ministries--including the emphases upon moral and religious reforms as conditions for a new spiritual rebirth among their people, with a renewed trust in their god's guidance and guardianship--another emphasis began after the Exile. This was looking forward to a new era, which was not oriented to human ingenuity, military intrigues and resources, but to a reign of divine sovereignty. In other words, an emphasis began in apocalytical hopes for a new age under a divine administration of justice.

One of the prophets of hope for the new age was Haggai, who was a contemporary of those who returned from the exile in Babylonia, to whom he directed his emphasis upon rebuilding the Temple, as an indication of another chapter in the history of his people, and one hopefully dedicated to their god, such as had been their failure, for which they were so severely punished. The prophet Zechariah was likewise active in inspiring his people about the rebirth of their culture, impaired by the tragic penalty for their infidelity to their god. The dates for both of these prophets is the early part of the sixth century (520 B.C.).

The historical order in which the prophets have been mentioned in the foregoing analysis differs from the traditional order in which they are listed in editions of the Bible. Amos and Hosea were considered as the earliest of the eighth century prophets, followed by Isaiah, then Micah, then Jeremiah, and Ezekiel. The traditional order of the Prophets in most editions of the Bible, on the other hand, begins with Isaiah, Jeremiah, and Ezekiel, with Amos, Hosea, Micah, etc., listed as "Minor Prophets". The only possible principle for the classifying of Amos and Hosea, for instance as "minor prophets", is that the record of their discourses, delivered as prophecies, is shorter than those credited to Isaiah, Jeremiah, and Ezekiel. By virtue of the shorter length of each of these twelve prophets' discourses, they are grouped together, without consideration in the above mentioned prophets for their historical dating.

Whereas all the prophets considered in the above analysis were conditioned by the social and political contexts in which they lived, and about whose conditions they spoke, there is no such contemporaneous character of the so-called "prophecy" of Jonah. Although this was written in the fourth century, it refers to the fall of Nineveh, the "great city", as a prediction or a prophetic foretelling, whereas Ninevah was destroyed in the seventh century B.C. (612).

The Book of Daniel likewise is not prophetic in the sense of predicting or foretelling, although its composition pretends to foretell the defeat of the Babylonians during the reigns of Nebuchadnezzar and Belshazzar. It was actually written several centuries after this historical time, the likely date of which writing is in the middle of the second century B.C. This dating is established on the basis of events to which reference is made that actually occurred during the time of Antiochus Epiphanes, which is before the Maccabaean revolt in 165 or 164 B.C.

6. Prophets regarded the established priesthood as unworthy of its authority in the life of the Israelites

A dominant emphasis in the prophetic tradition, between the eighth and sixth centuries, reaffirmed the command given to Abraham by his god, as this is stated in the first book of Scripture: "Maintain the way...by just and upright living"(18:19). Living uprightly and justly was the criterion affirmed by the Prophets for a life which alone was worthy of worshiping divine reality. Whereas this quality of life was often submerged under priestly procedures and emphases upon ritual and sacrifices, it was again affirmed in the fifty-first psalm, which is addressed to divine reality: "Thou hast no delight in sacrifice; if I brought thee an offering, thou woulds't not accept it. My sacrifice, O God, is a broken spirit; a wounded heart, O God, thou wilt not despise"(vs.1-17).

This affirmation of a spiritual criterion of life, which is comparble to the one affirmed in Genesis, was needed to remind the Israelites that there was a type of worship other than the one stressed by the priestly tradition, as this is recorded principally in Leviticus, but also in the later part of Exodus and in parts of Numbers. The one hundred and forty-sixth psalm, therefore, declares: "The Lord loves the righteous"(vs.9), which is an interpretation of the nature of divine reality and that defines the quality of life which the prophetic tradition stressed as a worship alone worthy of a life dedicated to its divine sovereign. It was the version of worship and religious life which Amos, historically one of the first in the prophetic tradition, stressed, when the prosperity of the Northern Kingdom's lavish "liturgical show disguised the lack of sound religion".**43** Preoccupied with their role in conducting such ritualistic ceremonial, the established priesthood dismissed the suffering of impoverished people as irrelevant to a religious institution's concern. Hence, as a spokesman for his god, the Prophet declared: "For crime after crime of Israel I will grant them no reprieve, because they sell the innocent for silver and the destitute for a pair of shoes. They grind the heads of the poor into the earth and thrust the humble out of their way" (2:6-7).

Directing himself to a condemnation of the contemporary priesthood for its indifference to the distress of impoverished people, he spoke as a prophet sent by God: "I hate, I spurn your pilgrim-feasts; I will not delight in your sacred ceremonies. When you present your sacrifices and offerings, I will not accept them, nor look on the buffaloes of your shared-offerings. Spare me the sound of your songs; I cannot endure the music of your lutes"(5:21-23). This is a disparagement of the priestly system of religion which had become sponsored by the wealthy, during the reign of Jeroboam II (783-743), in their indifference to those who suffered from injustices. As one concerned for their plight, and unimpressed with a ritualistic version of religion, which was developed and maintained by the priesthood, he could think of no other challenge more worthy for a life which was devoted to a just god than working for justice and righteousness, so that it would become a dominant character of society. Hence his appeal: "Let justice roll on like a river and righteousness like an ever-flowing stream"(5:24).

The prophet Hosea, a contemporary of Amos, stressed the same challenge to his people to turn their attention from the priestly version of ritualistic religion to a religion of a spiritual dedication to "knowledge of God", which would then reorient their lives in fidelity to their divine sovereign; and in this rededication of their lives, they would understand the irrelevance of "whole-offerings" to a devotion to such a reality. Hence, his creed of religious faith is a program for daily conduct: "Loyalty is my desire, not sacrifice, not whole-offerings but the knowledge of God"(6:6).

Then contrasting this spiritual type of a religious life with the liturgical procedures and ritualistic sacrifices at altars, he declared what he attributed to the voice of his god: "The more priests there are, the more they sin against me;...They feed on the sin of my people...But people and priest shall be treated alike. I will punish them for their conduct and repay them for their deeds"(4:8-9). His prophetic ministry to his people is then summed up in his appeal to them: "Turn back all of you by God's help; practise loyalty and justice"(12:6).

The central thesis of the prophetic appeal for a revitalization of the religious life of the Israelites was again affirmed in the ministry of Isaiah to his people, declaring to them that they should: "Cease to do evil and learn to do right, pursue justice and champion the oppressed; give the orphan his rights, plead the widow's cause"(1:17). Such a redirection of life was also demanded by Amos and Hosea as the only way to reestablish themselves in the favor of their god, as sharing with him his role as guardian of his people. These prophets insist that the weakness of their nation is basically a loss of its awareness that corporate health is the only politically effective condition for coping with challenges to national security, such as the priesthood and the rulers at the time were soon to learn in their tragic reverses.

When Isaiah declared that "Wisdom and knowledge are the assurance of salvation"(33:6), he spoke not only of individual salvation, but also of corporate or national defence against the inroads of others who could take advantage of a collective disunity, in which the "wrangling and strife" about the details of keeping fast-days, according to priestly presumptions, were weakening national stability. Hence his denunciation of such a preoccupation with relative trivia, when their nation was disintegrating by virtue of the lack of cohesion among its people: "Your feasting leads only to wrangling and strife"(58:3).

Instead of such a version of fasting on holy days, and instead of being preoccupied with what each individual

270

himself does without consideration for others, he, speaking for his god, declared: "Is not this what I require of you as a fast: to loose the fetters of injustice, to untie the knots of the yoke, and set free those who have been crushed? Is it not sharing your food with the hungry, taking the homeless poor into your house, clothing the naked when you meet them..."(58:6-7).

Isaiah, as well as Amos and Hosea, are no longer thinking within the strictures of a tutelary deity of a particular people. The challenges which they affirm are obligations to the god of mankind, thereby expanding the world of which an enlightened person should be aware as the scope of a cosmic creator. By virtue of the range of what should be included in a religious worship, the prophets are entitled to consider themselves as spokesmen for a universal divinity, such as Isaiah declares when he says: "Thus says the Lord, the creator of the heavens"(45:18)

The type of religion which he regards as alone worthy of the worship of divine reality is commensurate with a cosmic god, and not merely with a tutelary god of a particular people. Hence a person readily regards the declarations which he attributes to the god for whom he speaks, as commensurate with a universal god, worthy of the homage of mankind, and not only of a particular people: "Your countless sacrifices, what are they to me: says the Lord. I am sated with whole-offerings of rams and the fat of buffaloes; I have no desire for the blood of bulls, of sheep and of he-goats"(1:11).

The superstitious basis out of which sabbaths arose, determined by lunar phases, were regarded by the prophet, oriented to a universal god, as trivial considerations to take as seriously as did the priesthood of the Israelites. Such a version of religion, therefore, was disparaged by the Prophets, as spokesmen for a universal sovereign of humanity: "New moons and sabbaths and assemblies, sacred seasons and ceremonies, I cannot endure. I cannot tolerate your new moons and your festivals"(1:13-14).

A people, however, who did not have the developed spirituality, such as Isaiah had, regarded "sacred seasons and ceremonies", which he disparaged, as suitable worship for a reality, the range of which was defined for them by a priesthood, whose spiritual sensitivities were as undeveloped as theirs. It is to people of such an impoverished spiritual life that

Isaiah addresses himself, justifiably identifying himself as a witness for a universal divinity: "This people approach me with their mouths and honour me with their lips, while their hearts are far from me, and their religion is but a precept of men, learnt by rote"(29:13).

A comparable breadth of spirituality is evidence also in the prophetic pronouncements of Jeremiah. In spite of his tendencey too often to be preoccupied with injuries which he suffered from antagonisms to his ministry, he, nevertheless, opens the range of the limited world in which his contemporaries lived, challenging them to enter into a life richer than one restricted to the scope of their customary way of worship. The reality to which their priestly ritual oriented them was a tribal god, and not a universal god. Therefore, his ministry, as a true prophet, oriented to a universal sovereign over humanity, is the appeal to human beings to enter into a wider world of concerns than the limited scope with which their priesthoods were preoccupied.

Aware of the grave problems internal to the tragic times in which he lived, he accused the priests of the established order as being "frauds"; declaring that "every one of them...dress my people's wound, but only skin-deep"(6:13-14). In other words, they ignore the deep sickness of their society, accepting the rituals of the priesthood as a solution for a social malady that was brought about by the spiritual poverty of people's life. Aware of the gravity of their surface treatment of human ills, sanctioned by a priesthood that was content with its institutional advantages, he declared the prophecy, which was soon confirmed: "They shall fall with a great crash, and be brought to the ground on the day of...reckoning"(6:15).

He regarded such reckoning as divine judgment upon the low moral level of the life of his contemporaries which was glossed over by the superficial system of the established priesthood. The priesthood was preoccupied with animal sacrifices, rather than with making genuine moral sacrifices of aspects of their lives which were handicaps to enlightened living.

The severity of Jeremiah's censuring of his people and their priests accounts for their resentment and antagonism to him. He disparaged the priests as the presumed "shepherds of the people" as "mere brutes", who "never consult the Lord"(10:21). And he regarded

272

this deficiency in their priesthood as the basic cause for the plight of his people that "they do not prosper" as a people of a healthy nation would. And as flocks of poorly tended sheep are scattered and destroyed by the incompetency of negligent shepherds, so he predicated that would also be the future of his people, whose priests and leaders he compared to incompetent shepherds, unworthy of their assignment to guard and protect their people. The figure of "flocks at pasture" was for Jeremiah a prophecy of the future of his people: "All their flocks at pasture are scattered." And the diagnosis for this collective tragedy to his people is affirmed as a censuring of their unworthy version of worship: "My people", he declares, "do not know the ordinances of the Lord", and the blame for this is not entirely the fault of the misguided people, but basically, the fault of their dishonest representatives who, presuming to know "the law of the Lord", actually interpret it "with their lying pens", and thereby "have falsified it"(8:8).

Lamentations, whose prophetic author is Jeremiah, continues his indictment of the priesthood, which was preoccupied with animal sacrifices, and consequently, tolerated injustices to the poor, which the Prophet characterizes as "the blood of the righteous". According to his analysis of the plight of his people, it is "the iniquities of her priests"(4:13-14).

Ezekiel's denunciation of priests and their institution in the religious history of the Israelites is qualified by his own priestly background. He, therefore, distinguishes between priests who are unworthy of their priesthood, and those whose priesthood is a worthy version of worship. Yet, his kinship with prophets in the tradition of Amos, and those who followed him, is also his emphasis upon a spiritual version of priesthood, whose role is not confined to perfunctory liturgy and ritualistic ceremonials. He is critical, therefore, only of a type of priest who is indifferent to genuine sacredness, and is satisfied with purely customary observances of sacred days and festivals, declaring that the later type "profane what is sacred" to the divine sovereign of human beings. It was priests, such as these, who "have done violence" to the priestly institution of instructing people in a knowledge of what is rightly required of them by their god (22:26). They profane the sabbaths when they do not emphasize their purpose of directing wholehearted dedication to their god. This is the "constant refrain of his indictment of Israel".44 And it was because of this disregard for the worthy role of priesthood that he censured those priests whose "words are false and (whose) visions are a lie". It was "against" these, the Prophet declares that God would justifiably be opposed, and justifiably condemn as unworthy of his service in teaching people how they should worship. It is thus the deceptive character of priestly performances which he describes as "misleading" people who trust them "by saying that all is well when all is not well"(13:9-10).

The very qualified criticism which Ezekiel directs at priests is not a dispargement of the institution of priesthood in the religion of his people, since a considerble part of the scriptural account attributed to him is devoted to describing how priests should dress, such as "When they come to the gates of the inner court they shall dress in linen; they shall wear no wool...They shall not fasten their clothes with a belt". He specifies likewise that in the inner court "When they go out to the people...they shall take off the clothes they have worn while serving, leave then in the sacred rooms and put on other clothes; otherwise they will transmit the sacred influence to the people through their clothing"(44:17-19). His nonspiritual notion of "sacredness", which actually is a parallel of what it means to primitive people, is expressed when he states the reason for leaving their garments in such specified rooms.

For more than one reason, the spiritual level of Ezekiel's prophecy is inferior to his predecessors among the prophets who are mentioned in the previous discussion. His version of "purity" is not of the spiritual character of wholehearted, unqualified devotion to a way of living which is worthy of the Divine Sovereign over human life, but it is a "concern for legal purity and for ritual detail", such as "anticipates Pharisaism".<u>45</u> The book in Scripture which is attributed to him ends with his defense of Levitical priests. In this respect also, it is slanted toward the priestly version of religion, rather than the prophetic, such as is witnessed to by those whose emphases have been considered in the preceding analysis. Even though he stresses as a religious obligation of his people that they "get...a new heart and a new spirit"(18:31), this proposed requirement is a weak challenge by contrast with the confrontations of people by the previously mentioned prophets.

There are two types of priests and two types of

priesthoods from Ezekiel's point of view: One which is unworthy of their calling as servants of god; and one which is worthy of this dedication. So likewise, there are two types of temples of which he takes account: One which is staffed by unworthy priests, such as the temple of his time, whose priests he disparages; and a temple that would be worthy for a worship of the divine reality, whose priests are dedicated by a commitment of a devout life.

The Book of Jonah is traditionally included in prophetic history by virtue of Jonah's awareness of his ministry to Nineveh to "denounce it for its wickedness"(1:1-3).

The ministry of Micah to his people may be characterized in a comparable way, since it attacks the deceptions and dishonesty of their practices, in details such as their "false measures", as for example, "the accursed short bushel". The practice of using "false scales" with "a bag of light weights" indicates the direction which his criticism of his contemporaries took. Sound though these criticisms are of a society which was floundering under the judgment imposed by its own dishonesty, his ministry has a very different spiritual character than some of the other prophets. And by contrast to the powerful ministries of Isaiah and Jeremiah, Micah's role as a prophet is comparatively weak. It does, however, have one emphasis in common with them, which is his disparagement of the pseudo-spiritual function of the sacrifices even of "thousands of rams or ten thousand rivers of oil"(6:6-7). And what is also a reason for his inclusion in the prophetic tradition is his appeal for a new quality of spiritual life, which he maintains "the Lord" requires of those who would be faithful in his worship: "Act justly,...love loyalty, (and) walk wisely before your God"(vs.8). Yet, by contrast with most other prophets, his prophecy is indeed "minor" in a spiritual sense.

A comparable appraisal of the prophetic role of Zechariah would likely not be unfair, if his message may be summed up in the appeal which he regards as specifying "what (people) shall do": "Speak the truth to each other, administer true and sound justice in the city gate. Do not contrive any evil one against another, and do not love perjury." This, he declares, "is the very word of the Lord"(8:16-17).

An account of the spiritual emphasis in the two

centuries of the most active prophetic tradition surely should not end with a consideration only of the prophets so referred to in the Hebrew canon of Scripture. Other spokesmen for the same spiritual version of religion are also included in noncanonical scriptural writings, such as First and Second Esdras, in which the accusation is made that "The leaders of the people and the chief priests committed many wicked and lawless acts, outdoing even the heathen in sacrilege, and...defiled the holy temple of the Lord in Jerusalem"(I.1.49).

Second Esdras affirms a divine judgment of the same severity as those credited by Isaiah and Jeremiah to the divine reality: "I will toss you away. When you offer me sacrifice, I will turn from you; I have rejected your feasts, your new moons, and your circumcisions"(1:31). The appeal for charity to the poor and pity for their heavy burden of poverty, which Ezra makes, is equal in every regard to the appeals of Amos and Hosea to their people for assuming a guardianship of those who have needs for whose fulfilment they do not have sufficient resources: "Champion the widow, defend the cause of the fatherless, give to the poor, protect the orphan, clothe the naked. Care for the weak and the helpless, and do not mock at the cripple; watch over the disabled, and bring the blind to the vision of my brightness. Keep safe within your walls both old and young"(II.2:20-22). This quotation would be an appropriate way to conclude an analysis of the prophetic tradition, which as a spiritual emphasis in human history, is not confined to two centuries, but includes every earnest concern for those who are in need of help which they themselves cannot fulfil. Those who respond to such needs of others thus take part in a way of acting which was regarded by the early Israelites as the concern of their god for them. The scriptural tradition of prophecy universalizes this guardian property of a divine reality, interpreting the universal God with this providential role for mankind. Believing that this is the guardian role of the "Creator of the heavens and the earth", is affirming a religious faith which underlies the tradition of prophecy as this is recorded in the Old Testament, which dominanted two centuries of history, but which will always continue as one of the supreme concerns of spiritually sensitive human beings.

7. **Many social conditions among ancient Greeks may be**

Any attempt to consider parallels in the two religions from approximately the eighth to the sixth centuries would encounter very meager material, since there is no parallel of prophets among the Greeks who were internal to an established religion and were also severe critics of its practices. This type of criticism appears only among the philosophers and the playwrights of Greece. The earliest of such philosophers is Xenophanes, who was born about the middle of the sixth century (56[5]). Possibly the second most severe critic of Greek religions of the time was Heraclitus, who flourished about the end of the sixth century, during the 69th

Anaxagoras flourished approximately a half century later, since he was born about 500 B.C. He, however, cannot be regarded as a direct critic of popular religions, but rather by virtue of his high-minded metaphysic of Nous or the universal Mind, he affirms a way of interpreting the world and human life which is an alternative to the ways in which it was interpreted in religions of his time. The same may be said of the Atomists, Leucippus and Democritus: Their metaphysics imply a thoroughgoing rejection of any reality of a supranatural order, and consequently, any traditional procedures of the established religions.

The scriptural version of life, with a correspondingly high-minded interpretation of divine reality was affirmed by other philosophers who were later than those mentioned. But in most cases, their criticisms of popular religions must be inferred from their philosophies, which do not include specific criticisms of existing religions.

The one principal source of direct criticisms of the popular versions of religions is the playwrights, and the most serious of such reflective analyses of contemporary religions are the dramas of Euripides.

Notwithstanding the relatively meager sources of a direct criticism of religious practices current among the Greeks in a comparable period of the two centuries (8th to 6th), it is, nevertheless, possible to take account of aspects of Greek culture, such as were the targets of the Prophets among the Israelites, who were critics of the culture internal to which they lived.

(i) Social wrongs were of long standing among the Greeks

The prophets among the Israelites were profoundly troubled by the social injustices of their times, and the prophetic denunciations of these social evils dominated by the prophetic ministry to their people throughout the two centuries. Hesiod, who flourished during the eighth century was, therefore, a contemporary of Amos, Hosea, and Isaiah, and in his Works and Days, indicates his troubled reflecting about the social conditions of his times, such as when he addresses his contemporaries with the charge: "Attend thou with eye and ear, and make judgments straight with righteousness."46 He directly challenges nobles and rulers of his times, just as the Prophets addressed their political leaders, declaring: "Princes...make straight your judgments, you who devour bribes."47 No such statement would have been made had it not been directed against the same type of social injustices as were condemned by the early prophets among the Israelites.

Social abuses among the Greeks must have intensified during the following centuries, since in the beginning of the sixth century (594/3), Solon, according to tradition, introduced reforms which were directed to correcting the economic and social plight of Attic farmers, whose poverty was so extreme that they were in indebtedness which was equivalent to enslavement. The only consideration which prompted the wealthy to accept the land reforms proposed by Solon was fear of a revolution, in which they would lose all that they had. The reforms proposed by Solon, therefore, were necessary to avert a social catastrophe, such as Plato maintained, in the Republic, would be inevitable when there was no longer one state, but actually two--one, the very rich; and the other, the very poor, in which the rich feared the poor for eventually warring against them, and thereby challenging the constitution or the type of government of the existing oligarchies or aristocracies, and then bringing about some version of democracy, in the sense that the people or demos determined governmental policies.

The radical cleavage of society, which evidently

persisted from the time of Hesiod to the time of Solon
is certainly a parallel of the tragic economic and
social conditions which the Prophets challenged with
their condemnations of those who were responsible for
bringing about such acute maldistribution of the
essential goods for sustaining life at even a minimum
of tolerable well-being.

Although Aristophanes, the Athenian playwright, is
considerably later (448-380) than any of the prophets
during the two centuries of their social criticism,
what he has Chremylus affirm in his _Plutus_ could have
been said by any one, or rather by everyone of the
Prophets: "Does it not seem that everything is
extravagance in the world, or rather madness, when you
watch the way things go? A crowd of rogues enjoy
blessings they have won by sheer injustice, while more
honest folks are miserable, die in hunger, and spend
their whole lives with (poverty).[48]

Aeschylus (525-456), who was somewhat later then the
last of the prophets in the sixth century,
characterizes a way that many people live who are
indifferent to any religious reverence for divine
reality, and take account of it only under
circumstances of the most spectacular character. He
has the Messenger in _The Persians_ describe that when
the army entered Macedonia, an unexpected cold spell
set in which "froze the stream of the sacred Strymon,
from shore to shore". And then he says that "many a
man who had held the gods in no esteem, implored them
in supplication".[49] It was during unexpected
occurrences, such as an invasion of a powerful army,
which threatened to defeat the Israelites, that some,
who otherwise were unmindful of a divine reality,
became frightened at the time into appealing to the god
of their ancestors for help.

Even language, ordinarily having a religious meaning
may lose its last semblance of sacred associations,
such as in the case of the term "mysteria", which in
the "Athenian legal code...refers to the Eleusinian
Mysteries, but in Heraclitus' philosophy, it is used
with the denotative meaning of "night ramblers,
magicians, bacchants, maenads".[50] There is thus as vast
a difference between these two meanings of a term in a
discourse about religions as there is in the reference
which the Hebrew prophet Joel makes to the contrast
between "rend(ing) your hearts rather than your
garments"(2:13). One is a spiritual experience, and
the other is entirely without spiritual significance,

but is merely a bodily exercise, such as the hysterical behaviors of those who believed they too were participating in the "Mysteries".

The Prophets encountered many among their contemporaries who had positions of authority comparable to Agamemnon among the early Greeks, who responded to the Prophets in very much the same way that Agamemnon responded to the pronouncements of the prophet Calchas, as this is characterized in the Iliad: "Agamemnon lept up in anger", denouncing Calchas as "Prophet of evil (who) never yet (has) said a word to my advantage."51 The commander of the Achaian forces, just as many of the rulers among the Israelites, wanted the prophets to conform to his own desires, and resented the Prophets' criticisms.

(ii) **Much that was integral to the priesthoods among the Greeks was irrevelant to social and spiritual problems**

Kerenyi refers to a practice of a Greek priesthood on the temple staff of Hera representing "the mythical flight of the goddess", which was "manipulated by the temple staff" to reenact an archaic rite that had been performed eight centuries before, dating "to the time of the Ionian migration".52 Centuries removed from the culture in which it had some religious meaning, it was performed by priests in a culture in which it had lost its original meaning. The conservative character of Greek priesthoods, just as the conservative character of the priesthoods among the Israelites, clung to earlier ritual and ceremonies whose meanings had been completely lost, and yet, were performed without a shred of understanding by the people who looked on from the bewildered or indifferent sidelines.

Parke makes a generalization about the overall conservativism of Greek polytheism that it "tended to guarantee the continuance of cults even when they had lost importance with the people".53 This same generalization would be entirely applicable to the priesthood of the Israelites during the centuries of its severe criticism by the Prophets. The priesthoods of both peoples added rules to rules, making their role impressive to the uncritical people who were aware that only priests who were trained in the established order could know so much, about what the critical prophets regarded as less and less of religious importance.

MacDowell makes the comment on the tendency of "Athenian religion to have" so many rules that "its emphasis was more on practice than on conscience".54 Every prophet among the Israelites would have affirmed the same generalization about the established priesthoods. Their increasingly complex rules of liturgy entrenched them to Israelites other than the Prophets, who maintained the nonspiritual irrelevance of all such practices, which, nevertheless, dazzled those who were incapable of understanding the nature of a spiritual type of religion. The rules to which MacDowell refers among the Greeks were "mainly about sacrifices and other rituals" which were the aspect of the priesthoods that the Prophets depreciated as having no relation to enlightened worship. As MacDowell points out, the Greek priesthoods explained the origin, and therefore, the authority of such aspects of their version of religion, as the priesthoods among the Israelites did: "They were believed to have been made by gods, not by men." The only difference in the explanation is the Greek reference to a plurality of divine sources, rather than to the one divine ultimate, which the priesthoods of the Israelites presumed to represent.

The ritualistic procedures, and therefore, the rules which determined their correctness, were features of both priesthoods from considerable antiquity. The Iliad, for instance, mentions that Hector, the Trojan prince, addressed his mother, the queen of Ilium, with his acknowledgment: "Nor should I care to offer sparkling wine to Zeus with unwashed hands," declaring what he had been taught by the priests: "A man cannot pray (to Zeus) when his is bespattered" and has soiled hands.55

The highly esteemed Nestor from Pylos set an example to those in his company before Troy, when conforming to the ritual he had been taught by a priesthood in the Peloponnese, said: "First let someone fetch water for our hands...so that we may pray to Zeus and implore his grace."56 Such a ritual regarded as a religious procedure by both the priesthoods of the Greeks and the Israelites was dismissed as of no essential religious worth by the Prophets, whose appeal is for the quality of life, and not for what is a ritual practice. The same may be said of a "generalized formula of supplication" which became standardized, and consequently, could be recited without giving any thought to the appeal that was so directed in a routine procedure of worship. Such formulae were "typical of ancient prayers",57 and by virtue of the excessive conservatism of a priestly religion, continued to be respected as integral to religious practices.

A preoccupation in both cultures was with the spectacle of attire worn by the priests; and this concern, disparaged by the Prophets, was pronounced even in the Eleusinian services, which in its earliest expressions, would of all Greek religions, qualify as the most spiritual, according to the criteria of religion insisted upon the prophetic tradition of the Israelties. As Parke points out: "The vestments of the Eleusinian priest were...elaborate";58 and this fact is especially significant, since of all the religions among the Greeks, the Mysteries at Eleusis stressed a spiritual obligation of the mystai, as a qualification for their worthiness to participate in the rites.

The scrupulous care with which all the equipment was used in the annual Eleusinian rites, including the priestly vestments, expressed an attitude such as Ezekiel, in the role of a priest also expressed, when he insisted upon the precaution for treating the garments of the priests, lest their "sacredness" leave the garments. Hence, the priestly system, under whose charge the Eleusinian rites were conducted, regarded the attire and the related equipment as "Holy Things".

The hierophant or chief priest in the Mysteries was revered as a "revealer of the Sacred Things", whose position in this sacerdotal office was hereditary. The exclusive right to perform this role was explained by what likely was a myth that the chief priests descended from the ancient kings of Eleusis, just as the office of high priest in the established priesthood of the Israelites was explained as instituted by their god. A more credible explanation for chief priests as being especially qualified for their office is that a "comprehensive knowledge" of religious rites and the formulae for their appropriate performance was "possessed only by a few experts", and each of these "was supposed to pass on the knowledge to his successor".59 An explanation, such as this, would be a credible justification for an hereditary priestly office. It would thus have a defensible basis, such as Plato and Aristotle associated with a genuine aristoracy of qualifications for fulfilling the highest of political responsibilities. But as both of these philosophers were well aware, an hereditary aristocracy does not itself assure such qualifications. And the same may be said of the offices of the Hierophant. Spiritual qualifications for an office in a religious institution are not passed on by virtue of heredity; and the mistaken assumption that they are so transmitted accounted for misqualified people in the religious institution in both cultures. The matter of fact way that Herodotus declares this hereditary transmission of the highest of priestly offices itself seems to condemn it, as the Prophets would: "When a high priest dies his son succeeds to his office."60 The tragic fact which Plato expresses metaphorically that "Many a golden father has an iron son", was learned many times by the Israelites.

It may be that an awareness of the hazard of a hereditary succession of priesthood accounts for the long delay in establishing a priesthood in the worship of Zeus at Olympia, since it was not "until late in the history of Olympia" that there was an "official described as the priest of Zeus (Hiereus)". Sacrifices to the god which were made prior to a regular priesthood were performed by a temple personnel known as Manteis.61

(iii) Euripides was a principal fifth century B.C. critic of established Greek religions

Euripides directs a criticism against one of the most celebrated, if not the most celebrated, of Greek oracles, when the sister of Orestes maintained that the Delphian oracle "uttered that wrongful rede" which "decreed the death of my mother" at the hand of her own son, which Electra condemned as "a foul unnatural deed". Judging matricide as "unnatural" was, therefore, an indictment of the oracle for going counter to the Earth, as represented by the ancient goddess Gaia, who, according to Aeschylys, transferred the authority of the divine oracle to Themis, and therefore, it was against the prophetess of Themis that this criticism of Euripides was directed when Electra refered to what the oracle declared, "on the tripod of Themis".62 An extremely severe disparagement of this oracle, attributed to a divine source, is declared by the mother of Orestes in Euripides' Iphigenia in Aulis: "Surely must we deem the gods be fools, if we wish blessings upon murderers."63

In his Heracleidae, Euripides has the king of Argos disparage the sovereignty of Hera as inferior to oracles, when he declares that he had been mistaken to trust her, thinking she "was mightier far then any oracle, and would not betray" him.64 A disbelief in the dependability, therefore, both of oracle and deity expresses not only Euripides' point of view toward ancient Greek religions, but also the attitudes of the intelligent people of the fifth century.

What Kerenyi characterizes as "the vigorous youth of a culture",65 in which it had respect for religious beliefs and practices, was a dominant point of early Greek life, which had already undergone decline when the dramas of Euripides expressed what intelligent people themselves thought. Parke points out a specific indifference "in the classical period" when "most Athenians had ceased to feel very concerned"66 about the religious seriousness of some of the festivals, which from antiquity, had been dedicated to the gods. MacDowell likewise characterizes the attitude of Athenians "in the second half of the fifth century" as having less respect for "traditional religious belief" than in earlier centuries.

A total disbelief in the reality of gods--once a dominant aspect of Greek culture--became such a cause for governmental concern that a decree was "laid down that those who did not believe in the gods"67 would be subject to legal action. It was in this cultural context, therefore, that the dramas of Euripides were not isolated instances of an expression of disbelief in the soundness of earlier religious interpretations. Such a change in the Greeks' respect for religious practices and in their reverence for the gods worshiped in such practices, was not confined to religion, but extended also to the principles of traditional morality, which were disparaged as purely conventional. And the formulations of such principles of acting, as moral laws once regarded as having validity, were disparaged as no more than language itself. This disparagement of the validity or soundness of moral principles is declared by the Theban prince, Eteocles, in Euripides' The Phoenissae, who says: "Fairness and equality have no existence in this world beyond the name." And the Prince, speaking for Euripides, is clearly aware of the tragic consequences in this cultural phenomenon of disbelieving in the soundness of principles, which once were respected; and he maintains that "If all were at one in their ideas of honour and wisdom, there would have been no strife to make men disagree."68

The correlated disbelief in the validity of moral principles and in the existence of gods is expressed in the despondent assertion which Hippolytus utters at the end of his life, once dedicated to integrity and honor in his relation to others: "All vainly I revered God, and in vain unto man was I just."69 In deep sorrow, one of his last utterances in the tragedy of the same name is addressing "Great Zeus", asking the god, if he sees what has taken place in the false accusation which has discredited his life-long honor and brought about his death. He then asks if the god is aware of "Me, thy reverent worshiper, me who left all men behind in purity, plunged thus into yawning Hades 'neath the earth?'.70

The same correlation of disbelief in the existence of gods and disbelief that there are moral principles with validity, as ways for living which are more dependable for achieving worth in life than other principles, is also expressed by Orestes in Euripides' Electra: "We must believe no more in gods, if wrong shall triumph over right."71

A basic disbelief in the relation between genuine moral well-being, or blessedness in life, and the integrity of one's life is expressed by the Dioscuri in Euripides' Helen, when they acknowledge that although "for the noble souls hath the deity no dislike", nevertheless, "these oft suffer more than those of no account".72

Frederick Grant sums up the Hellenistic cultural phenomenon of a disbelief in the soundness or truth of traditional religious interpretations, and the thoroughgoing reliance of the disillusioned Greeks upon themselves: "Despair of divine intervention" was correlated with "an exclusive reliance upon human integrity or ability", and this correlation "was the last stage in the secularization of Greek religion.".73 This correlated religious disbelief and despondency about the worth of human life itself is affirmed in Euripides' Heracles: "Had the gods shown discernment and wisdom, as mortals count these things", there would have been "a visible mark of worth amongst" those of moral uprightness; and even "after death would these have retraced their steps once more to the sun-light, while the mean man would have had but a single portion of life; and thus would it have been possible to distinguish the good and the bad." This cynicism about a sound justification for the essential benefits of moral integrity in this life became also a total disbelief in any divine sovereignty over human beings. The Chorus then concludes: "But, as it is, the gods have set no certain boundary 'twixt good and bad"; and the expression of total disbelief is affirmed in declaring that "time's onward roll brings increase only to man's wealth", as if there is no other measure at all for the justification of life.74 This is the absolute dispair which is basic to all articulated cynicisms; and such cynicisms are summed up by the Chorus in Hippolytus, which expressed the attitude of many of the contemporaries of Euripides, and may well express his own: "I am angered with the gods; out upon them."75 In this particular case, the rejection of belief in any divine sovereignty over human life follows from the dispair of seeing no evidence in human relations for a consistent correlation between integrity and benefits which the upright alone enjoy. Others seem to "prosper" in getting the transient goods for which they sell they souls, and thereby destroy within themselves any sense of the justification for having lived. Their quality of life, however, is the moral penalty which is inescapably entailed in the moral poverty itself in their lives.

(iv) Sacrifices sanctioned by priesthoods were disparaged by Greek playwrights, as they also were disparaged by prophets among the Israelites

There is certainly an unequivocal parallel in the fifth century disparagement of priestly sacrifices by Sophocles and Euripides and the same type of disparagement by the Prophets of the Israelites. The Greek Teiresias denounced Creon, ruler of Thebes, for his refusal to permit the burial of the son of Oedipus, accusing him of a "wilful temper" which ails the State", from which "all (the) shrines and altars are profaned"; and in consequence of which "the angry gods abominate our litanies and our burnt offerings".76

This disparagement of such sacrifices was for the same reason that the priestly sacrifices among the Israelites were also disparaged by their prophets: The morality of a people and its rulers could not be sloughed off by sacrifices on an altar, such as soiled hands could be washed clean by water. This was a condemnation of the ancient assumption that priestly sacrifices had some magical efficacy which could absolve a ruler or his people from guilt for moral offences.

A motivation which was basic to the earliest animal
sacrifices among both the ancient Greeks and the
Israelites was an anthropopathic presumption that the
gods enjoyed the "savour" of burnt offerings, and
therefore, were dependent on human beings to make such
offerings for their benefit. It is this naively
anthropopathic interpretation of gods which is rejected
by Heracles, who addresses Theseus, legendary ruler of
Athens: "The deity, if he be really such, has no
wants."[77] This enlightened view of Euripides as
expressed in Heracles, was repeatedly affirmed by the
Prophets, who pointed out to their people that the god
who was creator of the world, and therefore, was
sovereign over all, needed nothing that could be
directed to him, which he did not already possess.

In two of Euripides' plays, the same disparagement of
sacrifices which are made by priests is also affirmed
by the Prophets to the Israelites. The Messenger to
Menelaus declares: "Nor is there after all aught
trustworthy in the blaze of sacrifice."[78] And Electra
laments that "No god...heeds the sacrifices offered by
my father long ago."[79]

A rejection of the appropriateness of sacrifices which
were conducted by priests was implied in the spiritual
version of the Eleusinian Mysteries before they became
adulterated by the inclusion of animal sacrifices,
which were a dominant part of contemporary religions.
But before this corruption occurred, a person who was
to be initiated into the Mysteries was required to have
"a soul conscious of no evil" and was to "have lived
well and justly".[80]

Chapter Eight

UNIVERSALITY OF AN ULTIMATE DIVINE REALITY

There was no ancient Greek religion internal to which developed a severe criticism of its nature, such as developed in the religious tradition of the Israelites during the two centuries of the Prophets, which have been mentioned in the foregoing discussion. There was, however, a comparable criticism of Greek religions by some who were not themselves internal to any established religious traditions. Among such critics were philosophers of the sixth and fifth centuries B.C., and their type of criticism continued throughout the following centuries.

The sixth century in the history of the prophetic tradition among the Israelites is a parallel of four influential philosophers in the history of Greek philosophy. Each of these philosophers was a critic of contemporary religion, such as the Prophets were of the religion of which they were contemporaries. But, as has been pointed out, these Greek philosophers were not internal to the religions of which they were also critics, such as was the case with the Prophets.

1. Fourth sixth and fifth century B.C. Greek philosophers rejected the popular religious versions of gods, and maintained instead that there is an ultimate reality which is universal and eternal

The first among the sixth century Greek philosophers to be a critic of the religion or religions of which he was a contemporary was Xenophanes (b.565 B.C.) who directed as severe a criticism against Homer and Hesiod, as the Prophets directed against the contemporary priesthoods, which perpetuated a version of religion that was conditioned by interpretations of divine reality which the Prophets censured. Although popular Greek religions were influenced by the anthropomorphic versions of the gods, as these were affirmed in both Homer and Hesiod, Xenophanes, nevertheless, was courageous enough to condemn such anthropomorphism, and consequently, to censure all that both of the poets maintained about the nature of the gods. He censured both of them for attributing characteristics to the gods which would be disreputable even if they were traits of human beings.[1] This criticism of the mythology of the two poets, who for centuries were highly esteemed by the Greeks, was for more than a disparagement of mythologies: It was also a condemnation of the morality of the Greeks which the poets projected onto the gods. Thus, in disparaging the popular mythology which the Greeks admired, Xenophanes condemned the low level of the morality of his contemporaries, just as the Prophets had done in their disparagement of the low moral level of their contemporaries.

Basic to his criticism of the religious and moral aspects of the culture of his contemporaries was his disparagement of the psychological conditioning of their concepts of gods, which were projections of their own characters. His acute insight into the phenomenon of people projecting their own natures, and therefore, their own moralities, onto their gods, is expressed in the shrewd comment that Ethiopians think only in images of gods, who like themselves, are "black and snub-nosed"; and Thracians, who have red hair and blue eyes, think their gods also have these same traits.[2]

Since Greeks in the established religions interpreted their gods after their own natures, they thought their gods were born, just as they themselves were. Hesiod also took this for granted in his Theogony, which accounts for the origins of the gods. Since they were thought of as having a beginning, they were thought of as having been born.[3] So likewise, as every human being moves from one place to another, so the Greeks thought their gods did. Whatever Xenophanes' contemporaries thought about their gods, thus conforming to the mythologies of Homer and Hesiod, Xenophanes disparaged as unworthy of the religious beliefs of intelligent people. In contrast to the popular opinion that gods "move about", he declared that the ultimate reality "abides", in the sense that it does not move.[4] The argument by which this metaphysic is defended is that there is one ultimate reality, rather than the almost countless divinities in whose plurality the Greeks believed. Xenophanes argues that there is one ultimate reality which has no origin; and since it is everything that is, it could not move into a so-called "space" that it already is not.

The gods of popular mythology and religions were regarded as ultimate, in the sense that everything in the world was explained in terms of them, and there was no other reality in terms of which they were explained. According to Xenophanes, reality is one, and therefore, is designated as the "Universe". As ultimate, it cannot be explained in terms of any reality other than itself. He uses the language of religion, however, with which to identify the Universe, speaking of it as "God"; and by virtue of this procedure in his analysis, maintains: "God is one."5 As such, he declares that it is "not like mortals in body or in mind". In other words, the reality which he identifies as "God" has no property in common with the gods of popular religion, other than that both are interpreted as "ultimate".

Since the notions of a god in popular religions include the property of "mind", so Xenophanes attributes "mind" to what he regards as "God". And furthermore, since human beings move or act according to their ideas of what they want or seek, so Xenophanes appropriates this version of "mind" to account for all motion in the world or universe. This becomes his metaphysics that the mind of ultimate reality "sets in motion all things",6 just as the mind of human beings activate them.

By virtue of identifying the totality of reality, or the universe, with the ultimate reality; and by virtue furthermore of identifying this with "God", Xenophanes proposed a reasoned metaphysic as the conceptual basis for an enlightened religion. By virtue, therefore, of this metaphysical interpretation of "God", he disparaged all popular religions as unworthy of enlightened human beings, just as the Prophets disparaged the popular versions of religion of their contemporaries.

According to tradition, Parmenides, who was born about a half century after Xenophanes (565 B.C.), became one of his pupils; and as Xenophanes, he too disparaged "the opinions of mortals, in which there is no true belief". Since ignorance is a common trait among people, this fact explains his disparagement also of their morality, declaring that "righteousness and justice" are "far from the trodden path of men".7 He thus declared a criticism of his contemporaries, which not only reaffirms the appraisal of Xenophanes, but also one which is comparable to the appraisal by the Prophets of their contemporaries. As Xenophanes offered a psychologial explanation for peoples' notions of gods as projections of their own nature, and so of their morality, Parmenides also gives a comparable explanation for common versions of religions. He maintains that they are expressions of "mortals, who knowing nothing", are correspondingly "helpless" to control their erroneous thinking; and as a consequence, live by thoughts of as low an order as "herds without discrimination"8. By virtue of their ignorance, and therefore, uncriticized beliefs by which they live, they interpret the nature of gods from their own ignorant perspective, thinking that they have a beginning, or were born, as people are born. But, following Xenophanes, he maintains that the ultimate reality is "without beginning".9 All temporal distinctions are inappropriate for speaking about it, and consequently, all that may defensibly be affirmed of it is that "it is". Implied in this predication is the inadmissibility of declaring that it has been or shall be.

All that popular religions believe about their gods as hearing their appeals, and taking notice of their sacrifices, are no more than expressions of ignorance, since the nature of ultimate reality is totally misinterpreted in such notions about gods.

The primary premise of Parmenides' metaphysic logically discredits the possibility of change, and therefore, any notion of an activity of gods is disparaged as irrationality or ignorance. The ultimate reality is what it is; or in other words, it is invariant; and implied in its invariance is that it could not have come into being. It is. And as the one reality, it logically follows that there is nothing other than what is, which is being. Such ultimate reality is knowable or intelligible only by intelligence, the criterion of which is logical consistency. On the other hand, all mythological versions of gods, which are basic to popular religions, are irrational. Mythological interpretation of gods consist of images, and images are particular. Such particular images are incapable of knowing universal reality, and therefore, are totally incompetent to interpret Being, whose universal nature is basic to all that is. In other words, whatever is, has being; but its individual being is not the universal Being. The universal Being is the eternal possibility for all particular instances of existing or being.

The only aspect of any human being which is capable of a true idea of universal reality is pure thought. Parmenides thus anticipates the Great Tradition in philosophy when he declares that "the object of thought" is "universal".10 Since Being is universal, as

291

the ultimate or the primary reality, it can be known by universal ideas. The thought, consequently, of those who are capable of universal ideas is the only knowledge which is possible of Reality; and such knowledge is foreign to every version of belief in gods which are interpreted with traits that have nothing in common with the ultimate, eternal Reality or Being. Being alone is invariant or changeless, such as active deities are not. Thus Permenides, on the basis of dialectic alone, disparages all popular versions of religions. The metaphysic, however, which he defends has little in common with the Prophet's versions of the Eternal, except that both maintain that the Eternal Reality is not worthily interpreted by anthropomorphically imagined deities, whose natures have no higher moral order than the priesthoods in their contemporary cultures.

The metaphysical premise of Parmenides is radically different from the theological premise of the Prophets, who maintain that God, the eternal reality, is the Creator, and the world is his creation. Parmenides, whose dialectic discredits the possibility for motion or acting, thus rejects the concept of a creator of the world, declaring that the Eternal, which is Being, is "motionless". Hence, he rejects a theological concept of a creator, maintaining that "creation" is only a "name that mortals have made", 11 who erroneously believe that there is "motion" or "change", whereas there is no possibility for it in pure Being, which eternally is what it is.

Although Parmenides criticizes the use of all analogies for interpreting Being, he, neverthless, inconsistently maintains that since Being is one, which is internally complete, it has a property of a sphere. But, suggesting this superficial similarity is indefensible, according to his own philosophy of Being as universal. A sphere is a particular instance of being, and is not pure Being.

Pure Being as Reality cannot be thought, although the term can be defined, and in this sense alone can be thought. Such a definition would indeed be "pure" thought, as nothing but thought. Parmenides, however, does not regard pure Being as only a concept or a "pure" thought. He regards it as Reality. He, therefore, makes the same mistake as extreme Idealists have made throughout the following centuries when he maintains that "Thinking and the thing for the sake of which we think are the same."12

Any attempted thinking of Being would be a particularizing of it; and any such noninterpreted reality would obviously have no parallel in any religious version of ultimate reality, even the most spiritual of its expressions.

The third person in the tradition of Greek philosophers who were critics of their contemporary religions is Heraclitus, a native of Ephesus, who flourished during the 69th Olympiad (505-500 B.C.). As a descendant of the royal line, he most likely inherited a high ranking position in the religious institution in which his family worshiped, but which he renounced. It may have had a moral level which he disparaged, as he did the Mysteries to which he refers as "celebrated in an unholy fashion".[13] The fact that human beings could believe that such a version of religion is a respectful worship of divine reality accounted for his embitterment of human beings, whom he describes as "not know(ing) what they do when awake, even as they forget what they do when asleep".[14] As totally insensitive to the nature of divine reality, they are as if they were "deaf" to any spiritual significance in reality; and in his total impatience with them, he refers to them as "fools".[15]

His disparagement of the low level of morality, and therefore, a concommitant low level of spirituality, is certainly very much the same appraisal which the Prophets affirmed of their contemporaries, both priests and lay alike.

As a Greek, he regards the world as uncreated. "This world", he declares, "neither any god nor any man shaped it". Reaffirming the Eleatic metaphysic, he maintains: "It ever was and is and shall be,"[16] which is a characterization of the property of being eternal. What he regards as the eternal nature of the world is what the Prophets regard as the nature of the Creator of the world. There is, therefore, no parallel in their two interpretations of the nature of the world, since it is not eternal according to the Prophets, but rather is a creation by an eternal reality, the Creator.

The world, according to Heraclitus, is ordered; and order is the property which Greek philosophers identify as the essential nature of law. Since the world is eternal, its order or lawful character is likewise eternal. Such a lawful order is an exemplification of Law, and consequently, Heraclitus maintains: "This Law holds forever."<u>17</u>

Whereas, according to him, the Law which orders the world is eternal, just as the world itself is, the Prophets argue likewise about the Law of God, maintaining that God, the Creator, is eternal, and his Law, therefore, as his nature, is eternal. The type of argument thus by which both the Greek philosopher and the Hebrew prophets infer that Law is eternal is the same, although both identify the reality very differently which determines the eternal property of Law. For Heraclitus, it is the world, and for the Prophets, it is the Creator of the world.

Both the Prophets and Heraclitus maintain, with comparable conviction, that "All things take place in accordance with (eternal) Law.<u>18</u> But the Law to which the Prophets refer is the Law of God, the Creator of the world; and the Law to which Heraclitus refers is integral to the lawful order of the world itself, which as eternal, is not created. Thus again, although both Philosopher and Prophets would define "eternal" and "lawful", as well as "Law", in comparable ways, the realities to which they predicate these properties are radically different. Heraclitus attributes them to an eternal world; and the Prophets, who do not consider the world as eternal, attribute them to the Creator of the world.

Pointing out this radical difference, not in analyses of properties, but in the realities to which they are predicated, stresses an indispensable caution which must be taken in ignoring differences in philosophies, when consideration is confined to their similarities.

The morally oriented criticism of the Prophets for the irreligious disregard of their contemporaries for the Law of God, as affirmed in the Decalogue, is an unmistakable parallel to the Philosopher's criticism of his contemporaries, when he declares that "the many live as if they had each a wisdom of his own", <u>19</u> rather than respecting the higher order of wisdom affirmed in Law. The religious Israelites interpret Law as the commandments communicated to them by Moses, but having their origin from God, which assures their validity or trustworthiness.

A reflective analysis of the relation of an eternal Law to its exemplifications in particular laws would likewise disclose a basic parallelism in which the Prophets thought of trustworthy moral instruction as a lawful directing of human life, and in what Heraclitus thought of the relation between eternal Law and genuinely lawful ordinances in human societies. He declares:"All human laws are fostered by one law, which is divine."20 In this comparable interpretation, both Prophets and Philosopher affirm moral philosophies which argue the same type of validity for trustworthy principles for ordering human life.

Both also maintain that the Law which establishes the validity of particular lawful directives, whether in human life or in the world, retains its identity in its particular exemplifications. Particular laws, whether in a moral order or in a physical order, are lawful by virtue of Law, as a universal reality, which is other than any of its exemplications, yet, is their essential condition.

By virtue of the identity of Law, as the condition for lawful particulars, such particulars participate in an eternal reality. A development of this metaphysic is obviously to the credit of Plato, and not to the credit of Heraclitus or the Prophets. Yet, both Heraclitus and Prophets regard the validity of particular laws as established by the nontemporal Law.

Such Law, according to both Heraclitus and the Prophets, was identified in Greek philosopies of the fifth and fourth centuries as Logos or the Word. According to both Philosopher and Prophets, the Word or Logos was interpreted as Wisdom. If the Prophets were to have engaged in philosophical analysis, as Heraclitus and subsequent Greek philosophers did, they would have identified the Logos or Word, with the Wisdom of God, such as was done in the Alexandrian philosophies of religion. As the Wisdom of God, it would then have been regarded by the Prophets as prior to, and distinguishable from, all instances of wisdom. This, however, is the philosophical analysis which Heraclitus maintains when he declares that "Wisdom is divided (i.e., distinguishable) from all (other) things",21 which are not ordered by Wisdom. He regards Wisdom as an expression of Mind, and also as a reality which has an identity, such as Mind does in dualistic metaphysics, when it is radically distinquished from matter, although there is no such dualism either in Heraclitus or in the Prophets. The Prophets regard the physical earth as created by God, and regard its order, or its lawful features, as established by the Wisdom of its Creator. They could, therefore, affirm of the ordered world, created by God, what Heraclitus says of "the mind by which all things are steered through all things".22 For the Prophets, this is the Mind or Wisdom of God. As such, it is eternal, and it is the property of its eternal nature that Heraclitus also attributes to the ordering factor in the world. A characteristic Greek term for such an eternal Mind or Wisdom is Nous; and Nous is the eternal reality which Heraclitus maintains is immanent in "all things" by which they "are steered through all things", by which he means are ordered; and in less impersonal terminology, are "guided" or "directed". This substitution of language then suggests a parallel to the ancient Israelites' belief that there is a divine guidance or directing of the affairs of human beings, just as there is in the physical order in which they live. No distorting, therefore, would be done in stressing this parallelism, because both Heraclitus and the Prophets believe there is an eternal Wisdom which orders the world, and in this sense, directs it. But again, in other respects, each interprets the world very differently. For one, it is created, and therefore, not eternal; and for the other, it is itself eternal because it is not created.

The "Wisdom" which both revere as eternal, although in other respects, interpret differently, would, nevertheless, be regarded by both, as it is characterized by Heraclitus: "Wisdom is a single thing."23 It is single in the sence that every particular thought or interpretation which has the property of being enlightened, or possessing "wisdom", is an expression of the nature of Wisdom. Both Heraclitus and the Prophets extend the role of such Wisdom to the world. Both likewise contrast such lawful or ordered aspects of the world as radically different from the disorder on the earth, which is brought about by disordered human beings, who live without the benefit of wisdom. Thus their disordered lives and their impact upon the earth express poverty of wisdom in all that they do.

It is at this point in Heraclitus' criticism of the low moral order of human bings that the Prophets certainly would concur. At this point, he specifically passes beyond the terminology of moral discourse into the language of religion, declaring that even "The wisest of men shows like an ape beside God."24 If this then is the disparity between the highest level of which human life is capable and the divine ultimate, or God, there would be no contrast that would adequately characterize the disparity between what most people do and are, and the criterion of Wisdom, whether identified with God or

regarded as itself the essential nature of whatever is
ordered, and therefore, is lawful.

This disparagement of all human beings, in contrast to
God, is fundamental in the entire religious tradition
of the Israelites. Wherever there is a confrontation
of any outstanding human being, such as Moses or Aaron,
there is always an acknowledgment of the propriety of
removing one's shoes as a token of awareness of
standing in a holy presence.

Since Heraclitus did not respect popular religions of
his contemporaries, he was disinclined to identify
ultimate wisdom with Zeus, the sovereign of the Greek
gods of popular religions. Yet, as a profoundly
religious person, he identified the ultimate and
eternal Mind with God, but not with Zeus, as
interpreted in the contemporary religions, which he
disparaged as "unholy". His religious inclination to
identify eternal Wisdom with God, but not with the
Greek version of Zeus, most likely is the meaning of
his assertion that "The one thing which alone is wise
is willing and unwilling to be called by the name of
Zeus."25 In so far as Zeus is regarded as the sovereign
of men and of gods, and therefore, in this sense is an
ultimate divine reality, the eternal wisdom could be
identified with him. But as having been born, he was
not an eternal reality, and for this reason, as well as
for moral reasons, he would not be worthy of being
equated with eternal Wisdom.

Heraclitus and the Prophets were keenly aware of the
antagonism to them by their contemporaries, whose ways
of living they criticized, and for whose morality they
had contempt. He declares that "many are bad, and few
good".26 Both he and the Prophets incurred the
antagonism of their contemporaries for their
disparagement of the irrational versions of ritual,
expressing the poverty of their spiritual life,"knowing
nothing" of divine reality,27 and therefore, engaging
in practices under the sanction of priestly orders,
which were an offence to intelligence, which Heraclitus
characterizes as presuming to purify themselves "by
defilement with blood, as if one were to step into mud
and wash it off with mud".28 The Prophets disparaged
the priestly versions of sacrifice as offensive to God,
declaring that they were irrelevant for making
themselves deserving of his tolerance, let alone of his
favor. Heraclitus condemned practices of his
contemporaries, under the sanction of an established
religion, such as the worship of Dionysus, as "most

shameless".<u>29</u> The Prophets regarded much of their contemporary religious practices and the immoralities of the priesthood in the same way, as "most shameless".

There are thus many aspects of Heraclitus' critique of the culture of his contemporaries which are identical with the Prophets' appraisal of their contemporaries' culture, both its religious and its moral aspects. There likewise are remarkable parallels in their interpretations of the ultimate reality, which as divine wisdom, confronts human life with a challenge of what the spiritual quality of life should be; and in so doing, condemns it for its deficiencies in not doing what it ought to do to be worthy of its relation to the divine ultimate, whose wisdom could enlighten life and ennoble it with an order that would be worthy of human beings, whose capacities could qualify them to live on a level of honor.

The fourth Greek philosopher who may be compared with the Prophets for affirming an interpretation of reality which contrasted radically with the intellectually and spiritually low level of the religious beliefs and practices of his contemporaries is Anaxagoras, who was born at the end of the sixth century, during the 70th Olympiad (50-497B.C.), and who flourished during the following century. Although a native of Thrace, he made his home in Athens, where he had the patronage of Pericles. But even this advantage did not prevent the Athenians from bringing him to trial on the charge of impiety, the actual ground of which charge was his vast intellectual superiority to the scientific ignorance of his contemporaries, whose ignorance of the nature of the world accounted also for their ignorant version of religious beliefs about the heavenly bodies, the stars, sun, and moon. Hence it was his nonreligious, but enlightened, interpretation of their nature which antagonized his less enlightened contemporaries, who defended their ignorance under the gloss of religion, maintaining that the bodies in the heavens are deities, whereas he maintained: "Sun and moon and all the stars are fiery stones."<u>30</u> Too unenlightened to understand his vastly superior naturalistic interpretation of the physical world, they charged him with impiety, which was a legal offence, for which he was forced to leave Athens, thereby impoverishing both its sciences and its religions.

Impressed with the order in the world, which he did not interpret in naturalistic concepts, he affirmed, as did Heraclitus, that such cosmic order is accounted for by an ultimate, eternal Mind (Nous). As intellectual Greeks before him had regarded the world as uncreated, and therefore as eternal, he argued that its lawful or ordered character could be accounted for only by an eternal Mind as the ordering factor in the world.

It is most unlikely that the third century Aristotelian, Theophrastus, understood what Anaxagoras maintained when he attributes to him the doctrine that "worlds were produced" by Nous. Aristotle also had a capacity, for the sake of refuting other philosophies, to misinterpret them, as his successor does in interpreting Anaxagoras, who declares the very opposite, maintaining that all that exists is ordered by Nous. In other words, the ordering of reality is coeternal with all that is ordered. This is an argument that ordering is not subsequent to an existing "chaos", such as mythologies maintain, which is the notion that he rejects. The profoundest aspect of his philosophy is an argument for defending the identity of Nous as independent of whatever it orders. If, as he argues, "things mingled with it", thereby altering its identity as separable from all that it orders, it would therby lose its eternal identity, and instead, acquire the nature of the reality which altered its identity. Such an alteration in its eternal identity "would prevent it from having power over anything in the same way that it does (when)... it is alone by itself".31

Even Plato, as well as Aristotle, underestimated the metaphysical significance of this argument, based on the premise that "mind is...mixed with nothing...it exists alone itself by itself". This is one more of many instances of the penalty which anyone must endure when his intellectual achievements and his spiritual quality of life are beyond the respectful appreciation of others, even though they may be intellectually of a high order. Jealousy and envy prevent even people of intellectual abilities from giving credit to others, lest they seem thereby to be surpassed in originality and creativity.

Aristotle, as a matter of fact, stresses as a fundamental feature of his own metaphysic that he accounts for motion, such as other philosophers had not, as an essential aspect of the eternal world. Yet, it is just this that Anaxagoras did, which Aristotle dismisses, and which Plato underestimates in his preoccupation with the formal character of reality. Whereas this insensitivity of philosophers, of the abilities of Plato and Aristotle, to acknowledge the philosophical importance of Anaxagoras' argument is difficult to understand, one, nevertheless, is faced with a comparable sense of bewilderment when he considers the rejection of the Prophets by their contemporaries, when the Prophets were spiritually so superior to them. Yet, it is a spiritual poverty which characterizes the level of religious life of both the Ancient Greeks and Israelites, who were contemporaries of those from whom they could have learned so much, but who refused to do so, and who, consequently, penalized themselves with their own perversity.

The philosophical argument which Anaxagoras offered for the necessity of respecting the identity of the ultimate source of order and movement in the world, as separable from, and in this sense, transcendent of, the cosmos which it moves and orders, could also have been affirmed by the Prophets, had their concern been philosophical, rather than a reform of a religion which had degenerated to a level of their contemporaries, who would not tolerate a religious proposal of a divine criterion as a moral obligation. This would have denied a depraved people of too much which they insisted on having, and therefore, they rejected the Prophets for challenging their religion, and disparaging them for being what the Prophets declared merited the stern judgment by God.

2. A consistent affirmation in the Old Testament of the universality of God is not earlier than the sixth century B.C.

A commentary in The Jerusalem Bible maintains that "the first time religious universalism receives clear expression"[32] is in the second part of the Book of Isaiah, chapters 40-55. This part of the Bible, which is also attributed to the Prophet, is, however, about two centuries later than the active ministry of the Prophet. If he was born about 765 B.C., this first consistent version of universalism would have been affirmed the time that Xenophanes was born (ca. 565 B.C.).

As has been pointed out, the first verse of Genesis, although affirming a genuine universalism of God as the Creator of "heaven and earth", nevertheless, was affirmed as the introduction of the Bible when the Pentateuch was formulated as a scriptural canon. Another affirmation in Genesis, in the thirty-fifth chapter, is of a very different type. Although it refers to "God almighty"(vs.11), its apparent universalism in interpreting the nature of divine reality is discredited by the following verse, which affirms that it was this god who declared: "The land which I gave to Abraham and Isaac, I give to you", referring to the "descendants" of the Patriarchs. It is also to this tutelary or guardian deity of the Israelites that Moses refers in Numbers (14:20), when he speaks of the god's "glory and signs that (were) worked in Egypt and in the wilderness". This specific identification of an occurrence in the history of the Israelites, therefore, indicates that the tribute to the deity as "the glory (which) fills all the earth" is to the guardian god of the Israelites, and does not indicate a belief in a god of the universe. This nonuniversal character of the god whose nature is interpreted in the Pentateuch is also unmistabably affirmed in Deuteronomy (4:7), when, speaking to his people, Moses asks them: "What great nation is there that has its gods so near as...our god is to us when we call to him?"

Although Amos, who is among the earliest prophets of the eighth century, regards the god whom he serves as the Creator--"he who made the Pleiades and Orion" (5:8)--he, nevertheless, indicates that he does not regard this divine reality as a universal sovereign of mankind when he refers to "Israel" as "you alone have I cared (for) among the nations of the world"(3:11). In light of this reference for one people, which is the scope of concern of a guardian or tutelary deity, it is difficult to understand how the scholarly commentary in The Jerusalem Bible could refer to the "doctrine of God", affirmed in the Book of Amos as a "universal lord", even though as a "defender of justice".33 There actually is no less unequivocal meaning in the nonuniversalism of Amos' concept of the ultimate divine reality than there is a reference of the prophet Joel, who, as spokesman for his god, declares: "I am present in Israel", and predicts that in the future, "my people (Israel) shall not again be brought to shame." This specifically restricted scope of divine providence cannot be glossed over by the subsequent prediction that after elevating his people, the Israelites, to an uncontested status of honor among nations, he then "will pour out (his) spirit on all mankind" (2:27-28). But this is not a genuine universalism of divine reality when one people is assured that after their discouragements and reverses, they will be elevated to a status among other nations, in relation to whom they shall not be inferior.

301

A universalism in this reference cannot defensibly be argued by maintaining, as a commentary in The Jerusalem Bible does, that in some instance, such as the Chronicles, the term "'Israel' means the community of God's faithful people with whom God made a covenant long ago".34 There is no reference in the Pentateuch to such a universal range of meaning of "covenant". The covenants which are referred to in the Pentateuch are established with the descendants of the Patriarchs, who are collectively denoted as "Israel". Reading meanings into critical terms in an historical study of the concepts which are affirmed in the Bible is not a contribution to the accuracy of such a study.

The vindictiveness of Jeremiah to those who rejected him as a prophet dominates his verion of divine reality to such an extent that he presumptuously addresses his god with the proposal that his god should treat people to whom the Prophet himself is antagonistic,by "Show(ing) them how hard thy heart can be, how little concern thou hast for them"(Lam.3:65). Even though he addresses his god as "Lord (of) thy heavens", he repudiates a genuine universality of sovereignty over all mankind, when he proposes that this divine reality should do as he himself does in relation to people against whom he has a grudge.

The same evident nonuniversality of a sovereign of mankind is affirmed by the prophet Nahum, who declares: "The Lord takes vengeance on his adversaries; against his enemies he directs his wrath; with skin scorched black, they are consumed like stubble that is parched"(1:9-11).

The same vindictiveness also dominates the prophet Habakkuk's anticipation of the future, when he declares: "I sigh for the day of distress to dawn over my assailants"(3:16). Hence, a god to whom such a vision of the future is admitted as his prophet's hope is certainly not a universal god, but rather is one with a nature which is regarded as vindictive, just as the Prophet's own nature is.

No part of the Old Testament surpasses the Psalms in regarding human vindictiveness as a property worthy of being attributed to the ultimate divine reality. Such a versiohn of deity thus discloses the nonuniversality which many of the Psalms regard as an appropriate interpretation of its nature. The retaliatory character of the Psalm which appeals to god to "turn back sevenfold on their own heads", "the contempt"

302

which the "neighbors" of the Israelites show for the Isrealites' guardian god, is incompatible with a concept of the universality of divine reality (79:12-13).

The Psalmist's vindictiveness, like some of the Prophets', is expressed in the concept of a god to whom an appeal is regarded as appropriate that the god "bring destruction on all who oppress" the Psalmist (56:7). Thus such a notion is consistent only with the nature of a tribal deity, and certainly not with a universal God of mankind. Another translation of this same verse makes this even more evident: "O god, in thy anger bring ruin on the nations." That this appeal is directed to a tutelary deity of the Israelites, and not to a universal god of mankind, is evident in a comparable request by the Psalmist that their god "cut off" all those who do not also acknowledge him as their god; and when this has been done, "then they will know that god is a ruler in Jacob, even to earth's farthest limits (59:13). The characterization of this deity as "ruler...even to earth's farthest limits", does not alter the identification of the deity as a "ruler in Jacob", which, of course, is Israel.

The sheer niggardliness of morality and spirituality of the Psalmist is expressed in his prayer to his god that "May his (enemies') children be fatherless"; May (they)...be vagabonds and beggars, driven from their homes"; and "May none have mercy on his fatherless children"(109:8-10). Such a low level of morality of any individual would make him totally incapable of comprehending the nature of a universal sovereign of mankind. The concept of a deity who would be capable of responding to such an appeal or proposal would have nature as contemptible as the one who makes it.

The sheer meanness of which some human beings are capable is also indicated in the Psalmist's interpretation of a god who "will gloat over his enemies"(112:8). And it is of such an interpreted deity that the Psalmist is assured that "The Lord is on (his) side" as his "helper", giving him strength also to "gloat over (his) enemies"(118:7). If the order of these references from the two psalms were reversed, it would be obvious that the vindictiveness of the Psalmist is objectified as the nature of the deity whom he presumes to interpret. Such a deity thus has no more universality of nature than the vindictive Psalmist himself has. Such a projection of the Psalmist's nature onto what he interprets as the nature of god is evident in his addressing the "Lord, thou god of vengeance"(94:1).

The Psalmist's belief that "the high praises of god be on (others') lips" is affirmed together with his belief that " a two-edged sword (be) in their hand, to wreak vengeance on the nations and to chastise the heathen"(149:6-7). The distinction of his own people, who worship the god for whom he speaks, and the heathen, as all who do not join in such worship, expresses the version of a tutelary or guardian deity of one people, and not of all nations or of all mankind.

The nonspiritual character of the Psalmist is manifested in his interpretation of "The righteous" who "shall rejoice that he has seen vengeance done and shall wash his feet in the blood of the wicked". And this he regards as the evidence which "the righteous" shall consider as evidence that "after all, there is a god that judges on earth"(58:10-11). The reference to "a god that judges on earth" evidently consoled those who read this psalm through the centuries, that by virtue of their own uprightness, they were spared this ordeal to which others evidently were entitled by virtue of the assurance by the Psalmist that this is divine judgment. But the divinity which is so characterized is actually the objectified nature of the Psalmist, whose restricted capacities for spirituality made it impossible for him to consider a world which was any wider than Canaan, and whose divine sovereignty would have qualifications only for such a limited locality, and not for the ruler of a universe.

3. References to a universal God occur in various books in the Old Testament

The first verse in Genesis, with which the Bible is introduced, is the clearest possible formulation of a theological explanation for the origin of the world, and therefore, for its contingent nature, being dependent for its existing upon an eternal divine reality: "In the beginning God created the heavens and the earth." There is no parallel of this concept of a creator of the universe--often characterized by the ancients as "heaven and earth"--in Greek religions. There is, however, comparable concepts in the religious literatures of the Egyptians, the Babylonians, and Canaanites. The Egyptian "Hymn to Amun" addresses the god: "Thou are the sole one, who madest (every)thing. The only sole one who madest what exists."35 The same concept is reaffirmed in the Egyptian "Hymn to Aten", which god during the reign of Akhenaten, superseded the divine sovereignty of Amun. Yet, the later religion also addresses the god: "Thou sole god, there is no other like thee! Thou didst create the earth according to thy will, being alone."36 By virtue of the divinity of the sun for the Egyptians, it is unwise to regard these hymns as affirming theologies comparable with the first verse in Genesis. A basis for this precaution is the characterization of the god Aten in this Hymn as "Lord of every land, who dost rise for them, Thou Aten of the day.37 Although the universalism affirmed in the Hymn may be beyond question, the reality to which the Hymn is addressed, whether the sun or a creator of the sun, is by no means unequivocal.

There may be less justifiable uncertainty about the Ras Shamra Texts, whose cultural background is also Semitic, when in "The Legend of Aqhat", the deity is addressed as "O Creator of Created Things".38 As stated, this would parallel the concept affirmed in the first verse of Genesis, since both acknowledge the universality of a divine sovereignty over all that exists, by virtue of its creative powers.

There may well be a justifiable hesitancy in regarding a parallelism of the concept of creator affirmed in the Babylonian "Epic of Creation" with the concept affirmed in the opening statement in the Bible, since the deity referred to in this epic may, as in the Babylonian "Hymn to Shamash", be identified with the sun. Such an identification is at least indisputable in addressing Shamash as "the giver of light".39

The Egyptian as well as the Babylonian hymn addressed to the ultimate source of life on the earth may well refer to the sun as the possibility for life, and in this sense, its source could justifiably be regarded as eternal, since Aten is addressed: "Thou lord of Eternity."40 The consideration, however, which is critical in these religious documents is what is considered to be the "first" of realities--the sun, upon which life depends, or the Creator of the sun itself, upon which, consequently, the sun is dependent for its existing.

Although the Ras Shamra Texts preserve the ancient Semitic notion of the god Baal as "Lord of the Earth",41 this in no way suggests a parallel concept of the creation of the earth. As the ultimate condition or cause for fertility on the earth, this deity may well have no other role than making life possible on the earth. And the same may be said about the Egyptian god Aten. If identified with the sun, and not with the Creator of the sun, it would be understandable that it should be characterized as "giving breath to sustain all thou dost make".42 Creatures on the earth could not come into being without the sun as its condition for their existing, and for this reason, all that is affirmed in the ancient religious texts leave the critical point insufficiently clear, such as it is not in the first verse of Genesis. This unequivocally declares that no existing reality has a being independent of God. This is the critical concept which distinguishes the theological doctrine of God as affirmed in Genesis and in subsequent biblical books, for which there is no parallel in the Greek, Babylonian, Egyptian, or even in the Semitic culture, in proximity to which the Israelites lived.

The order in which the creation of the earth and the life on it occurred, as this is stated in the following verses in Genesis, has very different significance from the theological significance of the first verse, and consequently, of the subsequent biblical reaffirmations of the same doctrine, that all that exists, other than the eternal Creator, depends upon the Creator for its nature. This is the concept which is reaffirmed in various ways throughout the biblical references to the universality of the Creator, whose being is the condition for every other reality, including the heavenly bodies. In addressing God, First Kings declares: "Heaven itself, the highest heaven, cannot contain thee"(8:27). This theological concept is implied in the concept that there is a Creator of the heavens, which in other than them, whose being is contingent upon a reality prior to them. Such a contingent status of the heavens means that they are not eternal in the same sense as is their Creator, and likewise, are not ultimate in the same sense.

The address which Nehemiah includes in his prayer, "Lord God of heaven"(1:5), is theologically equivalent to a concept that identifies God as having sovereignty over the heavens, which again, would be a version of the concept that as more ultimate than them, it is prior to them, and in this sense, may be thought of as the First upon whom their existing depends.

The concept which is credited to Eliphaz the Temanite,

a companion of Job, is theologically profounder than a concept which is affirmed by Job, when Eliphaz declares: "Surely God is at the zenith of the heavens and looks down on all the stars, high as they are"(22:12). Although this is expressed in a spatial imagery, it affirms a concept that God is of an order of being superior even to the stars. Although with very few exceptions, no Greek philosopher thinks of the stars in any other way than as eternal, and therefore, not as being subordinate to a divine sovereignty which is prior to them. Notwithstanding the particular imagery with which this concept is affirmed, it expresses a theology that attributes to god a priority of being antecedent to the stars, as the so-called "highest" order in the heavens. The poetic imagery with which Job interprets the relation of God to the heavens constitutes a handicap in knowing whether God is the creator of the "canopy of the sky", or merely uses it as a reality which is coeternal with God, such as evidentally is assumed in referring to "chaos" and "the void". The notion that there was an "abyss" or "void" prior to God's creating is a notion which is common in ancient cosmogonies, and therefore, having a very different metaphysical meaning from the first verse in Genesis.

The same incommensurate character of concepts is affirmed in some of the statements in Psalms, such as the declaration: "The heavens tell out the glory of God, the vault of heaven reveals his handiwork"(19:1). The second part of this statement has a theological or metaphysical meaning, such as the first part does not have. In the second part, the heavens are thought of as being the "handiwork" or the creation of God, and as such, God is prior to them, and therefore, the heavens are contingent upon his prior being. No such order or antecedence of God to the heavens, however, is indicated in affirming that "the heavens tell out (declare) the glory of God". When, of course, an interpretation is assumed, such as is stated in the second part, then the glory which is manifested in the heavens witnesses to a reality that confers such a property upon them. This interpretation is explicit in the Psalmist's addressing God, and characterizing the "heavens" as "the work of thy fingers". The antecedence of God to the Heavens, as his creation, is likewise explicitly affirmed in declaring that "the stars (were) set in their place by thee"(89:5), thus referring to the reality which accounts for their nature, and therefore, for their coming into being. The Psalmist affirms a theological interpretation, such

as is affirmed in the first verse of Genesis, referring
to "the Lord, maker of heaven and earth"(121:2); also
reaffirming this identical doctrine in another psalm
(134:3).

Although the shepherd Amos is not a theologian, he,
nevertheless, has a clear understanding of the biblical
concept of God as the Creator of the heavenly bodies,
referring to the Creator "who made the Pleiades and
Orion"(5:8). As their Creator, the stars are thus
regarded as having a status subordinate to their divine
sovereign.

The prophet Isaiah, who was a contemporary of the
eighth century Amos, is likewise consistent with
biblical theology that maintains there is a creator of
the world, which has a status such as the total world
does not have, as his creation. Regarding "the
everlasting God (as) creator of the wide world"(40:28),
the Prophet characterizes "the whole earth (as) full of
his glory"(6:3). The second part of the Book of
Isaiah, although attributed to the eighth century
prophet, was, nevertheless, written about two centuries
later, but it also affirms that the creator of the
world is "the Creator of the Heavens"(45:18). He
rephrases this same basic biblical doctrine when he
refers to God, "who stretched out the skies and founded
the earth"(51:13). This metaphorical version of the
same doctrine is, of course, of a lower philosophical
order than the less figurative, but also specific
formulation of the Creator of the heavens, whose being
was antecedent to the heavens which he created. This
more explicit theology is by no means intimidated by a
later theological quibble that there could be no
property of being a creator prior to creating, and
consequently, it is argued that the heavens are
coeternal with God. In spite of much that can soundly
be said in criticism of theological concepts in the
Bible, it is not cluttered up with such
pseudo-theological quibbles of sophistry.

Since social justice was a dominant emphasis of the
Prophets, rather than formulating developed theologies,
it is understandable that Isaiah maintains that
principles of justice are as eternal as the Creator,
and are integral to his creation of the earth and its
people. Hence he declares that "for the furtherance of
his justice", God established a law of justice with a
"surpassing majesty"(42:21) of the heavens themselves,
which also are his creations.

308

Jeremiah likewise emphasized in his ministry, which is directed to correcting social injustices, that the Creator requires justice of human beings, since as their "Lord", he has decreed there should be "justice and right upon the earth"(9:24). Such justice and right in human relations are, therefore, conditions in human life for their approval by their Creator, who "made the earth by his power; established the world...by his wisdom; unfurled the skies by his understanding" (10:12).

It is significant that the Prophet stresses the wisdom and understanding of the Creator of the earth and its people, since this is an implied argument that only their intelligence, which is expressed in their understanding of their obligations to each other will be tolerable to their Creator. And when they live with such understanding of their obligations to each other, they will also fulfill their obligations to God. And this type of life will constitute a wisdom which is essential to their worship of their God. Addressing himself to his people, as a spokesman for God, he directs the question to them: "Do I not fill heaven and earth?"(23:24), as if to challenge them with the presence of God in their lives, and therefore, attentive to them in their relations to their fellows, will hold them accountable for the injustices for which they are responsible.

This argument for God's judgment of human beings for their injustices to each other is, of course, basic to his ministry, and therefore, he does not affirm a theology which is unrelated to the moral judgment that, as a prophet, he maintains is as inescapable for human beings as is the justice itself which is integral to God's wisdom.

The highminded emphasis in the tradition of biblical prophecy made such an indelible impression upon the religious reflecting of Hebrews, centuries after the Prophets, that the Prophets' thoughts continue to be expressed in the following centuries.

Although First and Second Esdras are not included in the Hebrew canon of Scriptures, they, nevertheless, affirm theological concepts which are expressed in the prophetic tradition. Influenced by the theology of the canonical Hebrew Scriptures, their author, Ezra, characterizes God as "the king of heaven"(I.4:46). This characterization, of course, does not specify the nature of God as prior to the world, which is his creation, but another reference to God does specify this in referring to God as the "Lord, who dost inhabit eternity; to whom the...highest heavens belong"(II.8:20). This, therefore, is a theological concept which is consistent with the profoundest versions of the Prophets' interpretations of the priority of God, the Creator, to every reality other than his own identity.

The Book of Tobit is likewise not included in the Hebrew canon, although unlike the Second Book of Esdras, it is included in the Greek version of the Bible, which the Greek-speaking Jews in Egypt regarded as Sacred Scripture. Its author, Tobit, identifies himself as "taken captive in the time of Shalmaneser king of Assyria (1:2), and declares as the final statement in the Book: "The Lord God...lives for ever and ever"(14:15). Although this affirms the eternal nature of God, it does not specify the properties of God which are essential to the biblical theology that was formulated by the major prophets, such as Isaiah and Jeremiah. It is no more explicit a theological concept than is the canonical writings attributed to the prophet Habakkuk, who declares that "the earth" is resplendent with "the glory of the Lord"(2:14); or again, that "his splendour fills the earth", and "his radiance overspreads the skies"(3.3).

A more critical theological concept is affirmed by another so-called "Minor prophet", Jonah, who characterizes the "Lord" whom he worships, as "the God of heaven, who made both sea and land"(1:9). Yet, this likewise does not clarify the relation of the heavens to God, indicating whether they are created by God, such as is the earth, or whether they may be coeternal with the Creator of the earth. This critical theological doctrine, however, is specified in the apocryphal Book of Baruch, whose author identifies himself as living in Babylon, "in the fifth year after the Chaldaeans had captured and burnt Jerusalem"(1:2). In declaring that "The stars...shone for their Maker", he affirms the biblical doctrine of the major prophets that God is the Creator of the heavens, and this, as has been argued, is the critical theological doctrine in the uniqueness of the Prophet's version of God as prior to the heavens, which ancient religions that are referred to in the preceding discussion regard as uncreated, and in this sense, as not being contingent upon a creator for their existing or their being.

Possibly the most learned of the authors of the

Deuterocanonical books, is the author of Ecclesiasticus, who identifies himself as "Jesus Son of Sirach". It may be to his credit that he sums up the theological doctrines of the major prophets in a more complete and consistent manner than other authors of this category of writings. Actually, the theologically unique doctrine of this part of the Hebrew canon is affirmed by the learned writer of Ecclesiasticus, when he refers to God as "He who lives forever is the Creator of the whole universe"(18:1). No biblical doctrine which has been considered in the foregoing analysis can surpass, or even equal, the specificity of an entire metaphysics, such as is stated in this single assertion, which may be regarded as the primary premise of the biblical version of God that is affirmed by the principal prophets in the Old Testament. The doctrine that there is no qualification in the duration of the Creator's existing is affirmed in the characterization of God as "he who is from eternity to eternity"(42:21). And what relates the theology, which is so affirmed, to the prophetic emphasis is the concept that "God's majesty is equalled by his mercy"(2:18).

An emphasis upon the majesty and splendor of God is not peculiar to prophetic theology, but the concept that the majesty of his sovereignty is joined with his mercy the nature of God, the one ultimate reality.

An emphasis in prophetic theology which became dominant in later Wisdom literature is stressed in Ecclesiasticus, which maintains that God "has set in order the masterpieces of his wisdom"(42:21), thereby declaring that power and majesty are not the religiously significant properties of God, the Creator, but rather, the wisdom with which he creates and rules or directs his creation. A supremely profound metaphysical concept is then affirmed in attributing to God's wisdom or his "word", a cosmic role of integrating, which is affirmed in the remarkable passage that "by his word all things are held together"(43:26).

311

PREFACE

1. <u>Zeus</u> <u>and</u> <u>Hera</u>, trans. Christopher Holme, (Princeton, N.J.: Princeton University Press, Bollingen Series LXV 5, 1975), p.13.

2. C. Kerenyi, <u>The</u> <u>Religion</u> <u>of</u> <u>The</u> <u>Greeks</u> <u>and</u> <u>Romans</u>, trans. Christopher Holme, (New York: E.P. Dutton & Co.,Inc.,1962), p.15.

3. <u>Zeus</u> <u>and</u> <u>Hera</u>, p.38.

4. <u>The</u> <u>Odyssey</u>, trans. E.V.Rieu, (London: Methuen & Co.,1952),p.xi.

5. <u>Aeschylus</u>, <u>The</u> <u>Complete</u> <u>Greek</u> <u>Tragedies</u>, ed. by David Green and Richmond Lattimore, (Chicago and London: The University of Chicago Press, 1960), Vol. I, p.5.

6. Douglas M. MacDowell, <u>The</u> <u>Law</u> <u>In</u> <u>Classical</u> <u>Athens</u>, (Ithica, New York: Cornell University Press, 1978), p.17. Cf. Iliad 23.566-95.

7. <u>Iliad</u> , 2.683-685.

8. Frederic C. Grant, <u>Hellenistic</u> <u>Religions</u> (Indianapolis, Ne York: Bobbs-Merrill Company, Inc., The Library of Liberal Arts, 1953), p. xxxi.

9. Vincent Scully, <u>The</u> <u>Earth</u>, <u>the</u> <u>Temple</u>, <u>and</u> <u>the</u> <u>Gods</u>, (New Haven, Conneticut, Yale University Press, 1962; Revised edition, Frederick A. Praeger, Inc., 1969), p. 25.

10. <u>The</u> <u>New</u> <u>English</u> <u>Bible</u>, (New York: Oxford University Press, 1970), p. xvii.

11. John Allegro, <u>The</u> <u>Mystery</u> <u>of</u> <u>the</u> <u>Dead</u> <u>Sea</u> <u>Scrolls</u> <u>Revealed</u>, (New York: Gramercy Publishing Company, 1981), p. 62.

12. A. Dupont-Sommer, <u>The</u> <u>Essene</u> <u>Writings</u> <u>from</u> <u>Qumran</u>, trans. G Vermes, (Cleveland and New York: Meridan Books, World Publishing Company, 1962), p. 9.

13. <u>The</u> <u>New</u> <u>English</u> <u>Bible</u>, p. xvi.

14. <u>Documents</u> <u>from</u> <u>Old</u> <u>Testament</u> <u>Times</u>, ed. D. Winston Thomas, (New York: Harper and Row, Harper Torchbooks, 1961), p. 163.

15. ibid, p.v.

16. Herbert Weir Smyth, _Aeschylus_, (Cambridge, Massachusetts; Harvard University Press, Loeb Classical Library, No. 145, 1963), p. xi.

17. E.V. Rieu, _The Iliad_, (London: Methuen & Co., 1953), p. xviii.

18. ibid, p. xix.

19. Op. cit., p. 173.

20. _Herodotus_, trans. A.D. Godley, (Cambridge, Massachusetts: Harvard University Press, Loeb Classical Library, No. 117, 1966), Vol. I, p. x.

21. _The Iliad of Homer_, (Chicago and London: The University of Chicago, 1961), p. 20.

CHAPTER ONE

1. The Homeric Gods, trans. Moses Hadas, (New York: Pantheon Books, 1979), p. 287.

2. The Religion of the Greeks and Romans, p. 96.

3. The Homeric Gods , p. 7.

4. Benjamin Jowett, The Dialogues of Plato, (London: Oxford University Press, third edition, 1931), vol. I, p. 580-81.

5. Op. cit., p. 160.

6. Ibid., p. 16;10.

7. Ibid., p. 6.

8. The Oracles of Zeus, (Cambridge, Massachusetts: Harvard University Press, 1967), p. 27.

9. Op. cit., p. 160.

10. Vol. VIII, 11 and 13. No. 130, p. 13-15.

11. line 514, trans. H. Weir Smyth, (Loeb Classical Library, No. 145), p. 153.

12. line 5, ibid., p. 323.

13. Moira, (New York: Harper and Row, Harper Torchbooks, 1963) p. 138.

14. Walter F. Otto, op. cit., p. 135.

15. Walter F. Otto, "The Meaning of the Eleusinian Mysteries", The Mysteries, ed. Joseph Campbell (Princeton, N.J.: Princeton University Press, Bollingen Series XXX.2, 1978), p. 15.

16. The Odes of Pindar, Nemea 6, 1, trans. Richmond Lattimore, (Chicago: The University of Chicago Press, 1971), p. 111.

17. Psalm 8:5, The New English Bible, (NEB).

18. C. Kerenyi, Zeus and Hera, p. 133.

19. Judges 2:13, NEB.

20. I Samuel 7:3-4, NEB.

21. I. Kings 11:31-33, NEB.

22. Vincent Scully, op. cit., p. 26.

23. C. Kerenyi, _Zeus and Hera_, p. 115.

24. Ibid., p. 57.

25. _Iliad_, I. 36, trans. Richmond Lattimore, p. 60.

26. line 161, trans. E.P. Coleridge, The Complete Greek Drama, ed. Whitney J. Oates and Eugene O'Neil, Jr. (New York: Random House, 1938), vol. II, p. 115.

27. Walter F. Otto, op. cit., p. 133.

28. _Iliad_, I. 9f.

29. Ibid., I. 194f.

30. H.W. Parke, _Festivals of the Athenians_, (Ithaca: Cornell University Press, 1979), p. 128.

31. Ibid., p. 32-33.

32. Ibid., p. 135.

33. _The Religion of the Greeks and Romans_, p. 96.

34. _Festivals of the Athenians_, p. 22.

35. Ibid., p. 134.

36. _The Homeric Gods_, p. 166.

37. Hesiod, _Theogony_, 370f, trans. E.G. Evelyn-White, (Loeb Classical Library, No. 57, 1977), p. 107.

38. C. Kerenyi, _The Gods of the Greeks_, trans. Norman Cameron, (Thames and Hudson, 1979), p. 113.

39. _The Homeric Gods_, p. 3.

40. (123) _Epicurus, the Extant Remains_, trans. Cyril Bailey, quoted Frederick C. Grant, _Hellenistic Religions_, p. 157.

41. C. Kerenyi, _Zeus and Hera_, p. 63.

42. _The Religion of the Greeks and Romans_, p. 13.

CHAPTER TWO

1. <u>Moira</u>, p. 340.

2. <u>The Homeric Gods</u>, p. 154.

3. Ibid., p. 172.

4. Op. cit., p. 17.

5. Op. cit., p. 15.

6. <u>The Religion of the Greeks and Romans</u>, p. 98.

7. Ibid., p. 143.

8. Op. cit., p. 127.

9. Ibid., p. 213.

10. Trans. James Adam, <u>The Stoic and Epicurean Philosophers</u>, ed W.J. Oates (New York: Random House, 1940), p. 591.

11. <u>Zeus and Hera</u>, p. 100.

12. Op. cit., p. 174.

13. "Prometheus Bound", line 526, trans. H. Weir Smyth, (Loeb Classical Library, No. 145, 1963), p. 263.

14. <u>Greek Mythology</u>, p. 26.

15. line 62, trans. E.P. Coleridge, <u>The Complete Greek Drama</u>, Vol. I., p. 1018.

16. "The Madness of Hercules", line 62, trans. A.S. Way, (Loeb Classical Library, No. 11, 1971), p. 135.

17. line 570, trans. Robert Potter, <u>The Complete Greek Drama</u>, vol. I., p. 1079.

18. line 570-71, trans. A.S. Way, (Loeb Classical Library, No. 10, 1965), p. 329.

19. <u>The Laws of Classical Athens</u> , p. 246.

20. <u>Religion of the Greeks and Romans</u> p. 195.

21. "Works and Days", trans. H.G. Evelyn-White, op. cit., p. 17.

22. <u>Religion of the Greeks and Romans</u>, p. 195.

23. line 365f, trans. R. Storr, (Loeb Classical Library, No. 20, 1968), p. 343.

24. line 578, trans. Richmond Lattimore, The Odyssey of Homer, (Harper and Row, 1967), p. 136.

25. line 242, trans. E.V. Rieu, op. cit., p. 203.

26. Book VIII, line 570, trans. Richmond Lattimore, op. cit., p. 136.

27. C. Kerenyi, Zeus and Hera, p. 65.

28. "Works and Days", line 5f, op. cit., p. 3.

29. XXIV, line 527f.

30. III, line 164f, trans. E.V.Rieu, op. cit., p. 48.

31. IX, line 19f, trans. E.V. Rieu, ibid., p. 145.

32. I, line, 10, trans. E.V. Rieu, ibid., p. 1.

33. III, line 415, trans. E.V. Rieu, ibid., p. 55.

34. V, line 834, ibid., p. 97.

35. The Gods of the Greeks, p. 36.

36. XXX, line 6, trans. H.G. Evelyn-White, op. cit., p. 457.

37. II. line 146-148, ibid., p. 299.

38. Walter F. Otto, op. cit., p. 46.

39. XI, 1f, op. cit., p. 437.

40. IV, line 576, trans. Walter F. Otto, op. cit., p. 122.

41. I, 32, op. cit., p. 41.

42. line 345f, trans. H. Weir Smyth, op. cit. 139.

43. line 446f, trans. F. Storr, (Loeb Classical Library No. 21), p. 403.

44. line 225, trans. E.P. Coleridge, op. cit. I. p. 926.

45. William Chase Greene, Moira, p. 94.

46. Sophocles, (New York: A.S. Barnes & Company, Inc., 1961), 19.

47. Moira, p. 96.

48. "The Phoenician Maidens", line 1764, trans. A.S. Way, (Loeb Classical Library, No. 11), p. 491.

49. line 1285, trans. A.S. Way, (Loeb Classical library, No. 10), p. 513.

50. Op. cit., p. 591.

51. Fragment No. 11, Selections from Early Greek Philosophy, Milton C. Nahmn, (New York: Appleton-Century-Crofts, 1964), p. 84.

52. Fragment No. 16, ibid., p. 84.

53. Moira, p. 96.

54. The Jerusalem Bible, (Garden City New York: Doubleday and Company, Inc., 1966), p. 1128.

55. IV. 7, Documents from Old Testament Times, p. 8.

56. Ibid., p. 92.

57. Ibid., p. 196.

58. Die Philosophie des Als Ob, 1911.

59. Philosophy of the Unconscious ,1869, English trans. Couplan 1884.

60. line 54, Documents from Old Testament Times, p. 114.

61. The Mystery of the Dead Sea Scrolls Revealed, p. 103.

62. A. Dupont-Sommer, op. cit., p. 51.

63. XI(3) ibid., p. 101.

64. XI(17) ibid., p. 103.

65. IX(11) ibid., p. 231.

66. VII(24) ibid., p. 96.

67. IV, 94, trans. A.D. Godley, (Loeb Classical Library No. 118, 1963), p. 297.

68. <u>Iliad</u> <u>of</u> <u>Homer</u>, p. 31.

69. IV, line 44f, trans. E.V. Rieu, op. cit., p. 58.

70. line 205, trans. H. Weir Smyth, (Loeb Classical Library No. 145, 1963), p. 145.

71. I, line 194, trans. Richmond Lattimore, op. cit., p. 64.

72. VIII, line 314, trans. R.V. Rieu, op. cit., p. 137.

73. V, line 378, trans. R.V. Rieu, op. cit., p. 84.

74. V, line 378, trans. R.V. Rieu, op. cit., p. 138.

75. "The Seven Against Thebes", line 740, trans. H. Weir Smyth (Loeb Classical Library, No. 145), p. 385.

76. "Orestes", line 330, trans. A.S. Way (Loeb Classical Library, No. 10), p. 153.

77. "Ion", line 460, trans. A.S. Way, (Loeb Classical Library, No. 12), p. 47.

78. "Electra", line 708, trans. F. Storr, (Loeb Classical Library No. 21, 1967), p. 179.

79. C. Kerenyi, "The Mysteries of the Kaberiroi", The Mysteries, ed. Joseph Campbell, p. 46.

80. H.W. Parke, <u>Festivals</u> <u>of</u> <u>the</u> <u>Athenians</u>, p. 34.

81. IV(25), <u>Documents</u> <u>from</u> <u>Old</u> <u>Testament</u> <u>Times</u>, p. 85.

82. Ibid., p. 196.

83. C. Kerenyi, <u>The</u> <u>Gods</u> <u>of</u> <u>the</u> <u>Greeks</u>, p. 117.

84. <u>Zeus</u> <u>and</u> <u>Hera</u>, p. 19.

85. Ibid., p. 21.

86. H.W. Parke, <u>Festivals</u> <u>of</u> <u>the</u> <u>Athenians</u>, p. 29.

CHAPTER THREE

1. The Religion of the Greeks and Romans, p. 51.

2. Ibid., p. 61.

3. Ibid., p. 66.

4. The Meaning of God in Human Experience, (New Haven: Yale University Press, 1928), p. 79.

5. Op. cit., II. 42, p. 327.

6. Ibid., II. 144, p. 451.

7. "The Mysteries of the Kabeiroi", op. cit., p. 32.

8. Op. cit., II. 50, p. 339.

9. Documents from Old Testament Times, p. xviii.

10. The Jerusalem Bible, p. 81.

11. Ibid., 17b., p. 33.

12. Documents from Old Testament Times, p. 129.
13. Zeus and Hera, p. 78.

14. Description of Greece, "Arcadia", VIII.37.9, trans. W.H.S. Jones, (Loeb Classical Library, No. 297, 1965), p. 89. Cf. H. W. Parke, Festivals of the Athenians, p. 63.

15. Hesiod: The Homeric Hymns and Homerica, trans. H.G. Evelyn-White, (Loeb Classical Library, No. 57, 1977), note 1, p. 291.

16. Festivals of the Athenians, p. 141.

17. 385B, trans. Harold N. Fowler, (Loeb Classical Library, 1939), p. 11.

18. Documents from Old Testament Times, p. 143.

19. Ibid., VI 101, p. 13.

20. C. Kerenyi, The Gods of the Greeks, p. 67.

21. Documents from Old Testament Times, p. 90.

22. H.W. Parke, Festivals of the Athenians, p. 53.

23. Fragment 24, <u>Selections from Early Greek Philosophy</u>, Milton C. Nahm, (trans. Richmond Lattimore) (New York: Appleton-Century-Crofts, 1964), p. 85.

24. Ibid., p. 96, citing Aristotle´s, <u>Metaphysics</u>, I.5.986 b 18

25. Ibid., Meta. I.5.986 b 10.

26. Ibid., 8. p. 93.

27. <u>Metaphysic</u>, I.5.986 b 24, trans. Hippocrates G. Apostle, (Bloomington and London: Indiana University Press, 1966), p. 22.

28. cf. John Randall, Jr., <u>Aristotle</u>, "The Unmoved Mover", (New York: Columbia University Press, 1960), p. 37-144.

29. Ibid., p. 135.

30. Ibid., p. 136.

31. <u>The Gods of the Greeks</u>, p. 121.

32. Ibid., p. 116.

33. Ibid., p. 35.

34. H.W. Parke, <u>Festivals of the Athenians</u>, p. 73.

35. Ibid., p. 125.

36. <u>Zeus and Hera</u>, p. 89.

37. Fragment 19, op. cit., p. 89.

38. Fragment 65, ibid., p. 72.

39. Fragment 11, ibid., p. 86.

40. Fragment 23, ibid., p. 85.

41. "Iphigenia in Tauris", line 1026.

42. line 36, <u>Documents from Old Testament Times</u>, p. 146 (trans. R. J. Williams).

43. line, 74, ibid., p. 147.

44. line 101, ibid., p.148.

45. A. Dupont-Sommer, op. cit., p. 171.

46. The Mystery of the Dead Sea Scrolls Revealed, p. 76.

CHAPTER FOUR

1. C. Kerenyi, Zeus and Hera, p. 21.

2. Documents from Old Testament Times, notes, p. 14.

3. "Introduction to the Pentateuch", The Jerusalem Bible].p. 1

4. John Pinsent, Greek Mythology, (London, New York: Paul Hamlyn, 1969), p. 11.

5. Zeus and Hera, p. 38.

6. IV.471, trans. E.V. Rieu, p. 55.

7. IV.479, trans. Richard Lattimore, p. 77.

8. "The Legend of Aqhat, Son of Dan'el", line 8, 9, Documents from Old Testament Times, p. 124. (trans. J. Gray).

9. The Law in Classical Athens, p. 85; 99.

10. "Homer's Epigrams", VIII, trans. E.G. Evelyn-White, op. cit., p. 471.

11. "The Homeric Hymns", XXXIII, ibid., 461.

12. "The Babylonian Theodicy", line 297, Documents from Old Testament Times, p. 102. (trans. W. G. Lambert).

13. H.W. Parke, Festivals of the Athenians, p. 143.

14. Richard Patrick, Greek Mythology, p. 26.

15. line 687, trans. H. Weir Smyth, (Loeb Classical Library, No. 145), p. 71.

16. Zeus and Hera, p. 59.

17. Ibid., p. 58.

18. Walter F. Otto, The Homeric Gods, p. 153.

19. Vincent Scully, The Earth, the Temple, and the Gods, p. 133

20. The Odyssey, III, line 375, trans. Richmond Lattimore, p. 61.

21. line 375, trans. E.V. Rieu, p. 38.

22. The Odyssey of Homer, Richmond Lattimore, p. 6.

23. Richard Patrich, op. cit., p. 31.

24. "A Decree of Themistokles from Troizen", _Hesperia_, 29, 1960 198-223.

25. line 318, trans. Gilbert Murray, (The Complete Greek Drama), p. 362.

26. line 345, trans. H. Weir Smyth, (Loeb Classical Library, No. 145), p. 139.

27. line 825, trans. W. Weir Smyth and H. Lloyd-Jones (Loeb Classical Library, No. 146), p. 351.

28. "The Heracleidae", trans. E. P. Coleridge, (_The Complete Greek Drama_), p. 894.

29. _Documents from Old Testament Times_, notes, p. 153.

30. II.42, op. cit., p. 327.

31. Op. cit., VI.28, p. 3.

32. VII.53, p. 369.

33. Frederick C. Grant, _Hellenistic Religions_, p. 118.

34. IV.94, p. 297.

35. "Damascus Document III (2), A. Dupont-Sommer, _The Essene Writings from Qumran_, p. 124.

36. Walter F. Otto, op. cit., p. 23.

37. Op. Cit., p. 27.

38. _Documents from Old Testament Times_, notes, p. 41-42.

39. _Zeus and Hera_, p. 171.

40. _The Jerusalem Bible_, p. 269.

41. VII.53, p. 369.

42. line 471f, trans. H. Weir Smyth, (Loeb Classical Library, No. 145), p. 149.

43. Op. cit., p. 156.

44. I.54, trans. E.V. Rieu, op. cit., p. 2.

45. XIII.1, ibid., p. 222.

46. III.440, ibid., p. 56.

47. Documents from Old Testament Times, p. 92.

48. The Jerusalem Bible, p. 273.

49. Ibid., p. 492.

50. XVII.568, trans. E.V. Rieu, p. 325.

51. William Chase Greene, op. cit., p. 16.

52. Op. cit., p. 169.

53. Zeus and Hera, p. 51.

54. H.W. Parke, Festivals of the Athenians, p. 105.

55. Ibid., p. 149.

56. Ibid., p. 58.

57. Ibid., p. 24.

58. Documents from Old Testament Times, p. 144.

59. Ibid., p. 197. (trans. E. Ullendorff)

60. "The Rival of Baal", ibid., p. 131. (trans. J. Gray)

CHAPTER FIVE

1. "Babylonian Chronicle"(a), _Documents from Old Testament Times_, p. 72.

2. "Nineveh Prism of Esarhaddon"(b), ibid., p. 72.

3. "Rassam Cylinder of Ashurbanipal"(c), ibid., p. 72. (trans. D. J. Wiseman)

4. Act. III, Sc.1, line 81-2.

5. XI. 170, _Documents from Old Testament Times_, p. 23. (trans. J. V. Kinnier Wilson)

6. Ibid., p. 145.

7. Ibid., p. 141.

8. _Zeus and Hera_, p. 31.

9. Walter F. Otto, op. cit., p. 179.

10. _Zeus and Hera_, p. 41-42.

11. Douglas M. MacDowell, op. cit., p. 10.

12. 2.205-6.

13. 9.98-9.

14. line 19, trans. E.P. Coleridge, _The Complete Greek Drama_, p 919.

15. line 19, trans. A.S. Way, (Loeb Classical Library, No. 11), p. 499.

16. line 560f, trans. E.P. Coleridge, op. cit., p. 933.

17. line 798, trans. E.P. Coleridge, op. cit., p. 826.

18. Douglas M. MacDowell, op. cit., p. 8.

19. John Allegro, op. cit., p. 62.

20. _The Jerusalem Bible_, p. 8.

21. A. Dupont-Sommer, op. cit., p. 146.

22. Ibid., p. 147.

23. John Allegro, op. cit., p. 60.

24. "Scroll of the Rule", VIII(13), <u>The Essene Writings from Qumran</u>, p. 92.

25. Ibid., (21). p. 93.

26. Hymns (IX, 34-6), p. 52.

27. "The Legend of Aqhat, Son of Dan´el", line, 8-9, op. cit., p. 124.

28. <u>Documents from Old Testament Times</u>, p. xxx.

29. Ibid., p. xvi.

30. Ibid., p. xx.

31. IV.7, ibid., p. 8.

32. <u>Iliad</u>, I. 218, trans. Richmond Lattimore, op. cit., p. 65.

33. line 453, trans. William Nickerson Bates, (New York: A.S. Barnes & Company, 1940), p. 79.

34. Walter F. Otto, op. cit., p. 25.

35. Works and Days, line 184f, op. cit., p. 17.

36. David Greene and Richmond Lattimore, <u>Aeschylus</u>, p. 7.

37. line 119f, trans. F. Storr, (Loeb Classical Library, No. 10), p. 259.

38. line 71, trans. H. Weir Smyth and H. Lloyd-Jones, (Loeb Classical Library No. 146), p. 165.

39. line 366, op. cit., p. 315.

40. <u>The Iliad of Homer</u>, p. 54.

41. B. Vermes, <u>The Dead Sea Scrolls in English</u>, (Baltimore, Maryland: Penguin Books, 1966), p. 65.

42. Dupont-Sommer, op. cit., p. 401.

43. "Homer´s Epigrams", VIII, op. cit., p. 471.

44. "To Demeter", op. cit., II, p. 315.

45. <u>The Jerusalem Bible</u>, p. 269.

46. VIII.129, op. cit., p. 131.

47. The Jerusalem Bible, p. 9.

48. X(9), Dupont-Sommer, op. cit., p. 184.

49. "Agamemnon", line 45-46, trans. H. Weir Smyth and H. Lloyd-Jones, op. cit., p. 11.

50. IX, 117, trans. Richmond Lattimore, op. cit., p. 201.

51. IV, 39-43, ibid., p. 114.

52. Ibid., line 48, p. 114.

53. Ibid., III, 339, p. 112.

54. Ibid., IV, 129, p. 116.

55. Ibid., III, 370f, p. 110.

56. XVI, 170-171, The Odyssey of Homer, Richmond Lattimore, p. 244.

57. XIX, 51-52, ibid., p. 283.

58. I, 11, Iliad of Homer, Richmond Lattimore, p. 59.

59. V, 435-437, ibid., p. 139.

60. Xenophon, Hellenika, 1.7.9-10, quoted: Douglas M. MacDowel op. cit., p. 189.

CHAPTER SIX

1. <u>Zeus</u> <u>and</u> <u>Hera</u>, p. 74.

3. <u>Festivals</u> <u>of</u> <u>the</u> <u>Athenians</u>, p. 80.

4. II, 551.

5. II, 400, <u>The</u> <u>Iliad</u>, E.V. Rieu, p. 30.

6. III, 104, ibid., p. 47.

7. <u>The</u> <u>Iliad</u> <u>of</u> <u>Homer</u>, p. 103.

8. VI, 90, trans. E.V. Rieu, op. cit., p. 102.

9. XXII, 170, ibid., p. 399.

10. <u>Zeus</u> <u>and</u> <u>Hera</u>, p. 33.

11. 1,26, trans. E.V. Rieu, p. 2.

12. III, 178, trans. Richmond Lattimore, p. 55-56.

13. H.W. Parke, op. cit., p. 45.

14. Ibid., p. 45-46.

15. Ibid., p. 128.

16. line 535, trans. E.P. Coleridge, (<u>The</u> <u>Complete</u> <u>Greek</u> <u>Drama</u>) p. 777.

17. line 535, trans . A.S. Way, (Loeb Classical Library, No. 12), p. 205.

18. line 1197-1201, trans. E.P. Coleridge, op. cit., p. 951.

19. line 398f, trans. E.P. Coleridge, p. 895.

20. line 440, trans. E.P. Coleridge, p. 896.

21. line 440, trans. A.S. Way, (Loeb Classical Library, No. 11), p. 287.

22. <u>The</u> <u>Religion</u> <u>of</u> <u>the</u> <u>Greeks</u> <u>and</u> <u>Romans</u>, p. 104.

23. Spinoza, <u>The</u> <u>Ethics</u>,, note to Proposition XLII.

24. John Pinsent, op. cit., p. 47.

25. <u>Festivals of the Athenians</u>, p. 20-21.

26. John Pinsent, op. cit., p. 47.

27. I.66, trans. E.V. Rieu, p. 3.

28. I.66, trans. Richmond Lattimore, p. 61.

29. IV.48-49, trans. E.V. Rieu, p. 53.

30. XI.772, ibid., p. 205.

31. XXIV.70, ibid., p. 437.

32. XXIV.70, trans. Richmond Lattimore, p. 477.

33. XIV.422-23, trans. E.V. Rieu, op. cit., p. 208.

34. XIV.422-23, trans. Richmond Lattimore, p. 221.

35. <u>Festivals of the Athenians</u>, p. 19.

36. I.463, trans. Richmond Lattimore p. 71.

37. I.133, op. cit., p. 173.

38. <u>The Earth, the Temple, and the Gods</u>, p. 13.

39. line 535-38, trans. A.S. Way, (Loeb Classical Library, No. 12), p. 205.

40. line 1515-20, trans. Anonymous, (<u>The Complete Greek Drama</u>), p. 790-1.

41. <u>The Great Bronze Age of China</u>, ed., Wen Fong, (New York: Th Metropolitan Museum of Art; Alfred A. Knopf, Inc., 1980), p. 4.

42. Ibid., p. 56.

43. IV.26, op. cit., p. 225.

44. <u>Zeus and Hera</u>, p. 36.

45. Vincent Scully, op. cit., p. 134.

47. XXIII.22, trans. E.V. Rieu, op. cit., p. 409.

48. <u>Festivals of the Athenians</u>, p. 138.

49. "Agamemnon", line 205 f., trans. H. Weir Smyth and H.

Lloyd-Jones, (Loeb Classical Library, No. 146), p. 21.

50. Euripides, "Hecuba", line 632f, trans. E.P. Coleridge, (Complete Greek Drama), p. 819.

51. line 408, trans., E.P. Coleridge, ibid., p. 895.

52. line 911f, trans. E.P. Coleridge, (The Complete Greek Drama), vol.II, p. 196.

53. Zeus and Hera, p. 35.

54. Sextus Empiricus III.220, quoted Frederick C. Grant, op. cit., p. 100.

55. H.W. Parke, op. cit., p. 138.

56. The Epic Cycle: The Cypria, I., The Homeric Hymns and Homericay,trans. H.G. Evelyn-White, (Loeb Classical Librar No. 57) , p. 493.

57. line 27-29 , trans. Richmond Lattimore, (The Complete Greek Tragedies), vol.III, p. 346.

58. Frederick C. Grant, op. cit., p. 113.

59. Ibid., p. xxxvii.

60. H.W. Parke, op. cit., p. 20.

61. C. Kerenyi, Zeus and Hera, p. 23.

62. I.473, trans. Richmond Lattimore, op. cit., p. 71.

63. line 779-780, trans. Ralph Gladstone, (The Complete Greek Tragedies), vol.III, p. 146.

64. H.W. Parke, op. cit., p. 49.

65. Walter Wili, "The Orphic Mysteries and the Greek Spirit", The Mysteries, ed., Joseph Campbell, p. 69.

66. H.W. Parke, The Oracles of Zeus, (Cambridge, Massachusetts: Harvard University Press, 1967), p.119.

67. H.W. Parke, Festivals of the Athenians, p. 32-33.

68. C. Kerenyi, The Religion of the Greeks and Romans, p. 188.

69. The Varieties of Religious Experience, (New York, London: Longmans, Green and Co., 1928), p. 31.

70. Zeus and Hera, p. 150.

71. H.W. Parke, The Oracles of Zeus, p. 164.

72. Zeus and Hera, p. 116.

73. Ibid., p. 166.

74. Ibid., p. 150.

75. Greek Mythology, p. 126.

76. Zeus and Hera, p. 148.

77. C. Kerenyi, The Religion of the Greeks and Romans, p. 10.

78. H.W. Parke, Festivals of the Athenians, p. 33.

79. Ibid., p. 42.

80. Ibid., p. 22.

81. Ibid., p. 73.

82. Ibid., p. 137.

83. C. Kerenyi, The Religion of the Greeks and Romans, p. 183.

84. H.W. Parke, Festivals of the Athenians, p. 19.

85. IX.496-501, trans. E.V. Rieu, op. cit., p. 159.

86. I.382-386, ibid., p. 11.

87. IV.86-104, ibid., p. 60.

88. XVII.50-51, trans. Richmond Lattimore, op. cit., p. 254.

89. I.66-67, trans. Richmond Lattimore, The Iliad of Homer, p. 61.

90. Iliad, I.39-42, ibid., p. 60.

91. line 483-85, trans. H. Weir Smyth and H. Lloyd-Jones, op. cit., p. 207.

92. line 487-89, ibid., p. 207.

93. C. Kerenyi, The Religion of the Greeks and Romans, p. 106.

94. H.W. Parke, _Festivals of the Athenians_, p. 146.

95. Douglas M. MacDowell, _The Law in Classical Athens_, p. 109.

96. Ibid., p. 111.

97. Aeschylus, "Libation-Bearers", 1.15, trans. H. Weir Smyth and Lloyd- Jones, op. cit., p. 160.

98. _Description of Greece_ II.xvii.1, trans. W.H.S. Jones, (Loe Classical Library, No. 93, 1969), p. 333.

99. line 450, trans. H. Weir Smyth and H. Lloyd-Jones, op. cit., p. 315.

100. _Zeus and Hera_, p. 146.

101. _Festivals of the Athenians_, p. 63.

102. line 280, trans. H. Weir Smyth and H. Lloyd-Jones, op. cit., p. 299.

CHAPTER SEVEN

1. H.W. Parke, Festivals of the Athenians, p. 29.

2. Ibid., p. 51.

3. Ibid., p. 73 .

4. Ibid., p. 123.

6. C. Kerenyi, Zeus and Hera, p. 432.

7. C. Kerenyi, "The Mysteries of the Kabeiroi", op. cit., p. 40.

8. "The Heracleidae", 1.777-83. cf. C. Kerenyi, Zeus and Hera, p. 126.

9. C. Kerenyi, The Religion of the Greeks and Romans, p. 96-7.

10. H.W. Parke, Festivals of the Athenians, p. 75.

11. C. Kerenyi, The Religion of the Greeks and Romans, p. 179

12. 653, trans. B. Jowett, (London: Oxford University Press, 1931), v.p. 31.

13. H.W. Parke, op. cit., p. 155.

14. Douglas M. MacDowell, op. cit., p. 127.

15. Ibid., p. 197.

16. Ibid., p. 199.

17. Iliad, III, 385-88, trans. Richmond Lattimore, op. cit., p. 110.

18. Iliad, IV, 86, trans. E. V. Rieu, op. cit., p. 59.

19. Ibid., XIII, 355, p. 232.

20. Ibid., XXI, 285, p. 384.

21. Ibid., XX, 81, p. 363.

22. Ibid., XVII, 323, p. 318.

23. Ibid., XVII, 74, p. 311.

24. Ibid., XVII, 583, p. 325.

25. XVII, 485, trans. E.V. Rieu, op. cit., p. 255.

26. Ibid., I, 105, p. 4.

27. I, 323, trans. Richmond Lattimore, op. cit., p. 35.

28. II, 382-385, ibid., p. 49.

29. VII, 20, trans. E.V. Rieu, op. cit., p. 90.

30. VIII, 7-9, ibid., p. 100.

31. XIII, 221, ibid., p. 190.

32. XIII, 312-313, trans. Richmond Lattimore, op. cit. p. 206.

33. III, 371, ibid., p. 60.

34. XXII, 240, ibid., p. 327.

35. line 132, trans. H.G. Evelyn-White, op. cit., p. 333.

36. I, 85-87, trans. Richmond Lattimore, op. cit., p. 85-87.

37. Ibid., 385, p. 69.

38. XV, 252, trans. E.V. Rieu, op. cit., p. 219.

39. line 285-89, trans. F. Storr, (Loeb Classical Library, No. 20), p. 27.

40. line 300-303, ibid., p. 29.

41. line 766-68, trans. E.P. Coleridge, (The Complete Greek Drama), II.p. 192.

42. The Jerusalem Bible, p. 1118.

43. Ibid., p. 1134.

44. Ibid., p. 1130.

45. Ibid., p. 1131.

46. line 9-10, op. cit., p. 3.

47. line 264, ibid., p. 23.

48. line 501-03, trans. Anonymous, (The Complete Greek Drama), II.1086.

49. line 480-500, trans. H. Weir Smyth, (Loeb Classical Library, No. 145), p. 151.

50. Paul Schmitt, "The Ancient Mysteries in the Society of Their Time, Their Transformation and Most Recent Echoes", The Mysteries, p. 93.

51. I, 103, trans. E.V. Rieu, op. cit., p. 4.

52. Zeus and Hera, p. 152.

53. Festivals of the Athenians, p. 25.

54. The Law in Classical Athens, p. 192.

55. VI, 266, trans. E.V. Rieu, op. cit., p. 107.

56. Iliad, IX, 171, ibid., p. 150.

57. Festivals of the Athenians, p. 21.

58. Ibid., p. 58.

59. Douglas M. MacDowell, op. cit., p. 192.

60. II, 37, op. cit., p. 321.

61. H.W. Parke, The Oracles of Zeus p. 190.

62. "Orestes", 1.162, trans. A.S. Way, (Loeb Classical Library, No. 10), p. 139.

63. line 1189, trans. A.S. Way, (Loeb Classical Library, No. 9), p. 111.

64. line 1039, trans. E.P. Coleridge, (The Complete Greek Drama), I, p. 912.

65. The Religion of the Greeks and Romans, p. 14.

66. Festivals of the Athenians, p. 95.

67. Douglas M. MacDowell, op. cit., p. 200.

68. line 499f, trans. E.P. Coleridge, (The Complete Greek Drama), II, p. 183.

69. line 1369, trans. A.S. Way, (Loeb Classical Library, No. 12), p. 269.

70. line 1365f, trans. E.P. Coleridge, (The Complete Greek Drama), I, p. 797.

71. line 584, trans. A.S. Way, (Loeb Classical Library, No. 10), p. 53.

72. line 1678f, trans. E.P. Coleridge, (The Complete Greek Drama), II, p. 58.

73. Hellenistic Religions, p. xxiv.

74. line 655f, trans. E.P. Coleridge, (The Complete Greek Drama), I, p. 1031.

75. line 1145, trans. E.P. Coleridge, ibid., I, p. 792.

76. line 1016, trans. F. Storr, (Loeb Classical Library, No. 20), p. 391.

77. line 1345f, trans. E.P. Coleridge, (The Complete Greek Drama), I, p. 1050.

78. "Helen", 1. 745, ibid., II. p. 30.

79. Sophocles, Electra, 1. 198, ibid., II, p. 71.

80. Festivals of the Athenians, p. 60.

CHAPTER EIGHT

1. Fragment No. 11, Selections from Early Greek Philosophy, Milton C. Nahm, (New York: Appleton-Century-Crofts, 1964), p. 84.

2. Fragments 15 and 16, ibid., p. 84.

3. Fragment 14, ibid., p. 84.

4. Fragment 26, ibid., p. 85.

5. Fragment 25, ibid., p. 85.

6. Fragment 25, ibid., p. 85.

7. Fragment 1, ibid., p. 92.

8. Fragment 6, ibid., p. 93.

9. Fragment 8, ibid., p. 93.

10. "The Eleatic School", op. cit., p. 89.

11. Fragment 8, ibid., p. 94.

12. "The Way of Truth", 8, ibid., p. 94.

13. Fragment 125, ibid., p. 75.

14. Fragment 2, ibid., p. 68.

15. Fragment 3, ibid., p. 68.

16. Fragment 20, ibid., p`. 69.

17. Fragment 2, ibid., p. 68.

18. Ibid., p. 68.

19. Fragment 92, ibid., p. 73.

20. Fragment 91, ibid., p. 73.

21. Fragment 18, ibid., p. 69.

22. Fragment 19, ibid., p. 19.

23. Ibid., p. 19.

24. Fragment 98, ibid., p. 74.